Transforming World Politi

This book provides a critical understanding of contemporary world politics by arguing that the neoliberal approach to international relations seduces many of us into investing our lives in projects of power and alienation. These projects offer few options for emancipation; consequently, many feel they have little choice but to retaliate against violence with more violence.

The authors of this pioneering work articulate *worldism* as an alternative approach to world politics. It intertwines non-Western and Western traditions by drawing on Marxist, postcolonial, feminist and critical security approaches with Greek and Chinese theories of politics, broadly defined. The authors contend that contemporary world politics cannot be understood outside the legacies of these multiple worlds, including axes of power configured by gender, race, class, and nationality, which are themselves linked to earlier histories of colonizations and their contemporary formations. With fiction and poetry as exploratory methods, the authors build on their "multiple worlds" approach to consider different sites of world politics, arguing that a truly emancipatory understanding of world politics requires more than just a shift in ways of thinking; above all, it requires a shift in ways of being.

Transforming World Politics will be of vital interest to students and scholars of International Relations, Political Science, Postcolonial Studies, Social Theory, Women's Studies, Asian Studies, European Union and Mediterranean Studies, and Security Studies.

Anna M. Agathangelou is an Associate Professor in the Departments of Political Science and Women's Studies at York University, Canada and co-director of the Global Change Institute, Nicosia, Cyprus.

L.H.M. Ling is an Associate Professor in the Graduate Program in International Affairs at The New School, New York, USA.

This is a worldly and sophisticated antidote to so much that is sterile and narrow in today's International Relations. The authors have provided us with a literate and learned statement on how to view a complex world. It is an important early contribution to what **should** become the mainstream of International Relations.

Stephen Chan *Professor of International Relations,*
School of Oriental and African Studies (SOAS),
University of London, UK

In challenging historical erasures that have been carried through violence as desire and the desire for violence, as well as the framing of discourses and the incarceration of labour in property relations, *Transforming World Politics* makes us think about our diminished way of life under the neoliberal imperium. The authors make the bold claim that we need to interrogate and challenge not only the 'other' but ourselves, thus creating new possibilities of moving forward together.

Shirin M. Rai *Professor of Politics and International*
Studies, University of Warwick, UK

The New International Relations
Edited by Richard Little, *University of Bristol*, Iver B. Neumann, *Norwegian Institute of International Affairs (NUPI), Norway* and Jutta Weldes, *University of Bristol*.

The field of international relations has changed dramatically in recent years. This new series will cover the major issues that have emerged and reflect the latest academic thinking in this particular dynamic area.

International Law, Rights and Politics
Developments in Eastern Europe and the CIS
Rein Mullerson

The Logic of Internationalism
Coercion and accommodation
Kjell Goldmann

Russia and the Idea of Europe
A study in identity and international relations
Iver B. Neumann

The Future of International Relations
Masters in the making?
Edited by Iver B. Neumann and Ole Wæver

Constructing the World Polity
Essays on international institutionalization
John Gerard Ruggie

Realism in International Relations and International Political Economy
The continuing story of a death foretold
Stefano Guzzini

International Relations, Political Theory and the Problem of Order
Beyond international relations theory?
N.J. Rengger

War, Peace and World Orders in European History
Edited by Anja V. Hartmann and Beatrice Heuser

European Integration and National Identity
The challenge of the Nordic states
Edited by Lene Hansen and Ole Wæver

Shadow Globalization, Ethnic Conflicts and New Wars
A political economy of intra-state war
Dietrich Jung

Contemporary Security Analysis and Copenhagen Peace Research
Edited by Stefano Guzzini and Dietrich Jung

Observing International Relations
Niklas Luhmann and world politics
Edited by Mathias Albert and Lena Hilkermeier

Does China Matter? A Reassessment
Essays in memory of Gerald Segal
Edited by Barry Buzan and Rosemary Foot

European Approaches to International Relations Theory
A house with many mansions
Jörg Friedrichs

The Post-Cold War International System
Strategies, institutions and reflexivity
Ewan Harrison

States of Political Discourse
Words, regimes, seditions
Costas M. Constantinou

Transforming World Politics

From empire to multiple worlds

Anna M. Agathangelou
and L.H.M. Ling

Routledge
Taylor & Francis Group

LONDON AND NEW YORK

First published 2009
by Routledge
2 Park Square Milton Park Abingdon Oxon OX14 4RN

Simultaneously published in the USA and Canada
by Routledge
270 Madison Avenue, New York, NY 10016

Routledge is an imprint of the Taylor & Francis Group, an informa business.

Typeset in 10/12pt Sabon by Graphicraft Limited, Hong Kong
Printed and bound in Great Britain by TJ International Ltd, Padstow, Cornwall

British Library Cataloguing in Publication Data
A catalogue record for this book is available from the British Library

Library of Congress Cataloging in Publication Data
Agathangelou, Anna M.
   Transforming world politics : from empire to multiple worlds / Anna M. Agathangelou
and L.H.M. Ling.
      p. cm.
   Includes bibliographical references and index.
   1. International relations—Social aspects. 2. World politics—21st century. 3.
Neoliberalism. I. Ling, L. H. M. II. Title.
JZ1251.A33 2009
327—dc22

                                                                            2008040957

ISBN10: 0-415-77279-6 (hbk)
ISBN10: 0-415-77280-X (pbk)
ISBN10: 0-203-88033-1 (ebk)

ISBN13: 978-0-415-77279-2 (hbk)
ISBN13: 978-0-415-77280-8 (pbk)
ISBN13: 978-0-203-88033-3 (ebk)

to the next generation of multiple worlds

Mikael Lawrence, Aleksi Christos
and
Catherine, Emily, Mark, Sarah

Contents

Acknowledgements

Family, friends, colleagues, and students have helped us tremendously over the years. This book is very much a reflection of their love and support. We are grateful to you all.

We thank Rosemary Shinko for inviting us to present an early version of this book at the International Studies Association-Northeast Circle in 2005. We are most grateful to the Circle's discussants that year for their trenchant and insightful comments. Thanks, also, to the three anonymous reviewers who read the book proposal and provided us with excellent suggestions. We may not have followed up on every one, but their critiques have enriched this manuscript and our work more than they can imagine. Also thanks to Jutta Weldes and Heidi Bagtazo for working with us to see the book to fruition. And a special thanks to Cyril Ghosh who edited and proof-read the manuscript.

Anna is grateful to all the feminist and activist communities whose solidarity she has had along the years. She thanks more specifically: Sabah Alnasseri, Kristi Andersen, Apostolos Apostolou, Zehrat Arat, Morgan Bassichis, Pinar Bilgin, Shampa Biswas, Matt Bonham, Melissa Breton, Christine Chin, Lissa Chiu, Geeta Chowdhry, Carolyn Cross, Olga Demetriou, Gavan Duffy, Kostas and Phyta Evangelou, Helene Fuller, Sophia Georgiou, Barry Gills, Siba N. Grovogui, Suheir Hammad, Nadia Hasan, Marsha Henry, Paul Higate, Nikos Ilia, Naeem Inayatullah, Sarah Kaiksow, Barış Karaağaç, Barbara and Denny Keplinger, Kole Kilibarda, Anna Kim, Junji Koizumi, Abhinava Kumar, Eisei Kurimoto, Tae-Hwan Kwak, Nelson Lai, Robert Latham, Miqui Li, Derek Maisonville, David McNally, Ananya Mukherjee, Sheila Nair, Mustapha Kamal Pasha, Maria and Nikos Peristianis, Shirin Rai, Maita Sayo, Tamara Spira, Jennifer Sterling-Folker, Patrick Thaddeus-Jackson, Heather Turcotte, Sevgül Uludağ, Cindy Weber, Sandy Whitworth, Neshe Yashin, Magda Zenon, and a very special thanks to the whole department of Political Science at York University whose commitment to more viable and progressive politics embodies the connections and solidarities of multiple worlds.

Thanks also to my father and mother who consistently encourage me to continue struggles and work for the creation of multiple worlds and just polities. Their *agon* informs my own and instigates my commitment for justice. To my second set of parents, David and Sallie Killian, and sister, Kathy Killian, thanks for your presence in my life and your unwavering love and support. To my siblings, Christakis, Margarita, Maria, and their families: thanks for your love and great sense of humor and laughter which keeps me going! Thanks to my partner, friend and comrade, Kyle D. Killian for being there to encourage me to reach to greater heights and to be "free like the air." And, finally, but not least, I want to thank, out of the depths of my heart, my two sons – Mikael Lawrence and Aleksi Christos – who enable me to put things in perspective by reminding me of the relevance of that daily connection for forging any revolutionary solidarity. Otherwise, the struggle to a socio-ontological poetics of life remains just an idea.

Lily would like to mention the following:

Thanks to Mike Cohen, Jonathan Bach, Phil Akre, and Ashok Gurung for the congenial and productive working environment at the Graduate Program in International Affairs (GPIA) and the India China Institute (ICI) at The New School. They continue what is the best of The New School: its legacy of progressive, people-oriented politics.

Deep gratitude to the following for their intellectual, emotional, and psychic support: Bertha Kadenyi Amisi, Payal Banerjee, Pinar Bilgin, Stephen Chan, Boyu Chen, Fiona Chew, Geeta Chowdhry, Neta Crawford, Defne Turker Demir, Erica Dingman, Lucy Duddy, Tim Emmert, Katy Eppley, Cynthia Fagen, Volker Franke, Marianne Franklin, Nancy Fraser, Cyril Ghosh, Kasturi Gupta, Zac Hall, Marsha Henry, Paul Higate, Ginger C.C. Hwang, Habiba Jaffa, Rogan Kersh, Katarina Kozuchosvska-Duplessy, Maivân Clech Lâm, Steve Macedo, Michelle Materre, Yumiko Mikanagi, Maura Moynihan, Liane Newton, Timothy Pachirat, Valina Persaud, Eileen Raffo, Trix van der Schalk, Chih-yu Shih, Everita Silina, Ann Snitow, Gina Luria Walker, Bob Vitalis, Alys Willman, Hong Anh Thi Vu, Cindy Weber, I-Hsien Wu, Tina Yagjian, and Adriana Yoto.

An extra hug each to Patricia Robertson, Martha Bonham, and Shirin Rai: thanks for being there!

And to Gavan Duffy: it's beyond words.

Portions of this book have been published elsewhere:

- Agathangelou, Anna M. and Killian, Kyle D. (2006) "Epistemologies of peace: poetics, globalization, and the social justice movement," *Globalizations* 3(4): 459–483.
- Agathangelou, A.M. and Ling, L.H.M. (2005) "Power and play through *poisies*: reconstructing Self and Other in the 9/11 Commission Report," *Millennium: Journal of International Studies* 33(3): 827–853.
- Agathangelou, A.M. and Ling, L.H.M. (2004) "The House of IR: from family power politics to the *poisies* of worldism," *International Studies Review* 6(4) December: 21–49.
- Agathangelou, A.M. and Ling, L.H.M. (2004) "Power, borders, security, wealth: lessons of violence and desire from September 11," *International Studies Quarterly* 48(3) September: 517–538.

- Agathangelou, A.M. and Ling, L.H.M. (2003) "Desire industries: sex trafficking, UN peacekeeping, and the neo-liberal world order," *Brown Journal of World Affairs* 10(1) Summer/Fall: 133–148.
- Agathangelou, A.M. and Ling, L.H.M. (2002) "An unten(ur)able position: the politics of teaching for women of color," *International Feminist Journal of Politics* 4(3): 368–398.
- Hwang, C.C. and Ling, L.H.M. (2008) "The kitsch of war: misappropriating Sun Tzu for an American imperial hypermasculinity," in Bina D'Costa and Katrina Lee-Koo (eds) *Gender and Global Politics in the Asia Pacific*, London: Palgrave Macmillan.
- Ling, L.H.M. (2008) "Borderlands: a postcolonial-feminist approach to Self/Other relations under the neoliberal imperium," in Heike Brabandt, Bettina Rooss and Susanne Zwingel (eds) *Mehrheit am Rand? Geschlechterverhaeltnisse, globale Ungleichheit und transnationale Loesungsansaetze*. Wiesbaden: VS Verlag.

Series Editor's Preface

The final chapter of this volume, entitled "A play on worlds," concludes with a three-act play called "Othello's Journeys." The play begins with Othello, symbol of the classic subaltern man, "damned to eternal regret" by his murder of Desdemona and his own subsequent suicide. In a liminal after-death space, Othello encounters several unexpected interlocutors – the third-century philosopher Epicurus, the eighteenth-century feminist Vietnamese poet Hồ Xuân Hu'o'ng, the Greek mythological character Cassandra, and Lina, a twenty-first century professor of politics. By engaging with Othello and his despair and regret from their conspicuously diverse perspectives, his interlocutors encourage Othello to embrace his own location in multiple worlds and the attendant recognition that there are many different ways of understanding the world, and of being in it. Othello, transformed by the encounters, concludes: "Where once weak and broken, I am strong and whole!" As a result, Othello "sets forth with renewed vigor, confidence, and insight in himself and his multiple worlds." Interesting – quirky even – for an International Relations text, but what is this seemingly eccentric play-writing business all about?

This "play on worlds," drawing on Augusto Boals' notion of the theatre of the oppressed, "embodies what it claims to demonstrate," highlighting as it performs the dramatically distinctive approach to the analysis of world politics that Anna M. Agathangelou and L.H.M. Ling offer in *Transforming World Politics*. This approach, which they have dubbed "worldism," is unashamedly emancipatory: it wants to transform our way of understanding, and being in, world politics. In so doing, it challenges many of our most entrenched preconceptions about contemporary world politics as well as the most entrenched assumptions of the mainstream discipline of International Relations (IR). By starting with multiple worlds, particularly those of the subaltern, "it highlights the agency of all to participate in the making of their multiple worlds through multi- and trans-subjectivities, forming a community of syncretic growth, learning and co-transformation."

The target of *Transforming World Politics* is an IR discipline that the authors, like many others, find complicit in the savagery and injustice of contemporary world politics. As we are daily reminded, the practices of world politics seem to revolve around stark oppositions between "us" and "them" and the violences and injustices that such oppositions spawn. The

global "war on terror" that has been waged under U.S. guidance since
September 2001 is merely one recent, if in many ways shocking, case in
point. It exemplifies the unremitting cycles of violence and retribution that
come from an attitude that "they" must become, or be made to become,
like "us." Whether the mission is to civilise the barbarian, to counter total-
itarianism, to spread democracy, to bestow the benefits of market liberal-
isation, or to construct a global Ummah under Sharia law, the underlying
assumption is one of fundamental opposition. "We" are not safe, unless
"they" become like "us." Conventional IR scholarship reproduces this funda-
mentally binary vision of the world. With its underlying assumption of
oppositional relations between self and other, it both fosters and legitimizes
the dichotomous thinking that produces this unremitting violence. It takes
for granted that world politics is ultimately about struggles for power
and the preservation of "our" security against "them." As such, the authors
argue, the discipline of IR remains part of the problem, not the solution.
It cannot lead us towards peace and justice.

Agathangelou and Ling challenge this inherently violent vision of world
politics. Drawing on a wide range of critical social theory – notably
Marxism, Feminism, post-structuralism and post-colonialism, but also
Buddhism and Confucianism – their "worldist" approach begins with the
fundamental "entwinement" of, rather than the stark opposition between,
self and other. That is, it begins with the postcolonial insight that the contemporary world has been constructed, and continues to be constructed and
reconstructed, through intense and intimate relations between self and other.
While these relations are sometimes discordant and conflictual, they can
also be cooperative and sustainable. And they are always both complex
and mutable.

Part I of *Transforming World Politics* depicts and dissects the contemporary "neoliberal imperium." This neoliberal imperium, the authors
maintain, is a hegemonic project that both reflects and reproduces a complex set of social relations of power that encompass global capitalism,
the neoliberal state, the market economy, the patriarchal family and a
foundational ontology of Hobbesian fear and Lockean property. This form
of empire is based on particular constructions of race, gender, sexuality and
class, so that in the dominant U.S. discourse on the "war on terror," for
instance, the "civilization" that "we" must defend is "European, Christian,
white, capitalist, heterosexual, and patriarchal." This neoliberal imperium,
generally unchallenged by mainstream IR, pursues two goals: to become
the only world available to anyone anywhere and, simultaneously, to
expunge any and all alternative worlds.

Part II of *Transforming World Politics* presents worldism, an emancipatory project that seeks to bring about a "less violent, more global, and
sustainable world politics" by highlighting and celebrating multiple subjectivities and worlds. The ambitious goal of worldism is no less than to
"initiate a journey where agents of one world meet the horizons of those
from another, so negotiations could begin between 'us' and 'them' to build
a new 'we'." To achieve this goal, worldism offers distinctive ontological,

epistemological and methodological commitments that allow analysts to examine the social ontologies that comprise multiple worlds, to highlight interconnections and interdependencies, and to discover those "affinities and complementarities" that entwine multiple selves and worlds with each other. In making their arguments, the authors draw on such unusual and varied sources as the famous Chinese novel *Dream of the Red Chamber* and contemporary Greek poetry. The authors deploy worldism to rethink several significant contemporary international issues: the "Cyprus problem," U.S.-India-China relations, and the so-called "global war on terror."

While not all readers will be convinced, Agathangelou and Ling's *Transforming World Politics* offers an exciting alternative for those downhearted by the relentless violence and injustice of contemporary world politics, the traditional pessimism of conventional IR scholarship, and the sometimes stifling conventions of academic writing.

Jutta Weldes
University of Bristol

Introduction

"Hunt them down. Smoke 'em out."

George W. Bush, on the 9/11 attackers

"What the United States tastes today is a very small thing compared to what we have tasted for tens of years."

Osama bin Ladin, three weeks later

A binary of "Self" vs "Other" besets world politics, producing violence for all.[1] This binary convinces the Self that it has no option but to issue an ultimatum to the Other: convert or face discipline.[2] Under today's neoliberal imperium, conversion comes in the form of "liberalization," "democratization," "regime change," or "nation building." Discipline sometimes means outright military action. The latter may ensue even when the former succeeds.[3] Many who identify with the Other are, accordingly, fed up. They retaliate in kind, and this usually involves violence in a world already saturated with it.[4] Those who sympathize with the Self, in turn, seek more law and order, control and predictability. Efforts to convert/discipline the Other intensify and the cycle continues.

This book presents an alternative in worldism. It offers a vision of and approach to world politics based on a notion of "multiple worlds." These refer to the multiple relations, ways of being, and traditions of seeing and doing passed to us across generations. More than a postmodern sense of "difference," worldism registers the *entwinement* of multiple worlds: their contending structures, histories, memories, and political economies in the making of our contemporary world politics. These produce legacies of discord (e.g., Self vs Other) as well as complicity (e.g., selves in others, others in selves). Both account for the context of social relations that make world politics what it is. World politics thus serves as a site of multiple worlds where we can learn much about today's conflicts and challenges, as well as cooperation and sustainability.

We do not idealize multiple worlds or their consequences. Rather, we politicize them. Worldism acknowledges violence and oppression as central features of power politics. Yet this recognition compels us to embrace worldism even more. Despite all the carnage and chaos, death and destruction, the world lives on – not through the Self's conversions or disciplining of the Other, but the unending struggles, connections, adaptations, and innovations made by the Other to survive hegemony. This requires integrating what seems impossible to integrate – e.g., languages, norms, institutions, practices, and political economies – especially when such integration is prohibited by ruling elites. Indeed, ordinary peoples have been struggling in multiple worlds ever since first encountering one another. From the ancient silk roads to the central African trading empires to Alexander the Great's armies, we have been mixing, merging, and moving. The latest formations can be traced back almost 500 years ago when Europe's merchant ships, equipped with guns and bibles intended for trading, later turned into conquests of non-European Others, and eventually produced communities and subjectivities rife with violence ambiguity, endurance, and surprise.

Worldism aims not to counter the neoliberal imperium nor withdraw from it. Rather, worldism seeks to disrupt the imperium's hegemonic ontology and its socio-political practices – to demystify them – by demonstrating the existence of grander, more profound possibilities cumulated from a wider range of human experiences than the reductive, abstracted binary of Self vs Other. Reading the world with worldist lenses, we access the *intimacies* that bind selves and others, including those that battle within ourselves, so that we may recover and reconstruct for another day for another generation.

MAJOR CONCEPTS AND TERMS

Key to worldism are the following concepts and terms:

1 The Neoliberal Imperium. We refer to the neoliberal imperium as an overarching hegemonic project. It encompasses states, governments, classes, and sets of ideologies that work in tandem to validate one another. Specifically, the neoliberal imperium reflects and sustains a set of *social relations of power* expressed through daily interactions and the institutions that support them (e.g., global capitalism, the neoliberal state and its market, the patriarchal family, complicit knowledge production in the academy, an ontology of fear and property). On this basis, the imperium draws on and legitimizes neocolonial strategies of power based on race, gender, sexuality, and class to privilege the few at the expense of the many, despite the continuous exploitation of the latter to sustain the former.

Our treatment of empire differs significantly from that of Hardt and Negri's *Empire* (2000). Where they see empire as secure, universalizable, and certain, run by a self-regulating capitalist system, we present empire as a socio-political formation that attempts two goals simultaneously: (1) to establish itself as the only available possibility for all, and (2) to deny, dismiss, or erase other worlds. Hegemony thus is not just collusion between state and civil society institutions to preserve elite interests, as Gramsci theorized (Femia 1987), but also a systematic effort to wipe out all other ways of seeing, doing, being, and relating in the world. In particular, empire prohibits any admission that other worlds could have contributed to the making of its own world. Indeed, this understanding of empire accounts for why Hardt and Negri's *Empire* could become so popular among the bourgeois elite. As discussed in Chapter Three, an intellectual infrastructure that renders human agency invisible in producing empire relieves the imperium's leaders and managers, not to mention teachers and students, from assuming any culpability for the violent conduct and consequences that we face in world politics today.

2   **Race, Gender, Sexuality, and Class.** Issues of race, gender, sexuality, and class provide substantive *and* analytical centrality in worldism. Both are needed to understand how social relations structure institutions of power. For example, we look at a racial construction like "whiteness" and its ability to convey a sense of entitlement to the Self such that all Others fall short by default.[5] Not simply a cultural artifact, this "production of whiteness" reflects an economic and political infrastructure that connects the personal with the local, national, regional, international, and global. For this reason, the "global war on terror" becomes, as President George W. Bush declared on 22 August 2007, not just a "clash of civilizations" but a "struggle *for* civilization."[6] It would be fair to say that, for Bush, this means one "civilization" in particular and it is his: i.e., European, Christian, white, capitalist, heterosexual, and patriarchal. With the 2008 election of Barack Obama, the first African-American President of the US, we will have to see how this civilizational approach to the "global war on terror" will continue, if at all;

3   **Hypermasculinities/Hyperfemininities.** Ashis Nandy (1988) first diagnosed "hypermasculinity" as a cultural pathology under colonialism. To justify colonialism's "civilizing mission," the upper classes in England glorified acts of aggression, competition, power, and production as "manly" and denigrated "womanly" features like welfare, nurturing, kindness, contemplation, and consumption. In turn, elites in India, yoked by foreign occupation yet wanting to preserve their local hierarchies over domestic Others, sought to demonstrate India's own credentials for hypermasculinity. In this way, Nandy concluded, both colonizer and colonized suffered from a common "undeveloped heart." It infected each with racism, sexism, and a false sense of cultural homogeneity that, invariably, would erupt into daily, banal violence.

Here, hypermasculinity refers to a reactionary form of "hegemonic masculinity" (Connell 1995), flaring whenever it senses threat. Hegemonic masculinity comes from customary norms and practices. When agents of hegemonic masculinity feel threatened by outside forces, hypermasculinity arises by inflating, exaggerating, or otherwise distorting conventional understandings of masculinity. These eventually merge into a new strain of hegemonic masculinity. Bouts of hypermasculinity occur when patriarchal elites goad each other on, escalating the inflations, exaggerations, and distortions with each round.

Hypermasculinity *needs* hyperfemininity to perform but does not acknowledge this dependence and devalues it at the same time. Like hypermasculinity, hyperfemininity refers to a reactionary, radicalized version of conventional femininity when it seems under threat. Also like hypermasculinity, hyperfemininity eventually reformulates hegemonic femininity. During times of conflict, this process consolidates into a "moral economy of war" (Weber 2002) that leaves women, immigrants, and minorities with the worst jobs at the lowest pay (Sassen 1998). They also face the most abusive and systematic forms of collective violence, especially at urban sites undergoing rapid "development" (Holston and Appadurai 1996). As discussed in Chapter Two, hypermasculinity and hyperfemininity rationalize an "undeveloped heart" in the neoliberal imperium by satiating desire with violence, supplementing development with "desire industries," and security with militarization (Agathangelou 2004b, 2006).

Worldism does not ignore the allures of power. Rather, worldism opens up spaces for alternative ways of being, living, and doing that take us beyond the narrow confines of Self/Other, conversion/discipline, hypermasculinity/hyperfemininity. Doing so breaks down neoliberalism's insular sovereignty and its fixation on property and profits. On this basis, world politics can begin to shift from the seductions of empire to multiple worlds.

4 Postcolonial Theory and Worldism. Our analytical framework owes deep intellectual debts to Marxist and postcolonial theorizations. Worldism, however, also departs from them in significant ways. Chapter Five elaborates upon these convergences and divergences but we highlight a few points here.

A streak of Marxism runs through postcolonial theorizing. Postcolonial studies benefit from Marx's insights into the structural, material forces that shape society and its ideologies (Marx 1968, 1978). Marx's political commitment to a life with justice and dignity has inspired, also, generations of postcolonial theorists. In particular, worldism draws on two of Marx's critiques of the contradictions of capitalism: (a) the class and racial antagonisms that rationalize exploitation as employment, allowing profits to far exceed wages, and (b) capitalism's promises of material comforts at the cost of physical and emotional well-being for individuals as well as societies. As informed by Marx, alienation in worldism reflects "historically specific instances" of a "whole complex of social relations" rather than simply an economic byproduct (Rupert 1995: 15).

Contra Marx, however, worldism theorizes about the colonial condition and its aftermath, (neo)colonial and postcolonial legacies.[7] Colonialism and imperialism are not simply instruments of counter-capitalist revolution,as Marx considered them. Rather, worldism centralizes colonialism and imperialism as instigators of capitalist social relations that became embroiled with pre-capitalist ways of living and understanding to produce what we have today: an enduring mix of both. To analyze this mélange of cultures and structures, worldism turns to postcolonial studies.

Postcolonial studies originated in Literary and Cultural Studies in the 1980s. Since then, it has moved into the "soft" social sciences like History, Sociology, and Anthropology more easily than the "hard" ones like Political Science, International Relations (IR), or Economics. In particular, the

Subaltern Studies Group, composed mainly of scholars from South Asia, articulated a postcolonial historiography of British colonialism in India that turned inside-out mainstream understandings of this relationship, this period, and its significance for us today.[8]

Postcolonial theorizations retell the story of empire as the *relationship* between colonizer and colonized. Viewed dialogically, this perspective holds both colonizer and colonized accountable for the colonial condition that brought unanticipated consequences for both. More pointedly, post-colonial studies document the continuing legacies of the colonizer's relations with the colonized, showing the relevance of the past not only for the present but also for its implications for the future. Postcolonial theorists link the private (e.g., "household") with the public (e.g., "governance"); upstairs (e.g., "masters") with downstairs (e.g., "servants"); insiders (e.g., "pure breds") with outsiders (e.g., "hybrids"); the micro-personal (e.g., "sex") with the macro-structural (e.g., "power"); and today (e.g., "modernity") in relation to yesterday (e.g., "tradition") and tomorrow (e.g., "aspirations"). Categories such as "North," "South," "race," "gender," and so on are dis-assembled to help us understand and eventually transform the transnational forces that shape their formations in the first place.

IR theorists have applied postcolonial theory to film and other forms of cultural analysis (see Paolini 1999). While insightful, these treatments represent global life as text only and fall short of addressing its more concrete and pressing problems. Not content to limit postcolonial theory to historical and cultural critique, a new generation of postcolonial scholars in IR questions institutions of power more directly (Persaud 2001; Ling 2002b; Chowdhry and Nair 2002; Edkins 2003; Agathangelou 2004b; Franklin 2005). For example, they ask: How would postcolonial theory explain poverty and exploitation, racialized and sexualized class relations, war and insecurity within as well as across national borders? What kind of transformative politics and policies could a postcolonial understanding of race, gender, sexuality, and class offer?

Worldism signals a possible next step. It makes explicit the multiple worlds presumed by postcolonial theorizing. That is, the multi- and trans-subjectivities embodied by selves and others, most recently, in the colonies but coming from older encounters as well like those on the Silk Roads (fourth century BC–sixteenth century AD). Worldism inquires even further. It examines the social ontologies that comprise these multiple worlds and the legacies of power and survival they leave behind through discourses, insti-tutions, structures, and practices. Ontologically, worldism springs from and points to the multiple social ontologies that give meaning to social relations and account for their contestations entwinements, and transformations.

Epistemologically, worldism draws on the Greek notion of *poisies*. The term generally refers to "creativity" and/or "poetic inspiration" in the English-speaking world. We return *poisies* to another construction preval-ent in Greek thought: that is, the self reverberates with others to construct their mutual subjectivities communally. We use *poisies* here as a site, a kind of social relation, and a socio-ontological formation (Agathangelou and

Killian 2006). Similar treatments can be found in other traditions as well, such as Buddhism's *pratītyasamutpāda* ("co-dependent arising") and Confucianism's *ren* ("humaneness," "sociality"). These dialectical traditions give insight into how syncretic engagements take place. Like hermeneutics, syncretic engagements initiate a journey where agents of one world meet the horizons of those from another, so negotiations could begin between "us" and "them" to build a new "we." In this way, not just one, abstract definition of community but multiple, *lived* ones emerge in daily intercourse, affirming multiple worlds.

Methodologically, worldism focuses on the social relations that make worlds.[9] We coin the term "relational materialism" (Agathangelou 2004b). Like its Marxist precedent of historical materialism, relational materialism grounds world-making in the materiality of human struggles for survival both at the micro-personal level (e.g., "worker" and "capitalist") as well as macro-structural ones (e.g., "global capitalism"). Our reference to relational materialism, though, is not restricted to what Marx called the "relations of production" – that is, those social formations that emerge from structures of capitalist production. Rather, relational materialism emphasizes that *all* history-making, whether capitalist or pre-, micro-personal or macro-structural, derive from a socially-constructed material base. Put differently, economic structures are themselves instantiations of social relations just as social relations come into being and are perpetuated by material structures. One cannot operate in isolation from the other.

Worldism thus bears two dimensions: a descriptive process of daily life and an analytical project for an emancipatory world politics.[10] As a descriptive process, worldism involves the following:

1   *multi-* and *trans-subjectivities* that emerge from reverberations between selves and others,
2   *agency* in all parties to make the world, including relations of inequality and injustice as well as recovery and reconstruction,
3   *syncretic engagements* that enable the "border crossings" (Mignolo 2000) or "interstitial learning" (Ling 2002b) needed to develop new ways of thinking, doing, being, and relating, and
4   *community-building* that integrates and sustains multiple worlds despite barriers imposed by hegemony's leaders and managers.

As an analytical project, worldism adds three qualifiers:

1   *accountability* marks worldist inquiry to ensure
2   an internal *criticality* to question, contest, and challenge hegemony, so that worldist approaches to world politics could
3   disrupt strategies of empire or any other kind of hegemony to ensure *emancipatory reconstructions* even as we recover new, less violent worlds.

Fiction and poetry help us express these worldist commitments. Just as Edward Said found politics in art and literature so we draw on art and literature to articulate politics – especially its socio-ontologies – where connections, struggles, and solidarity matter more than separations and dominance. Fiction and poetry provide a space to critique *and* reconstruct our worlds by voicing, seeing, understanding, and bridging the differential locations and subjectivities of selves and others. Of course, fiction and poetry can also serve hegemonic purposes. Rudyard Kipling's life work immediately comes to mind. Worldism, however, helps us read fiction and poetry in ways that reveal the ontological legacies that give meaning to social relations and their interaction. Specifically, a worldist reading of fiction and poetry helps us politicize social relations *critically*, thereby unleashing creative possibilities for change previously unimagined.

OUTLINE OF BOOK

This book proceeds in two parts. Part I identifies the neoliberal imperium: what it is and why it can seduce us into accepting, if not submitting to, its violence. Part II presents worldism: what it is and how it can bring about a less violent, more global, and sustainable world politics.

Chapter One focuses on the politics of erasure that come from the binary of Self vs Other. The attacks on 11 September 2001 (hereafter "9/11") exemplify the retaliatory spiral that can result, even for a global hegemon like the US, when the Self believes it has only one option toward the Other: conversion and/or discipline. We show, for example, reactive[11] jousts between US President George W. Bush and al Qaeda leader Osama bin Ladin and how this hypermasculine competition affects the rank and file in their respective communities. International organizations like the United Nations (UN) seek to broker peace but offer no mechanism, in language or principle, to negotiate with Others. In recognizing only one world – its own – the neoliberal imperium demands that all Others adhere to its principles, norms, rhetoric, and practices. Other traditions matter only so long as they demonstrate the imperium's claims of tolerance, pluralism, and fair representation. As an example, this chapter dissects the "debate" at the UN between the US and Iraq on the eve of the former's invasion of the latter. We conclude with an analysis of the 9/11 Commission Report (2004). It demonstrates, again, the politics of erasure by affirming the need to convert/discipline the Islamic Other, initially through education and, if that fails, then military might. This chapter ends with a query: Why do we allow the politics of erasure to prevail?

Chapter Two stresses: neoliberal desire accounts for neoliberal violence. Promises of the good life secure compliance from elites and masses alike despite the imperium's resort to systematic coercion. Even al Qaeda, which vows to destroy the "Great Satan" US, borrows guerrilla tactics from the neoliberal world market. Indeed, desire's critical role in sustaining the imperium fans "desire industries" throughout the globe, especially as the state militarizes and securitizes against those very Others who populate these sectors: e.g., the migrant workers who toil in homes, fields, factories, offices, "entertainment establishments," even military bases. As the imperium's guards, UN peacekeeping missions facilitate and use these "desire industries," turning bodies, not just geographies, into frontiers of neoliberal–neocolonial plunder (Agathangelou 2009). Still, what accounts for the *normalization* of neoliberal desire and violence in the global political economy and our daily lives?

Chapter Three examines complicity with empire at one site of knowledge production: the academy. In particular, we focus on the field of IR. Looking at the social relations behind the field's main schools of thought, we analogize IR to a colonial household: i.e., it erects borders between a Western, enlightened, and patriarchal Self against all Others. "Acceptable" Others are relegated to the House's downstairs quarters, serving as "native informants" for the upstairs "theorists" who draw on these resources selectively and expeditiously (e.g., when "crises" erupt) to theorize for all. "Non-acceptable" Others are exiled outside the House despite intimate relations with and contributions to members inside the House. Like its colonial counterpart, the House of IR seems more solid than it actually is. The need to prevent underlying relations from dismantling and redefining the House requires a constant upkeep that, invariably, falters over time. Even so, why does the House of IR command such intellectual tenacity?

Chapter Four unearths the ontological origins of the House of IR: i.e., Hobbesian fear and Lockean property. From its classical forbears in realism and liberalism to contemporary advocates of neoliberalism, the ontology of fear and property aims to domesticate the Other by assimilating it into the Self's standards for civilization, accumulation, and progress. Kipling's "White Man's Burden" (1899) epitomized this rationale. Neoliberalism updates it with a cooler, hipper façade as represented by the 2006 slogan of a global icon of corporate capital: "Welcome to the Coke side of Life."[12] Economic crises expose the neoliberal imperium's brio for violence. This chapter notes, for example, how neoliberal institutions in North America and Western Europe immediately indicted Asia's former "miracle" economies for "crony capitalism" during their financial meltdown in 1997–98. At the same time, these same institutions applauded the US government and corporate sector for "facing down" widespread corruption scandals, exposed in Enron's wake, two months after 9/11. Since the wars in Iraq and Afghanistan, multi-billion dollar contracts have rehabilitated many of these same corporations to install "regime change" and "nation-building."

Part II introduces worldism.

Chapter Five articulates a *relational ontology* for worldism. Specifically, worldism reflects the relations among multiple worlds and their social ontologies. Their interactions give rise to world politics as a site of solidarities and alternatives alongside and despite conflicts and contestations.[13] This chapter also explains worldism's epistemology in *poisies* (as well as other traditions) and methodology in relational materialism. In delineating worldism's main features, we identify their immediate intellectual precedents in constructivism, postmodernism, and postcolonial-feminism. An older lineage pertains as well. Here, worldism learns *poietically* from the insights and trials of philosophers and revolutionaries from China, Greece, India, and Japan, as well as other sites of colonial/imperialist violence, who attempted to reconcile multiple worlds/civilizations in world politics. Given all this, what does worldism look like and how do we actualize it?

Chapter Six forwards fiction and poetry as an exploratory method for worldism. We begin with China's most famous novel, *Dream of the Red Chamber* or *Honglou meng* (circa 1750s) to illustrate worldist logics. Excerpts from contemporary Greek poetry extend such logics to show how social relations can be reconstituted to disrupt hegemonic violence. This chapter also discusses recent calls for a "linguistic" or "artistic" turn in IR. It argues that onto-poetics, specifically, and aesthetics, generally, shape the world while describing it. Worldism elaborates upon this insight. From our readings of *Honglou meng* and Greek poetry, we locate selves and others interacting with one another reverberatively, contrapuntally, rotationally, oppositionally, and iteratively. These types of social relations reveal the "affinities and complementarities" that bind even seemingly die-hard opposites like Self and Other, providing the potential for less violent change and reconstruction. How do these principles and their insights work in world politics?

Chapter Seven applies worldism to three sites of contemporary world politics: (a) the "Cyprus problem," (b) US–India–China "triangulation," and (c) the "global war on terror." Convention considers each an intractable conflict between mutually hostile, if not alienated, subjects. With worldism to provide analytical guidelines, we suggest possibilities for (re)seeing, (re)feeling, and (re)thinking. We do so by locating and expanding upon the multi- and trans-subjectivities that exist within each site, the agency of each community to rebuild despite hypermasculine desires for revenge or retribution, and the syncretic engagements that draw upon complicity for change rather than reject the complicity as simply reinforcement for the *status quo*. Of course, we do not – and cannot – claim to present the field with a complete, polished template to solve the world's problems. Such a proposition is not only absurd but would repudiate the very principle of open-ended, deliberative engagement that worldism represents. Rather, we propose worldism as a vision, an orientation, a method, a set of epistemes even, that we hope will spur much creative thinking and doing.

What now of the neoliberal imperium? How does worldism make a difference?

Chapter Eight returns to those issues raised in Part I. With worldist lenses on, we take a second look at the imperium's politics of erasure, its justification of violence with promises to satiate desire, the complicities of knowledge production, and the imperium's foundation in an ontology of fear and property. We realize that the neoliberal imperium cannot deliver on what it promises. It limits us to a worldview and a way of life that curtails our own creativity, energies, and possibilities for change, emancipation, and freedom. Worldism offers an alternative to empire not by discarding or dismissing it. Rather, we seek to engage the imperium to show that the binary of Self vs Other occupies but one small corner of humanity. In so doing, we disrupt the imperium's violences, thereby opening the opportunity to transform it.

In this spirit, we engage Parts I and II of the book *poietically*, in the form of a play. It allows us to address the seductions of empire without centering it. Our play focuses on Shakespeare's *Othello*. For us, Othello symbolizes the classical Subaltern Man, a character forged by empire's racialized power and damned to eternal regret due to the violence committed onto and by him. In our play, Othello enters the Liminal Realm after having murdered his love, Desdemona, and killed himself ("*O miserable and eternal brute, I have killed that which I loved most!*"). Othello self-justifies that at least he had serviced his state ("*I smote that malignant Ottomite, the Turk*").[14] Still, he admits to defeat, pain, and shame ("*I remain perplex'd in the extreme*"). But Othello is not alone. The third century philosopher, Epicurus, and an eighteenth century feminist poet from Vietnam, Hồ Xuân Hu'o'ng, appear to help Othello journey from his "demise" to flourish in a more connected and loving alternative to life and power, especially for the next time around. Other characters like Cassandra, and Lina, a twenty-first century professor of politics, also appear to engage with Othello on the major issues that plagued his life. Othello thus sets forth with renewed vigor, confidence, and insight in himself and his multiple worlds.

We are ready for this reassessment. Not by pure coincidence do we see an embodiment of multiple worlds in Barack Obama, an heir to but not imprisoned by Othello's legacy. Instead, Obama is a socio-political phenomenon paved by the struggles of others, as noted in his autobiography *Dreams from My Father*, yet open-ended to the struggles still to come.

A PERSONAL NOTE

Worldism is not just an abstraction for us. It is about our own political biographies as well as those of generations who came before and those who will follow. Though derived from specific civilizational locations (Greek and Chinese), our experiences speak to all those identities and histories deemed "peripheral" to contemporary world politics due to their "traditional" ("non-Western") attributes. We challenge the notion that only "modern" ("Western") assimilations can qualify for full participation in world politics. At the same time, we contest the idea that all we need to do is return "traditional" ideas and practices to world politics, for these bear their own share of alienation, violence, and abuse. Again, we know this only too well, having grown up in geopolitical and cultural sites (Cyprus and Taiwan) considered "peripheral" to what convention construes as their "glorious" originals.

In the field of IR, specifically, we have experienced first-hand the alienation and erasures that come from a one-world perspective: e.g., our attempts to forge community in a discipline that views scholarship as an individualized endeavor, produce new thinking in a knowledge field that favors the mainstream, and present alternative visions and practices in a world polity that prefers to carry on "as usual."

We need a world-rich paradigm for world politics, one that accounts for all who make our worlds. At the same time, this world-rich paradigm must acknowledge that silencing may still occur; accordingly, it must be checked with a criticality that stems from the *relations* among multiple worlds, not a hierarchical and violent positioning of one over others. We seek, then, a world politics that builds communities not break them down, that produces ways of celebrating life not violating it, that connects in solidarity to speak truth to power not excuse it, and that creates alternatives for future generations not condemn them to war and destruction.

Part I
The neoliberal imperium

1 Politics of erasure

> there have been no words.
> i have not written one word.
> . . . .
> not one word.
>
> Suheir Hammad, "first writing since" (2001)[1]

World politics reels with hegemony. Mainstream analysts typically cite Thucydides' line as warrant: "The strong do what they can, the weak suffer what they must." Relations in world politics thus fall into two distinct categories: the (strong) Self sets "the rules of the game" for the (weak) Other to play. Should compliance fail to ensue, or worse, should outright violation occur, the Self must discipline the Other. "The Athenians killed all the men and enslaved all the women and children" – so ends the chapter on Melos in the *History*. Realists and liberals use these few lines to justify our contemporary world politics under the neoliberal imperium. Some push "soft power" (Nye 2004) to sweeten the promises of prosperity and equality in a "capitalist peace" (Gartzke 2007). Still, the fundamental stricture of Self vs Other remains.

International institutions like the UN cannot help. Supposedly an arbiter of fair representation, free speech, due process, and democratic voting for the world community, the UN actually proxies for the neoliberal imperium by centering liberal internationalism as the institution's only, legitimate discourse for debate.[2] Other norms, practices, and traditions cannot participate as equal sources of consideration or impact. This flush of imperialist victory, however, fades even as it begins. The exiled now vows to redeem glory and dignity with more violence. These jousts of vanity and power invariably take on the form and structure of hypermasculine competition, exploiting the same pool of subjugated and marginalized populations: e.g., women, children, workers, peasants, and other "minorities."

This chapter discusses three recent instances of the politics of erasure: (a) Bush and bin Ladin in the aftermath of 9/11, (b) the US/Iraq "debate" at the UN, one month before the US invaded Iraq, and (c) the 9/11 Commission Report (2004). Each exemplifies the violent consequences of the Self's attempts to erase the Other.

We begin with 9/11.

NINE ELEVEN

> ... Today is a week, and seven is of heavens, gods, science.
>   evident out my kitchen window is an abstract reality.
>   sky where once was steel.
>   smoke where once was flesh ...

On 11 September 2001, terrorists struck at the heart of the capitalist world order. The attack and its targets demonstrated with horrendous efficiency that neither global wealth (World Trade Center) nor military might (the Pentagon) defends against low-tech, human sacrifices when the latter are mobilized. For this reason, some US leaders have used 9/11 to generalize a sense of insecurity across the globe. Three conventions established after the end of the Cold War now seem suspect: viz., "US power reigns supreme," "borders dissolve in a globalized world," and "liberal capitalism secures prosperity, democracy, and stability for all." The rest of the world has always asked, "Whom can we trust?" Now, those at the center of the capitalist world order wonder: "How can we feel secure again?"

We must rethink "international relations." The charred remains of the World Trade Center (WTC) and Pentagon compel us to review power as more than just economic or military superiority. Had the terrorists restricted themselves to this traditional, realist notion, they would have needed the backing of a state[3] or access to huge arsenals of military hardware to execute their plan. They relied, instead, on box-cutters and a suicidal guerrilla tactic. Their comrades in the caves of Afghanistan brandished little more than outdated American and Soviet firepower.

Many also declared borders are obsolete under the state-straddling, market-binding strategies of neoliberal globalization. Yet 9/11 dramatized the sovereignty of borders in our minds. The terrorists attacked US hegemony to "protect" but really to isolate Islamic culture and religion; likewise, the tragedies in New York and Washington, DC, have reinscribed borders in the popular American imaginary, now translated into a "global war on terror." Assumptions about national security and national wealth also crumbled in light of 9/11. How could the world's richest, most heavily-armed state – the only global superpower – be so *vulnerable*?

9/11 legitimates what has always swarmed world politics: hypermasculine competition. It comes through reactive discourses as well as tit-for-tat displays of power, as demonstrated by Bush and bin Ladin, respectively, representing the US and al Qaeda. Each camp draws on a common pool of hyperfeminized resources to produce more fodder for their competition, whether it is through breeding more babies for war or, paraphrasing Gayatri Spivak, having white women "liberate" brown women from brown men for white people. Meanwhile, dissent is censored as "unpatriotic" or "unfaithful," depending on the patriarchal community in question. A Self-involved, Self-delusional consumerist politics follows, turning on its head what constitutes "legitimate" violence. Bombings of whole nations, for example, do not qualify as using weapons of mass destruction (WMDs). Similarly, goading young people to undertake suicide bombings for particular political causes turn into acts of faith and fidelity.

A caveat: we recognize that Bush and bin Ladin, along with their respective allies, do not occupy parallel levels of or access to violence in world politics. Al Qaeda cannot match the economic, political, and military resources possessed by the US state. What binds Bush and bin Ladin, instead, are their mutually-embedded, retaliatory strategies of hypermasculine competition in world politics.

Hypermasculine competition for violence

Bush and bin Ladin

Nine days after the 9/11 attacks, President George W. Bush addressed a joint session of Congress to outline America's "global war on terror" and to finger Osama bin Ladin as its chief suspect. bin Ladin responded with a videotape broadcast on 7 October 2001 by Al-Jazeera television based in Qatar.

The two speeches share remarkable similarities. Each leader targets the Other as the cause of violence and destruction in the world, generally, and against his own country or people, specifically. They declare that the Other must be defeated or killed. Each leader presents the collective Self as innocent, victimized, virtuous, moral, and rational; the enemy Other, as demonic, murderous, and barbaric. Both leaders conclude that militarization must be transnationalized. A moral imperative to national or communal security, each proclaims, is to take care of one's own.

Note these six common themes:

1. Virtue, Truth, and Centrality vs Murderous Envy. For each camp, the Self's virtue, truth, and centrality incite a murderous envy in the Other. The terrorists hate America, Bush explained, because of their sense of *lack*:

   > They hate what we see right here in this chamber, a democratically elected government. Their leaders are self-appointed. They hate our freedoms – our freedom of religion, our freedom of speech, our freedom to vote and assemble and disagree with each other.
   > (Bush 2001a)

   For bin Ladin, "infidels" seek to destroy what they cannot possess: that is, an unwavering, Islamic Self who is endowed with Truth. America is "morally depraved" because it "champion[s] falsehood, support[s] the butcher against the victim, the oppressor against the innocent child" (bin Ladin 2001b). bin Ladin further suggest that the US consolidates its hegemony by clubbing all Others, including non-Arabs, non-Muslims. Referring to the US atomic bombings of Hiroshima and

Nagasaki, bin Ladin charged that "[h]undreds of thousands of people, young and old, were killed in the farthest point on earth in Japan. [For the Americans] this is not a crime, but rather a debatable issue" (bin Ladin 2001b). But the faithful will prevail despite the infidels' evil tricks. "He whom God guides is rightly guided but he whom God leaves to stray, for him wilt thou find no protector to lead him to the right way" (bin Ladin 2001b);

2. Innocent Victim vs Irrational Barbarity. Victimization by this envious, irrational Other demands retributive justice. Bush referred, of course, to the official tally of 2,801 dead or missing on 9/11.[4] The US is an innocent bystander to world affairs he told the nation but time has come for military action: "Tonight we are a country awakened to danger and called to defend freedom" (Bush 2001a). Once roused, the American giant will spare no means to punish its offenders.

    bin Ladin portrayed all Muslims as innocent victims of US aggression. Conveniently discarded from the world's public memory, America's acts of aggression are *for no apparent reason* other than to exert raw power, thoughtlessly applied. For example:

    > [Islam's] sons are being killed, its blood is being shed, its holy places are being attacked, and it is not being ruled according to what God has decreed. Despite this, nobody cares.

    > One million Iraqi children have thus far died in Iraq although they did not do anything wrong.

    > [I]sraeli tanks and tracked vehicles also enter to wreak havoc in Palestine, in Jenin, Ramallah, Rafah, Beit Jala, and other Islamic areas and we hear no voices raised or moves made.

    > [The Americans] bombed Iraq and considered that a debatable issue.
    > (bin Ladin 2001b)

3. Rationality vs Radicalism. For Bush, the terrorists personify Evil. They seek to shatter the secure, prosperous world-order that America upholds. If the terrorists have a goal, then it is for the abominable purpose of remaking the world in their radical self-image:

    > These terrorists kill not merely to end lives, but to disrupt and end a way of life . . . Al Qaeda is to terror what the mafia is to crime. But its goal is not making money; its goal is remaking the world, and imposing its radical beliefs on people everywhere.
    > (Bush 2001a)

    Bush carefully distinguished Good Arabs/Muslims from Bad Arabs/Muslims. The former are America's "many Arab friends;" the latter, "a radical network of terrorists and every government that supports them" (Bush 2001a). He recuperated "good Arabs" as those who comply with his version of the law; "bad Arabs" are those who violate it.

Furthermore, according to Bush, al Qaeda's terrorists "blaspheme the name of Allah" (Bush 2001a) by perverting their own people and society in the name of religion:

> Afghanistan's people have been brutalized; many are starving and many have fled. Women are not allowed to attend school. You can be jailed for owning a television. Religion can be practiced only as their leaders dictate. A man can be jailed in Afghanistan if his beard is not long enough.
>
> (Bush 2001a)

bin Ladin denounced the American Demon categorically. There are only bad Americans and they pollute the world with an arrogance and hypocrisy that know no bounds:

> They came out in arrogance with their men and horses and instigated even those countries that belong to Islam against us.
>
> They came out to fight this group of people who declared their faith in God and refused to abandon their religion.
>
> They came out to fight Islam in the name of terrorism.
>
> (bin Ladin 2001b)

4. The World Must Choose. Each camp demanded an unequivocal decision from the world: the righteous "Self" vs the murderous "Other," "civilization" vs "barbarity," "the faithful" vs "the infidels."

> Either you are with us, or you are with the terrorists.
>
> (Bush 2001a)

> [There is] one [world] of faith where there is no hypocrisy and another of infidelity, from which we hope God will protect us.
>
> (bin Ladin 2001b)

5. Globalized Militarization is a Moral Imperative. Both camps justified globalizing militarization as a *moral/cultural* imperative for attaining their respective desires ("national security" for Bush; "Islamic honor and integrity" for bin Ladin). For Bush, Al Qaeda's attack on America recalls one Sunday in 1941" (Bush 2001a).

For bin Ladin, the US deserves 9/11. He praised the attackers as a "successful . . . convoy of Muslims, the vanguards of Islam [whom God] allowed . . . to destroy the United States" (bin Ladin 2001b). For this reason, justice in any form is acceptable: "May God mete them the punishment they deserve" (bin Ladin 2001b). Let the American Demon now suffer what the Islamic Self has had to endure since colonial times:

> What the United States tastes today is a very small thing compared to what we have tasted for tens of years. Our nation has been tasting this humiliation and contempt for more than 80 years.
>
> (bin Ladin 2001b)

bin Ladin issued a promise and a threat:

> As for the United States, I tell it and its people these few words: I swear by Almighty God who raised the heavens without pillars that neither the United States nor he who lives in the United States will enjoy security before we can see it as a reality in Palestine and before all the infidel armies leave the land of Mohammed, may God's peace and blessing be upon him.
>
> (bin Ladin 2001b)

6. We Take Care of Our Own. Bush established a new cabinet-level office, Department of Homeland Security, to protect America and Americans from future terrorist attacks. Evoking a sense of national unity reminiscent of World War II and the Great Depression, the President appealed to the American people to normalize their lives with the following guidelines:

    a. *Take care of your family.* "I ask you to live your lives and hug your children."
    b. *Stay loyal.* "I ask you to uphold the values of America, and remember why so many have come here."
    c. *Be tolerant of Others.* "We are in a fight for our principles, and our first responsibility is to live by them. No one should be singled out for unfair treatment or unkind words because of their ethnic background or religious faith."
    d. *Donate time and money.* "I ask you to continue to support the victims of this tragedy with your contributions."
    e. *Cooperate with law and order.* "The thousands of FBI agents who are now at work in this investigation may need your cooperation, and I ask you to give it."
    f. *Comply with those who seek to protect you.* "I ask for your patience, with the delays and inconveniences that may accompany tighter security – and for your patience in what will be a long struggle."
    g. *Help the economy by spending money.* "I ask your continued participation and confidence in the American economy. Terrorists attacked a symbol of American prosperity. They did not touch its source."
    h. *Pray for victims, the military, and the country.* "Finally, please continue praying for the victims of terror and their families, for those in uniform, and for our great country."

    (Bush 2001a)

bin Ladin urged ". . . every Muslim [to] rush to defend his religion." He commended the terrorists for sacrificing themselves for their "oppressed sons, brothers, and sisters in Palestine and in many Islamic countries." He concluded: "I ask God Almighty to elevate their [the terrorists'] status and grant them Paradise. He is the one who is capable to do so" (bin Ladin 2001b).

In sum, Bush and bin Ladin affirmed that the Self is irreconcilably opposed to the Other. This allowed for a massive deployment on *moral* grounds for militarization on a transnational scale since, as with all dichotomies, the superiority of the first term (Self) justifies dominance over the second (Other). Logic required, then, for Bush to call for a "war on terror;" and for bin Ladin, a "global *jihad*." Each sought to increase national/communal security but, as the next chapters will show, just the opposite resulted given the binary of Self vs Other.

The UN could not adjudicate between these reactive camps of hypermasculine competition. The organization itself was confined to one discursive tradition and its practices: i.e., liberal internationalism.

DEBATE AT THE UN

> today it is ten days. last night bush waged war on a man once
> openly funded by the
> cia. i do not know who is responsible. read too many books, know
> too many people to believe what i am told.

Hammad urges us to have a more nuanced understanding of different peoples. But the UN can hear only one voice and that is the Anglo-American, liberal one. Founded on classical liberal principles and staffed with those vested in the neoliberal imperium, the UN inherently favors this tradition over others. Those from different juridico-political and ethical traditions such as Islamic law, for example, may speak but they cannot be heard *on their own terms*. The "debate" between former US Secretary of State Colin Powell and then Iraqi Ambassador to the UN, Mohamed Aldouri, on the eve of the US invasion of Iraq, serves as a case in point.

"A web of lies"

"It is all a web of lies."[5] On 5 February 2003, US Secretary of State Colin Powell accused Iraq of guilt and duplicity: that is, Iraq possessed WMDs in direct violation of UN agreements and sought to hide this fact. Lasting about an hour and a half, Powell drew on "solid sources" that disclosed "disturbing patterns of behavior." He began with taped phone recordings of Iraqi military personnel, supposedly plotting to hide WMDs, then moved to US satellite pictures of so-called mobile WMD factories on the ground, eyewitness accounts from detainees and informants of Iraqi manipulations and maneuverings to cover up their WMDs, and UN inspectors' reports.

Powell began with the following premises:

1. Iraq had *consistently* duped the world. ("This effort to hide things from the inspectors is not one or two isolated events, quite the contrary. This is part and parcel of a policy of evasion and deception that goes back 12 years, a policy set at the highest levels of the Iraqi regime."); and,
2. Saddam Hussein was evil because:

a. he lied ("Saddam Hussein and his regime are not just trying to conceal weapons, they're also trying to hide people").

b. he *had* WMDs ("There can be no doubt that Saddam Hussein has biological weapons and the capability to rapidly produce more, many more").

c. he had used them before and on his own people ("Saddam Hussein's use of mustard and nerve gas against the Kurds in 1988 was one of the 20th century's most horrible atrocities; 5,000 men, women and children died").

d. Saddam also had nuclear weapons ("[W]e have more than a decade of proof that he remains determined to acquire nuclear weapons").

e. Saddam's government was as corrupt as he was ("We know that Saddam's son, Qusay, ordered the removal of all prohibited weapons from Saddam's numerous palace complexes. We know that Iraqi government officials, members of the ruling Baath Party and scientists have hidden prohibited items in their homes. Other key files from military and scientific establishments have been placed in cars that are being driven around the countryside by Iraqi intelligence agents to avoid detection . . . Yet, to this day, Iraq denies it had ever weaponized . . .").

f. Saddam had experimented on people ("[S]ince the 1980s, Saddam's regime has been experimenting on human beings to perfect its biological or chemical weapons").

Powell set Iraq against the US, the UN, and the world with the following dichotomies:

1. Bad Iraq vs Good UN. Iraq's guilt was presumed and not open to examination. ("Resolution 1441 was not dealing with an innocent party, but a regime this council has repeatedly convicted over the years.") Powell referred to Iraq's failure over the years to comply with international demands for a full accounting of its military capability. ("They failed that test. By this standard, the standard of this operative paragraph, I believe that Iraq is now in further material breach of its obligations. I believe this conclusion is irrefutable and undeniable.") In contrast, the UN represented the common good. Its inspectors had no political agenda. They were "impartial experts." ("We laid down tough standards for Iraq to meet to allow the inspectors to do their job.") But if the UN did not take action, Powell warned, it risked becoming irrelevant. ("[T]his body places itself in danger of irrelevance if it allows Iraq to continue to defy its will without responding effectively and immediately.");

2. Cooperative Disarmament vs Noncooperative Armament. Since "the international community" had decided that Iraq's disarmament would indicate cooperation, then a reverse judgment also applied: that was, a lack of such cooperation *necessarily* meant that Iraq was re-arming

or hiding its WMDs. ("Everything we have seen and heard indicates that, instead of cooperating actively with the inspectors to ensure the success of their mission, Saddam Hussein and his regime are busy doing all they possibly can to ensure that inspectors succeed in finding absolutely nothing");

3. US Sovereignty vs Iraqi Sovereignty. Any act of Iraqi sovereignty thus violates international law. ("The regime only allows interviews with inspectors in the presence of an Iraqi official, a minder. The official Iraqi organization charged with facilitating inspections announced, announced publicly and announced ominously, that, quote, 'Nobody is ready to leave Iraq to be interviewed'.") In contrast, the US *is* international law by authoring it. ("We wrote 1441 not in order to go to war, we wrote 1441 to try to preserve the peace. We wrote 1441 to give Iraq one last chance. Iraq is not so far taking that one last chance");

4. Mature US vs Puerile Iraq. Iraq did not deserve sovereignty. It was an *enfant terrible* that threatened itself, the region, and the world. Powell nested these subsidiary arguments within the main one:

   a. Iraq jeopardized itself. Saddam's ambition threatened his own country and people. ("Nothing points more clearly to Saddam Hussein's dangerous intentions and the threat he poses to all of us than his calculated cruelty to his own citizens and to his neighbors. Clearly, Saddam Hussein and his regime will stop at nothing until something stops him.")

   b. Iraq jeopardized the region. Saddam's ambition also threatened to engulf the entire Middle East. ("For more than 20 years, by word and by deed Saddam Hussein has pursued his ambition to dominate Iraq and the broader Middle East using the only means he knows, intimidation, coercion and annihilation of all those who might stand in his way.")

   c. Iraq jeopardized the world. Not just the citizens of Iraq or the Middle East, but the whole world had suffered from Saddam and his terrorist cronies. ("Our concern is not just about these illicit weapons. It's the way that these illicit weapons can be connected to terrorists and terrorist organizations that have no compunction about using such devices against innocent people around the world.") Citing these examples, Powell argued that Iraq lacked the maturity and rationality to handle WMDs. In contrast, Powell underscored the maturity of the US as a global power. It alone knew what was "really" going on inside Iraq. For this reason, Powell allied the US with the UN on one side, as defenders of global justice, and Iraq with terrorist organizations like al Qaeda, on the other, as instigators of global injustice;

5. UN/US/Global Justice vs Iraq/al Qaeda/Global Injustice. Powell began by proclaiming an affinity between Iraq and various terrorist organizations, especially al Qaeda. Saddam Hussein's Iraq, Powell charged, gave

safe haven to al Qaeda, the group responsible for the 9/11 attacks. Powell dismissed critics who claimed that the secularist regime in Iraq could not ally with ultra-religious organizatons like al Qaeda (Lander and Cowell 2003; Miller and Preston 2003). "Ambition and hatred are enough to bring Iraq and Al Qaeda together," he declared. Powell insisted that Iraq supported other terrorist groups that threatened the peace and stability of "the international community." ("Hamas, for example, opened an office in Baghdad in 1999, and Iraq has hosted conferences attended by Palestine Islamic Jihad. These groups are at the forefront of sponsoring suicide attacks against Israel.") These affinities are contrasted with those that substitute the US for the UN, representing global justice. At first, Powell paid homage to the UN as the final arbiter of the case. ("[H]ow much longer are we willing to put up with Iraq's noncompliance before we, as a council, we, as the United Nations, say: 'Enough. Enough'?") Then he explicitly equated the US with UN interests, thereby portraying them as one and the same. ("My colleagues, we have an obligation to our citizens, we have an obligation to this body to see that our resolutions are complied with.") Powell ended with a call to shared duties and obligation for global justice. ("We must not shrink from whatever is ahead of us. We must not fail in our duty and our responsibility to the citizens of the countries that are represented by this body.")

Powell effectively negated the Iraqi Other with the US/UN Self. His testimony placed a law-abiding, mature US/UN concerned with global justice in direct contradiction to an abusive, infantile Iraq that could not understand its responsibilities to the world community. Such logic required, accordingly, an act of discipline and containment by the US/UN Self against the Iraqi Other. Though unsuccessful in obtaining official UN support for military action against Iraq, Powell did succeed in persuading the US Congress to vote in favor of unilateral action against Saddam's regime.

The US dropped 3,000 bombs and missiles on Baghdad within the first 48 hours of its invasion on 20 March 2003 (Coile 2003). Civilian casualties mushroomed, Saddam fled, and Iraq collapsed six weeks later.

"Incorrect allegations"

The Iraqi rebuttal was brief.[6] "We had wished we were granted sufficient time," so began Iraq's ambassador to the UN, Mohammed Aldouri. "Nevertheless," he continued, "Iraq will provide detailed and technical responses to the allegations made in that statement."

Aldouri denied Powell's allegations:

1. Iraq never possessed WMDs. US Secretary of State Colin Powell's charges, Aldouri retorted, were full of "incorrect allegations, unnamed sources, unknown sources." For evidence, Aldouri cited Saddam Hussein.

("His excellency, President Saddam Hussein, reiterated in his interview granted yesterday to former British minister Tony Benn that Iraq is totally free of weapons of mass destruction, a statement written by numerous Iraqi officials for over a decade.");

2. Iraq was neither guilty nor duplicitous. Aldouri emphasized that Iraq had complied with UN demands for full disclosure of its military arsenal. ("Iraq submitted an accurate, comprehensive and updated declaration of 12,000 pages, including detailed information on previous Iraq programs, as well as updated information on Iraqi industries in various fields.") These inspections had been thorough. ("As of February 4th of this year, the inspection teams had conducted 575 inspections all over Iraq, covering 321 sites.") They demonstrated Iraq's "innocence." ("This confirms Iraq's declaration that it is free from weapons of mass destruction and that its declaration is truthful and accurate.");

3. Iraq did not support al Qaeda. Aldouri rejected any connection between Iraq and al Qaeda. Again, he cited Saddam Hussein for evidence. ("As for the supposed relationship between Iraq and the al Qaeda organization, I would note what his excellency, President Saddam Hussein, said. I quote: 'If we had a relationship with al Qaeda and we believe in that relationship, we would not be ashamed to admit it. We have no relationship with Al Qaeda', end of quote.") The US Central Intelligence Agency (CIA) and British intelligence, Aldouri noted, had confirmed Iraq's lack of connection with al Qaeda; and,

4. The US was not the UN. Aldouri distinguished the UN from the US. He tried to emphasize that the UN could operate on its internationalist mandate whereas the US sought to interfere and manipulate. ("[Powell] could've left the inspectors to work in peace and quiet to ascertain without media pressure.") Aldouri counter-charged that the US and the UK deliberately sabotaged the case against Iraq before the world community. ("Ongoing inspections have shown that previous allegations and reports from the United States and Britain were false.") Indeed, Aldouri declared, the US lied. Powell's so-called "facts," he dismissed, were specious at best. ("It is important for me to remind that programs for weapons of mass destruction are not like an aspirin pill, easily hidden. They require huge production facilities, starting from research and development facilities, to factories, to weaponization, then deployment. Such things cannot be concealed. Inspectors have crisscrossed all of Iraq and have found none of that"). US interest, Aldouri further charged, was world domination starting with Iraq:

> [T]he clear goal behind holding this meeting, behind the presentation of the secretary of state of the United States of false allegations before this council today, is to sell the idea of war and aggression against my country, Iraq, without any legal, moral or political justification. It is an attempt to convince American public opinion first and world public opinion in general to launch a hostile war against Iraq.

Aldouri concluded with two affirmations. Iraq, he stated, "offers security and peace," a characterization exactly counter to that presented by the US. Aldouri reiterated Iraq's commitment to cooperate with the UN inspection teams so they could verify Iraq's good standing ("free of weapons of mass destruction"). He asked that the UN release Iraq from undue punishment ("lift the unjust sanctions . . . [and] ensure respect of [Iraq's] national security and ensure regional security") and confront, instead, the *real* threat in the region ("the huge arsenal of weapons of mass destruction in Israel"). Aldouri ended by calling for compliance with UN strictures for legitimate action ("the provisions of paragraph 14 of Security Council resolution 687 of 1991").

Despite the spirited language, Aldouri's arguments were defeated from the start. In his own words, his argument could only focus on "detailed and technical responses." Aldouri had no alternative normative discourse to dislodge what he recognized, along with the rest of the world: that the US allegations were pretexts to war. Equally important, Aldouri did not have the discourse to differentiate *how* Iraq's arguments differed from the Anglo-American liberal ones or the structural leverage to explain *why* negotiations were needed across these normative divides.

Aldouri could not alter the Self vs Other discourse imposed by the US. He could only contest and deny the allegations against Iraq. On the two occasions when Aldouri cited Saddam Hussein, the very person "on trial" at the UN, as the source for his evidence, the Iraqi ambassador irrevocably damaged his case. Aldouri also tried to differentiate the UN from the US: the former as a forum for the international community; the latter, one state only. This was an understandable strategy given that he was making his case before the former. But his narrative failed to persuade on two counts. First, as the world's only superpower, the US enjoyed an overwhelming structural and discursive advantage at the UN; accordingly, it set the context and criteria for the debate, thereby influencing its outcome. Aldouri's counter-accusations of US malfeasance and Israel's openly-acknowledged arsenal of WMDs, among others, seemed a distraction at best. Second, Aldouri's attempt to demonstrate Iraq's compliance with UN inspections could not counter US allegations of noncompliance given the latter's access to its own, highly sophisticated technology and "expert" resources, as demonstrated by Powell's presentation. Powerful US satellites far outweighed whatever the UN inspectors could find on the ground, knocking from door to door. Clearly, underlying power relations overdetermined the US invasion of Iraq despite making it jump through the hoops of "reporting" its WMDs to the "international community." Not surprisingly, the "debate" between these two asymmetrically-located yet politically-equated subjects turned into a one-sided performance of US power.

Member states at the UN vetoed the US demand for military action. But given the discursive hegemony of liberal internationalism, they could reason only within the boundaries of this discourse. France cited "respect for law," "defense of freedom and justice," and "spirit of dialogue and tolerance" to account for its veto.[7] China simply refrained from formal statements. The public record thus retained the singular voice of Anglo-American liberalism.

The *9/11 Commission Report* (hereafter "the Report") reproduced the same institutional deafness to Others, this time through policy recommendations.

The 9/11 Commission Report (2004)

> and when the networks air footage of palestinians dancing in the street, there is no apology that hungry children are bribed with sweets that turn their teeth brown. that correspondents edit images. that archives are there to facilitate lazy and inaccurate journalism.
>
> and when we talk about holy books and hooded men and death, why do we never mention the kkk?

The Report sought to explain why a bunch of stateless terrorists, wielding low-tech weapons, were able to wreak havoc on the world's sole super-power. The Report concluded on a seemingly magnanimous note that the Islamic world needs more and better education about America and Americans. Once "they" know "us" better, the Report reasoned, the "war on terror" could be won (The Report 2004: 367, 375–378). Any and all venues should be used: radio, television, textbooks, scholarships, exchange programs, foreign aid.

Violence, however, undergirds the Report, particularly in its construction of Self/Other relations. It presented the Muslim terrorist Other accordingly:[8]

1. Arabs and Muslims are sorely "uninformed" about the US due to cartoonish stereotypes inundating the region. They need proper inculcation in the Anglo-American liberal virtues of "[t]olerance, the rule of law, political and economic openness, the extension of greater opportunities to women" (The Report 2004: 362–363);
2. bin Ladin and al Qaeda are categorically evil and maniacal. At the same time, they are yahoos and bumblers. An incurable irrationality undermines whatever diabolical plans they may have. Even sympathetic governments in the region have expelled them (The Report 2004: 55–63);
3. bin Ladin is a rich, spoiled charlatan. He's valued more for his money than his leadership or religious devotion (The Report 2004: 55); and,
4. Followers of bin Ladin/al Qaeda are similarly misled, mistaken, or misguided, at best, or deranged, at worst. They like to blame the US, the "Great Satan," for all their problems when they should look closer to home. These frustrated, underemployed young men really need jobs but are frenzied into a mob by greedy, irresponsible governments/leaders (The Report 2004: 52–54, 63, 362). It is the story of eccentric and violent ideas sprouting in the fertile ground of political and social turmoil (The Report 2004: 48).

The US Self, in contrast, was portrayed as innocent, peaceful, and global:

1. The US is an innocent bystander to world politics even though it is the world's largest economy and only superpower. Indeed, the US has little to do with the political, economic, and social violence experienced by generations in the Arab/Muslim world (The Report 2004: 51) "To us, Afghanistan seemed very far away. To members of Al Qaeda, America seemed very close. In a sense, they were more globalized than we were" (The Report 2004: 340);
2. America reflects the world. "[T]he American homeland is the planet" (The Report 2004: 362). The US seeks order and peace by "engaging other nations in developing a comprehensive coalition strategy against Islamist terrorism . . . The most important policies should be discussed and coordinated in a flexible contact group of leading coalition governments" (The Report 2004: 379); and,
3. The US *has done nothing wrong*. Grievances against the US have no validity. Whatever complaints the terrorists have qualify more as the pent-up frustrations of the unemployed, the envious, and the uneducated (The Report 2004: 340). They are the "losers" of globalization whereas, the US is the all-time winner. But America's good fortune has made these malcontents turn envy into rage, rage into hatred, and hatred into terrorism. The US is the victim of not just a physical attack but also a moral injustice. America's "openness" and "generosity" have been repaid with wanton destruction. The Islamic terrorist Other must be out of his [sic] mind, out of control, and/or simply out of it (The Report 2004: 362).

Implemented or not, the Report's recommendations reinforce the binary of Self vs Other. Unfettered by governmental regulation or accountability, the private sector in US-occupied Iraq and Afghanistan take Self vs Other to its logical extent (see Calaguas 2006). Note, for example, the indiscriminate killing of Iraqi civilians by guards employed by Blackwater USA, a private military firm (Glanz and Tavernise 2007). Such actions predictably provoke anger from locals. Many now take up arms against the US occupiers. In January 2005, Iraq's director of intelligence services revealed that insurgents numbered as many as 200,000, outnumbering US military troops in the country (Hider 2005). He explained:

> People are fed up with no security, no electricity, people feel they have to do something. The army (dissolved by the American occupation authority) was hundreds of thousands. You'd expect some veterans would join with their relatives, each one has sons and brothers.
>
> (Hider 2005)

The Bush Administration's "surge" of 20,000 in 2007 increased US troops in Iraq to 200,000 (Cordesman 2007). A related "surge" in Iraqi troops, however, "has lagged badly in effectiveness, if not in numbers" (Cordesman 2007: 17). As of November 2006, attacks by insurgents and/or terrorists in Iraq have increased to almost 200 strikes per day.[9] As of 4 March 2008, US military casualties in Iraq, both wounded and dead, numbered 29,320 according to official statistics (but estimated at 23,000–100,000 by unofficial sources), an increase of almost 7 percent since the war began in 2003.[10] The same applies to Afghanistan. "In the spring of 2006," the *New York Times* reports, "the Taliban carried out their [sic] largest offensive since 2001," resulting in a quintupling of suicide bombings and doubling of roadside bombings (Rohde and Sanger 2007: 1, 12–13). "All told," the report continues, "191 American and NATO troops died in 2006, a 20 percent increase over the 2005 toll" (Rohde and Sanger 2007: 13).

The US Department of Defense claims the insurgents are either self-interested mercenaries or victims of local warlords (Garamone 2007). But a small article in the 5 August 2007 issue of the *New York Times* suggests there might be another motivation at play. It notes that the Army convicted a US soldier of a March 2006 rape and murder of a 14-year-old Iraqi girl, including the murders of her parents and younger sister. After raping the girl, the soldier (one of five conspirators) "poured kerosene on her body and set it on fire in an attempt to hide evidence of the crime" (von Zielbauer 2007). Given the history of US military atrocities, especially rape, in locales like Okinawa, South Korea, the Philippines, and other parts of East and Southeast Asia during the Cold War (see Ling 2002b), it is not hard to imagine why both men and women in Iraq and Afghanistan, not to mention the rest of the Islamic world, would support hypermasculinity as the standard of the day. As Osama bin Ladin declared on 7 October 2001: "What the United States tastes today is a very small thing compared to what we have tasted for tens of years."[11]

CONCLUSION

... over there is over here ...

but i know for sure who will pay.

in the world, it will be women, mostly colored and poor. women will have to bury children, and support themselves through grief. "either you are with us, or with the terrorists" – meaning keep your people under control and your resistance censored. meaning we got the loot and the nukes.

The UN could not give a fair hearing to Iraq. US discursive and structural hegemony ensured a condition that Foucault called "constitutive exteriority" (Deleuze 1988: 43). Others *must* speak, act, and think in terms of exterior (i.e., neoliberal) rules, norms, values, and rhetoric. By definition, then, Iraq became exiled as war-mongering, noncompliant, and irrational. No other definitions or possibilities could be aired, leaving issues of social inequity and injustice conveniently silenced for the leaders, managers, and generals of global capital.

The outcast Other, then, takes its struggle for respect, if not parity, "outside." There, a reactive-parallel discourse of hypermasculine rivalry rages on. Five years of war and occupation, insurgencies and bombings, thousands of lives and billions of dollars later, what do we find? Certainly not WMDs in Iraq. Nor is there any evidence, as determined by the 9/11 Commission Report, of links between Saddam Hussein and al Qaeda.

Yet, the neoliberal imperium beats on. Despite all the violence, neoliberal elites manage to expand the imperium's reach. The 9/11 Commission Report is but one example. How do they do it? Equally important, why do "we," the imperium's object-subjects, let them get away with it? Neoliberal desire, we suggest.

2 Desire and violence

> I think the whole world addicted to the drama
> Only attracted to things that'll bring you trauma
>
> Black Eyed Peas, "Where is the Love?" (2003)[1]

The politics of erasure benefits a global political economy of desire and violence. It peddles race, gender, sexuality, class, and nationality for a supposedly better world and life through neocolonial images, means, and social relations. As noted by the Black Eyed Peas, a rap-rock group, "the whole world [is] addicted to the drama [of] things that'll bring you trauma." In these brief, two lines, they highlight how contemporary capitalism intersects with desire and security to produce mesmerizing, spectacular possibilities that are intertwined with suffering, hatred, and despair. Consequently, we are diverted from asking "Why?" This chapter amends this lack of attention.

The imperium of neoliberal globalization promises to deliver equality, prosperity, and happiness to all but on one, unequivocal condition: i.e., the Other must emulate the Self (but never really catch up). To ensure this ideological and structural double move, the neoliberal imperium relies on linking various kinds and levels of violence – physical, institutional, cultural – to cull consent while claiming to satiate desire.

This chapter examines the militarizing of daily life now officially sanctioned after 9/11. A gendered and racialized division of labor, both domestically and internationally, turns the bodies of men and women into frontlines of neoliberal globalization. These easily shade into sex trafficking and other "desire industries" that now proliferate throughout the globe. The connection between sex and security becomes most explicit when UN peacekeepers facilitate and participate in sex trafficking.[2] These activities do not operate in a vacuum. They draw on a prior history of socio-cultural constructions of race, gender, sexuality, and class in world politics. They prepare colonizers and colonized alike for exploitation, demonstrating more than any single activity or industry the central relations of capital to power in the constitution of empire.

MILITARIZING DAILY LIFE

Transnationalizing insecurity militarizes daily life. The state or community looms large like a garrisoned, patriarchal household that claims to protect women, children, and other subjugated ("weak") subjects from rapacious "outsiders." Yet it is precisely the silent, hyperfeminized labor and surplus resources of women and subjugated subjects that enable such hypermasculinized security in the first place. Racializing and gendering labor further contains dissent by shackling men and women, physically and ideologically, to imperial rule. Since 9/11, Bush and bin Ladin have deployed this kind of empire-building in parallel ways: i.e., the former in neoliberal terms; the latter, in fundamentalist, religious ones.

Hypermasculinity/hyperfemininity: neoliberal and fundamentalist-Islamic versions

As mentioned in Chapter One, Bush invoked eight guidelines for the American people to remain "normal." These recall traditional maxims to the law-abiding housewife, concubine, or mistress. Her mission in life: to maintain a happy home for husband and children. Who could disparage such a cozy scenario? Other politicians jumped onto the same thematic bandwagon: "go shopping" (former New York City Mayor Rudolph Giuliani), "buy that car" (Senate Majority Leader Tom Daschle), or "take that trip" (US Senator John Kerry). A television commercial shown shortly after 9/11, sponsored by the Travel Industry Association of America, superimposed images of "ordinary folks" from hotels, restaurants, airlines – all the tourism industries that suffered from the attacks – repeating Bush's line that economic consumption "takes care" of the national family.

The national-security state thus pushes and lulls citizens into sacrificing for it. They are asked to spend scarce resources despite increased income disparities and rising unemployment in the face of unprecedented corporate profits, especially in the oil industry. And these trends have continued, if not deepened. The *New York Times* reported on 29 March 2007 that "income inequality [in the US] grew significantly in 2005, with the top 1 percent of Americans – those with incomes that year of more than $348,000 – receiving their largest share of national income since 1928" (Johnston 2007), one year before the stock market crash that triggered the Great Depression. Similarly, *The Guardian* noted on 3 July 2008 that US unemployment was at its worst since 2002 (Seager 2008). Yet profits for oil industry giants like Exxon Mobil soared to $40.6 billion in 2007, according to the 1 February 2008 issue of *US News & World Report* (Lavelle 2008).

Likewise, bin Ladin claims to preserve the "true" Islamic nation. His sovereign homeland comes from a way of life guided by conservative Islam. But nowhere in his speeches, interviews, videotapes, or pronouncements does he offer an alternative to oppression, exploitation, hierarchy, intolerance, or poverty. Nor does he articulate an Islamic path to economic development that will improve people's lives. He suggests only an other-worldly vision of Islamic "paradise" attained through "*jihad*." For this earthly domain, he seeks a modern, technically-sophisticated economy (especially drawn from the global arms trade) but delinked from the West.

Both camps brand their agendas of hypermasculine/hyperfeminine competition on the bodies of men and women.

Men's bodies

The battlefield affects men's bodies most directly but first come notions of masculinity. Since 9/11, America's newfound concern for Afghan women has been accompanied by a swelling re-appreciation, announced in the *New York Times*, for "[b]rawny, heroic, manly men" (Brown 2001: 5). These are exemplified by ". . . stoic, muscle-bound [firefighters and police officers] . . . exuding competence from every pore . . ." (Brown 2001: 5).[3] The venerable newspaper quoted what seemed to be a growing, national sentiment: "[T]here's a longing for manliness. People want to regain what we had in World War II. They want to believe in big, strapping American boys" (Brown 2001: 5). Given the military's racial segregation during World War II and mainstream America's general neglect of heroic duty undertaken by its "colored troops," both African and Asian-American, these images implicitly evoke "big, [white] strapping American boys."[4]

bin Ladin's call for "martyrdom" makes a parallel historical erasure. Men contribute their physical lives to reorder the chaos wreaked by centuries of imperial desires from the West. Simultaneously, bin Ladin wants to reclaim Islam's injured masculinity from the West:

> [O]ur brothers who fought in Somalia . . . saw wonders about the weakness, feebleness, and cowardliness of the US soldier . . . They want to deprive us of our manhood. We believe that we are men, Muslim men who must defend the greatest place in existence, the Holy Ka'ab. We want to have the honour of defending it. We do not want American women soldiers . . . defending the grandchildren of [Muslim leaders] . . . The rulers in that region have been deprived of their manhood. And they think that the people are women. By God, Muslim women refuse to be defended by these American and Jewish prostitutes.
>
> (Ramazani 2001)

bin Ladin decries the West as "depriving" Islam of its manhood. At the same time, he hypersexualizes American and Jewish women soldiers by concocting them into "prostitutes." bin Ladin shifts from his seeming concern for Islamic manhood to assigning women to serve his version of the greater Islamic good, rather than their empowerment or welfare.

> [Death] takes on a meaning suffused with "masculinity" because death, power, and political representation are closely intertwined. While death has always been an important motif, in the context of political oppression it becomes a dramatized scene of subjectivity and empowerment

... It is through the "otherness" of femininity and its domestication that men gain subjectivity and agency in the scene of martyrdom ... Women enter the fundamentalist reconstruction of the past always in the form of wives, mothers, daughters, not as individuals.

(Moallem 1999: 336–337)

Women's bodies

Women's bodies are used, additionally, to mystify elite privilege. Bush appropriated a liberal feminist understanding of woman to bolster his case against the woman-hating bin Ladin/al Qaeda/Taliban (Bumiller 2001b: B2).[5] Yet no such commitment preoccupied the Administration before 9/11, despite mounting evidence of Taliban misogyny.[6] Afghanistan's underground women's organization, the Revolutionary Association of Afghan Women (RAWA), charged the US government with turning a blind eye to the Taliban's fundamentalism and misogyny, perhaps even abetted it, to expel the Soviet occupation of Afghanistan and secure an oil pipeline through Central Asia (RAWA 2001).[7] The Bush Administration itself admitted that women comprised 50 percent of government workers, 70 percent of school teachers, and 40 percent of doctors in pre-Taliban Afghanistan (Bumiller 2001a: B2).

Despite all this liberating, the female Other remains a silent, inscrutable object of desire. Notwithstanding the Bush administration's promises, no women were represented at the post-Taliban, nation-building talks held in Bonn, Germany, in November–December 2001, although two women were appointed to a post-Taliban government.[8] Indeed, contemporary media outlets like *National Geographic* have popularized an image of the Muslim woman as a half-veiled, muted waif, eyeing the white-male world beseechingly and remotely. This motif reflects a longstanding, Orientalist tradition of treating the female Other as young (underdeveloped), appreciative (subordinate), and tantalizingly mysterious (inscrutable) (see Ling 1999).

al Qaeda exploits a more particular form of femininity: i.e., woman as reproductive machine. bin Ladin and his cohorts assume without question that committed women of Islam would supply human fodder for their cause. Note this quote from a 35-year-old conservative Muslim mother, speaking defiantly to a US journalist shortly after the 9/11 attacks:

> In the name of God, I will sacrifice my son, and I don't care if he is my most beloved thing. For all of my six sons, I wanted them to be *mujahedeen*. If they get killed it is nothing. This world is very short. I myself want to be a *mujahid*. What will I do in this world? I could be in heaven, have a weekly meeting with God.

(Addario 2001: 38)

One wonders, after the journalist leaves, what this mother really thinks and feels.

Hypermasculine certainty masks an underlying insecurity. Muslim women's very status as objects of desire – that is, as mothers who reproduce sons – renders them vulnerable to rape by "infidels." As Patricia Molloy (1999: 306) has noted, "it is through desire, [understood as] the self's relation with the Other, that security is lived . . . [W]arfare functions as not only a gendered, but a racialized practice of securing desire."

An unspoken logic ensues. The more radical conservatives like bin Ladin and the Taliban reduce women to little more than baby-breeders, the more they need to war against a mythologized, rapist white-male West/ America.[9] So much for bin Ladin's terrorism campaign veiled as the path to "paradise." A reverse logic operates as well. The more the West and America demonize radical Islam as full of mythical misogynists, the more they find themselves compelled to "liberate" not just women but whole societies. So much for Western/American colonialism reframed as "secularization," "democratization," "regime change," and "nation building."

MILITARIZED, SEXUALIZED GLOBALIZATION

Neoliberal globalization militarizes and sexualizes life in general.[10] Chang and Ling (2000) note that globalization's "public," hypermasculinized face of "techno-muscular" developments in production, technology, media, and finance rely on and yet marginalize its supply of "private," hyperfeminized globalization: i.e., a "regime of labor intimacy" focused on the home and other reproductive economies fueled by the migration of predominantly women workers from poorer to richer economies. In 2006, 200 million migrants sent home $300 billion in remittances amounting to "nearly three times the world's foreign-aid budgets combined" (DeParle 2007: 52). In the Philippines, the country with the longest and most extensive policy of labor exportation for development, migrants account for a seventh of the country's gross domestic product ($15 billion/year).[11] A World Bank study finds that remittances to developing countries increased from $31.2 billion in 1990 to $167 billion in 2005, roughly double that of official aid flows.[12]

Militarized features show up most blatantly at peripheral sites of neoliberal production. The Mexican government's "new economy" combined with forced migration has led to the mechanization, fragmentation, and compartmentalization of indigenous and feminized subjects (*campesinos*) in US/Mexico export processing zones (EPZs) (Agathangelou 2004a). As feminized and racialized workers are driven to the border from economic necessity, they are moved into forms of labor that objectify and mechanize their bodies. One method of gender surveillance, for example, is a constant "pregnancy check": i.e., those found pregnant are fired or laid off (Staudt 2006). Additionally, countless women have been murdered or raped in Ciudad Juarez, one of Mexico's largest *maquiladora* factories.[13] Lacking protection from the state, their employers, or even basic infrastructure such as lit roads from factory to home, *campesinos* in southern and rural Mexico endure violence on a daily basis while, at the same time, facing increased obsolescence at the hands of Mexico's neoliberal developmental program. Yet international and multinational interests continue to collaborate with state militaries and paramilitaries, overrunning regions such as Chiapas, to "stabilize" their mutual investments.[14]

Indigenous women in war-torn countries like Guatemala are affected in yet another way. Fearful of being identified as "dissidents," "guerrillas," or "terrorists," they opt for anonymity, which makes them vulnerable to sex trafficking, especially in frontier areas (Norwegian Refugee Council 2001). Women are caught between a lack of proof of "citizenship," which they need to get reparations for "damages" (the term used in government documents), and a fear of having to reveal their identity as Indians, or non-whites, that would expose them to discriminatory treatment from the very governmental agencies mandated to protect them (Willman-Navarro 2006).

Local patriarchal elites seethe against "injustices" from the West but they excuse their own form of gender/sexual exploitation in the name of "tradition," "religion," "development," or "entitlement." National indus-trialization strategies institutionalize this regime of female exploitation by selling women as "docile," "cheap," and "expendable" labor – whether for a factory at home, a household overseas, or a brothel anywhere. One rationale overrides all objections: the patriarchal family/state must be saved from personal or national debt (Brown 2007). That this is accom-plished through direct, bodily sacrifice by generations of women around the world underscores the dualities of hypermasculinity and hyperfemininity that constitute the neoliberal world order. Many of these women and girls now believe that this is the way things are and always will be, making them prime targets for sex trafficking.

SEX TRAFFICKING

"Crises" expose intersections of race, gender, sexuality, and class in neoliberal globalization. After the fall of the Soviet Union in the late 1980s, for example, women accounted for two-thirds of the unemployed in Russia and the former Soviet republics (Bridger, Kay, and Pinnick 1996). Underemployed in the formal economy, women were "ripe" for sexual exploitation in the informal sector. Large and small-scale trafficking net-works mushroomed to recruit women and girls from both urban and rural areas throughout the region. Hotels, airlines, and charter companies often colluded with the state, directly or indirectly, to facilitate the trafficking of women. Advertising, the Internet, magazines, and tourism brochures, also aided in the process.

The International Organization for Migration (IOM) estimates that "up to 500,000 women a year are brought into Western Europe and forced into the sex industry. Other estimates place the figure as high as one million" (Hyland 2000).[15] Where former socialist economies once provided cradle-to-grave welfare, newly capitalist enterprises now seek to streamline their budgets by eliminating workers deemed too old, inadequately skilled, and/or requiring maternity leaves and child-care expenses. Such cuts largely target women. Even those women who could find employment in the formal economy face unequal wages, job discrimination, and outright sexism in the workplace.

An \$8 billion/year global business, sex trafficking prostitutes almost four million women, girls, and boys daily (*Trafficking in Persons Report* 2005). The United Nations Children's Fund (UNICEF) reports that 33,000 children work in the sex industry in Cambodia,[16] for instance, abetted by an explosion of tourism in recent years.[17] "[Using] up women, physically and emotionally, [sex trafficking] necessitat[es] fresh supplies of women on a regular basis [to keep] the recruitment and trafficking of women so profitable" (Hughes 2000: 6). Lately, trafficking travels both ways: clients find sex workers by going "out there" (Mullings 2000) as much as sex workers seek clients by coming "in here," as "entertainers," "artists," and "mail-order brides," or under some other rubric (Captive Daughters 2005).

Race is trafficked along with sex. Capital's constant search for more sources of cheap labor alters the subjects of sexual branding and their internal hierarchies. Russian women in the Mediterranean, for example, command higher prices for sex work than earlier waves of prostitutes primarily from South and Southeast Asia. Clients who, twenty years ago, considered the bodies of Filipinas, Arabs, and Latin Americans as "exotic" and "desirable" now view them as "black," good enough only for domestic work (Agathangelou 2004b, 2006).

Officials seek to deflect their complicity with sex trafficking by claiming it is under control, if not eradicated. In 1999, for example, local police in Ukraine busted a prostitution ring between Eastern Europe and the Mediterranean where 200 Ukrainian women and girls, aged 13–25, were being shipped to Turkey, Greece, and Cyprus for the sex industry. Traffickers received \$2,000 for each woman. The women were held in bondage until they repaid their expenses. If they complained, their debt was tripled (Hughes 2000). All three states remain complicit in sex trafficking through migration laws and importation of domestic and sex workers. Yet the trafficked persons – the ones usually deprived of all this money-making – are blamed for the violence, coercion, and exploitation that they endure daily.

How do the trafficked themselves see their role in the desire industries? We hear from three trafficked women in Cyprus, a Mediterranean gateway for prostitution and sex trafficking. Their voices underscore the coercion, desperation, and assault on human dignity that sex trafficking entails:

> I met an impressario through a friend of mine who worked in Greece before. I went to him – he asked me to pay him \$2,000 dollars and he promised me a lot of money in three months. And here I was in this cabaret with an old man. He wanted me to go with clients for "consummation," he said. When I realized what he meant I said "I do not want to." He screamed at me, "What do you want to do? Just sit around?"

I entered Turkey along with 13 other women. We came here with a Russian guy who knew where to take us through the port of Trabzon. Once we arrived at the border, two Turkish guys took us to a cabaret where guys walked in and picked us up for . . . you-know-what.

Several of us women from Russia, Georgia, and the Ukraine were told that if we wanted to go to Turkey we could make a lot of money. We just had to pay $2,500 to this Chechen guy and he can get us visas. That's what we did. And I ended up in Laleli with 20 other women forced to work in a hotel without any freedom. I worked there for 2 months and then I escaped. I made enough money, but I hated my boss who charged the clients so much money because I was Russian and he gave me 1/3 of what I was earning.

(quoted in Agathangelou 2004b: 56–57)

State agencies tend to focus more on crime and "violated" borders rather than the conditions of work for migrant women (Agathangelou 2006). This criminalization of migration makes it more dangerous for women while, at the same time, failing to protect them from daily violence. They are forced to depend on the very institutions that already see and treat them as a problem in civil society (Lindo 2006). This dilemma sharpens in "transitional" and "post-conflict" societies.

SEX AND PEACEKEEPING

"Transitional" and "post-conflict" societies are especially ripe for sex trafficking and peacekeeping. They have the demand (the presence of large and long-staying peacekeeping troops), supply (surplus women workers), and *need* ("underdeveloped economies"). The United Nations Transitional Authority in Cambodia (UNTAC), for instance, increased local prostitution in Phnom Penh 3.5 times in two years (1992–93), with 25 percent of its peacekeepers returning home HIV positive (Byrne, Marcus, and Power-Stevens 1996). These peacekeepers left behind a generation of children who, due to their mixed parentage, are often rejected by their own communities and thereby subject to the sex trade. Sex networks now mushroom throughout the globe (see Lindstrom 2004). In 2001, the Associated Press in Eastern Europe reported: "[UN] officers [secretly] forged documents for trafficked women, aided their illegal transport through border checkpoints into Bosnia, and tipped off sex club owners ahead of raids" (Kole and Cerkez-Robinson 2001). Apparently, Serbs and Albanians in the region could overcome political-ethnic differences to collaborate in sex trafficking, grossing $1.5 million per week (Kelmendi 2001).

Similar scenarios recur throughout the UN peacekeeping network.[18] These raise apprehension within the UN about peacekeeping's internal management as well as public relations. Today, the annual UN peacekeeping budget amounts to $4 billion to cover 17 global missions; its central office includes a mandate to handle illegal activities like sex trafficking (Porteus 2005). But some within the peacekeeping high command still tend to excuse prostitution and its related businesses (e.g., sex trafficking) with the attitude that "boys will be boys."

Military personnel undermine the very notion of security when they globalize sex and violence. First, sex trafficking itself involves a high degree of militarization. Crime cartels utilize high-tech equipment, including weapons of war, to defend this lucrative trade. Local patriarchal interests (including women participants) also use the same set of racial and sexual double standards to punish local women for violating nationalistic norms of "purity," even as their earnings provide for the family and the community (Samarasinghe 2007). During UN missions to Somalia, for instance, the local community broadcast all over the world pictures of a Somali woman who seemed "too friendly" to the French soldiers (Byrne, Marcus and Power-Stevens 1996). Second, sex trafficking and prostitution obviate borders. Not only persons but also diseases cross borders. HIV/AIDS, other STDs, child prostitution, and other legacies of sex trafficking now afflict those "at home" as much as those "over there." Moreover, peacekeeping's involvement in sex trafficking undermines its mission. The mission's local clients have suffered the traumas of war, poverty, genocide, and dislocation along with disintegrations of government and society. In many cases, international organizations like the UN remain their only hope for a stable, responsive civil society. When this last resource fails, where can they turn? What kind of global governance is the international community licensing, then, in the name of peace, justice, and order when women, girls, and boys are trafficked daily for pleasure and profit, often resulting in their death?

Peacekeeping: a neocolonial relationship

Peacekeeping is no exception to a neocolonial relationship. Peacekeeping by multilateral agencies like the UN or individual states like Canada may provide a crucial service by protecting people from violence, at least temporarily, in conflict-ridden societies. But these agencies also reinforce a world order that is, "on the whole . . . de-historicized, leaving in place an old colonial script in which the West saves hapless refugees from their fates" (Malkii, cited in Razack 2000: 5). That peacekeeping forces are populated primarily by men who are themselves racialized, genderized, and sexualized does not militate against their doing the same to Others. As Sherene Razack (2004) has shown, minority men in Canada's peacekeeping forces externalized the prejudices they have been subjected to in order to distinguish themselves from the (inferior, "third-world") locality where they were situated so they could fit in with the (superior, "first-world") transnational order that they represented. An Aboriginal peacekeeper in the Canadian mission, for instance, rationalized his killing of Somalis through two orders of racialized hypermasculinity: "The white man feared the Indian. So, too, will the black man" (Hall 1997: 5–6). For these peacekeepers, with uncertain access to dominance in the colonial hierarchy of race, gender, sex, class, and nation,

enactments of violence showed that they, too, qualified as (first-world) men
(Olsson and Tryggestad 2001).

Indeed, UN peacekeeping itself retains a racial and developmental
hierarchy. Ever since the disastrous intervention of US peacekeeping in
Somalia in 1993, when gleeful Somali bandits dragged the corpse of a US
soldier through the streets of Mogadishu, industrialized economies have been
reluctant to send in their own troops for peacekeeping missions. In 2001,
African Business reported that "[d]eveloping nations now contribute more
than 75 percent of the 30,000 troops involved in 15 missions worldwide
while the US, Japan and the European countries – supplying scant numbers
of ground troops – pay 85 percent of the UN's US$3 billion peacekeeping
budget."[19] In effect, cash-rich, first-world governments are subcontracting
cash-poor, third-world states to provide troops for peacekeeping operations
that sustain, basically, first-world geopolitics driven by first-world material
interests (Ghebali 2007).

As always, women's bodies serve as a convenient outlet for these power
relations. For Ronald Hyam (1991), colonialism's greatest bonus for the
ordinary British soldier and administrator were the local women. During
the "long" Cold War and the "short" Korean and Vietnam Wars, Asian
capitals like Tokyo, Bangkok, Manila, and Taipei were turned into "rest
and recreation" (prostitution) centers, for the US military (Truong 1990;
Pettman 1996; Ling 2002b). The South Korean government even negotiated militarized prostitution as a foreign policy enticement to keep US troops
on the peninsula (Moon 1997). In this way, the US effectively institution-
alized what Japan's imperial army tried to coerce during World War II
– a geographically diverse distribution of "comfort women" (see *positions*
1997; Yoshiaki 1999).

Mainstream analysts use world order as justification. Sex trafficking, they
reason, must be subordinated to what they consider higher priorities: e.g.,
global terrorism, weapons of mass destruction, rogue states, balance of power,
and (formal) trade. Accordingly, mainstream analysts typically exile sex
trafficking to related but subsidiary domains of research such as "women's
studies," "third-world development," and/or "area studies." These studies
typically devolve into a series of discrete, policy problems for "developing"
economies/societies "out there," effectively erasing from view the international system's complicity in sex trafficking, its proliferation throughout
the globe, and its integral relationship to "more important" security issues
like global terrorism. In this way, sex trafficking becomes reified as a
description only where clients exploit for pleasure; pimps, for profit; and
trafficked women are just plain victims.

Disappeared are the *real* power politics behind the militarizing and sexu-
alizing of our daily lives. That is, the neoliberal imperium's construction of
subordinate identities that obscures global inequalities, thereby producing the
need for greater militarization. Only with this process of systematic identity
formation could such blatant asymmetries in profits and exploitation, hypermasculinity and hyperfemininity be tolerated, maintained, and perpetuated.

NEOCOLONIAL IDENTITIES

Peacekeeping "keeps peace" for the neoliberal imperium. This requires configuring a whole range of identities and social relations accordingly. When UN peacekeepers find themselves in receiving countries, observes Razack (2000: 2), they "draw . . . on and sustain . . . a national mythology in which bodies of color are imagined as outside the nation and white men become the normative citizens." For some peacekeepers, "race is a form of pleasure in one's body that is articulated by [and] through humiliation of the Other" (Farley 1997: 464). Humanitarian efforts, for example, easily flare into naked aggression when peacekeepers perceive their "clients" as insufficiently grateful. Note these comments by Canadian peacekeepers on why they killed so many Somalis, the very people they were sent to protect:

> "I never saw a starving Somali. I never saw a grateful Somali."

> "We were sent to help them, and they did nothing to help us."

> "They were not even appreciative of the work we were doing for them. They just kept destroying everything we're building and I think that was the turning point really, for me anyhow. It was one of the big turning points against the Somalis, around mid February. I went from feeling sorry for them down to being fed up, thinking, 'Let's get out'. They brought it all on themselves."
>
> (quoted in Winslow 1997: 237–238)

The protector/colonizer, in short, requires constant adulation. If it is lacking, then the victim/colonized must be disciplined. "Hunt them down," George W. Bush proclaimed famously about the 9/11 attackers. "Smoke 'em out." bin Ladin and his followers are "Wanted: Dead or Alive." This hunting metaphor bears closer examination. What does it *really* mean? Brian Luke has deconstructed the psycho-social-sexual implications of hunting for the hunter. He finds a pattern of "anticipation, desire, pursuit, excitement, penetration, climax, and satiation" (Luke 1998: 635). As an example, he cites this dream from an all-time elk hunter:

> I see elk before me, around me, moving everywhere, big dark shapes in the trees, along with their calves of the year. I raise the rifle, wanting to fire, but also wanting to wait . . . I walk among them. They aren't afraid, and behind me one of the cows rubs her flank against me. She doesn't smell like elk – dry and musky. She smells washed and clean. When I turn around she drops her coat and becomes a naked woman, pressing herself to me and pushing me down. Her skin is the creamy color of wapiti rump, her breasts are small . . . As she bends her head to my chest and tries to take off my shirt, I lift her chin. Her eyes are wet and shining, and I can't tell if she is about to laugh or to cry. I

put my hand behind her head pulling her face toward me for a kiss, when I see the elk hide under my nose in the dawn.

(quoted in Luke 1998: 637)

The prey, in short, allows a manly life for the hunter. But consummation comes only when the hunter annihilates his prey, thereby sealing the hunter's manliness and its end at the same time. This cycle of love and extinction dooms the hunter to remain forever unrequited, pathologically chasing his elusive object of desire. No less a psychologically-adept, powermonger like Adolf Hitler acknowledged as much: i.e., the insecurity behind manly hunting due to the hunter's dependency on his prey. Hitler even projected ridicule from prey to hunter, as revealed in a conversation taped by Martin Bormann (*Hitler's Table Talk*). Hitler joked that while "[t]he joy of killing brings men together [i]t's lucky we don't understand the language of hares. They might talk about you something like this: 'He couldn't run at all, the fat hog!'" (Hitler, quoted in Boxer 2001: 5).

When placed in a colonial context, hunting's anxious eroticism exposes the trappings of racialized privilege. The "great white hunter," armed with his killing technologies, must rely on "natives" to carry his equipment, set up camp, scout the territory, track the prey, then skin it for display and/or butcher it for eating. The "great white hunter" simply shoots the animal. Given this precarious asymmetry, the "great white hunter" must convince himself – and the natives who outnumber him – that only he can use the killing technologies. The natives must be convinced that they are too primitive, stupid, irresponsible, or scared to take up the gun, the grenade, the gas, or the bomb. Otherwise, the native could direct these killing technologies at the "great white hunter" just as easily as the hapless prey.

Now, the prey-Other also wants blood. Too long the emasculated prize of predatory colonizers, he, too, trucks in violence and desire, security and insecurity to declare his public hypermasculinity. bin Ladin is motivated less by fleshly consummation in the here-and-now than by the promise of that final, orgiastic bliss in Paradise with "72 black-eyed virgins." Note this Pakistani man's regret at the end of the Taliban regime:

We went to the *jihad* filled with joy, and I would go again tomorrow ... If Allah had chosen me to die, I would have been in paradise, eating honey and watermelons and grapes, and resting with beautiful virgins, just as it is promised in the Koran. Instead, my fate was to remain amid the unhappiness here on earth.

(quoted in Burns 2002: A1)

For this reason,

[t]he death of a martyr is routinely announced in the Palestinian press not as an obituary but as a wedding. "The Wedding of the Martyr Ali Khadr Al-Yassini to the Black-Eyed in Eternal Paradise," said an invitation carried a few weeks ago in lieu of a death notice in Al-Hayat

Al-Jadida, an Arafat-controlled paper. The same nuptial theme emerges in the eve-of-battle instructions presumed to have been written by Mohamed Atta, a supposed leader of the Sept.11 attacks. "You should feel complete tranquillity, because the time between you and your marriage in heaven is very short," Atta assured his accomplices.

(Lelyveld 2001: 51)

This sense of hypermasculinity is "haunted by the phantoms and monsters of modernity . . . with their own horizons and contradictions" (Moallem 1999: 339). Bush's rhetoric celebrates modernity while bin Ladin's seeks to destroy it. Yet both aim to "contain and make manageable the chaotic situation arising from the basic contradictions of the same modernity" (Moallem 1999: 339). Partha Chatterjee critiques the same of peacekeeping. It is, he writes, a "moral-cultural drive to spread 'modernity' throughout the world" (Chatterjee 1998: 70). Peacekeeping, for Chatterjee, constitutes "a global civil society assessing the incomplete modernity of particular national political formations" (Chatterjee 1998: 67). Razack bluntly calls peacekeeping a "civilizing mission" whose "moral terrain" is firmly anchored in the first world (Razack 2000: 5).

DESIRE AND VIOLENCE IN MODERNITY

As a signpost of "modernity," international relations have long been inscribed with race, gender, sex, and class. Abouali Farmanfarmaian (1992: 116) explores this legacy of "colonialism, whiteness, identity" in the senior Bush's 1992 Gulf War. Sire to today's "war on terror"/"*jihad*" in more ways than one, the Gulf War replays a "national fantasy, with all its fears, anxieties, desires, and excitements" (Farmanfarmaian 1992: 111). Centering on themes of "miscegenation, family, and manhood," this national fantasy (like today's wars in Afghanistan and Iraq) pitches the US as a "righteous protector of the world against 'Iraq as an evil destructive force'" (Farmanfarmaian 1992: 112, 113). Rape becomes the overwhelming motif. The "rape of Kuwait" becomes an effective slogan for the first Gulf War, rendering the US in the triple manly role as lover, savior, and policeman to feminized Kuwait and Kuwaitis (Jeffords 1991).

Modernity, however, straddles generations and so does its sense of desire and violence. Sankaran Krishna (2006) finds colonization-through-language for the native populations of the "new" and "old" worlds. With the "Indians" of the "new world," European colonizers equated their lack of an alphabetized and written language with "naked savage[ry] . . . lack[ing] science, literature, and civility" (Krishna 2006: 99). With "Indians" from the "old world," however, the colonizers could not assign the same labels since the subcontinent more than matched the colonizers' own standards of archived knowledge. Instead, the British enacted another hierarchy. In valorizing "abstract" knowledge, they "intimately connected [it] with the reigning belief that what distinguished the orderly mind of the

British was precisely this genius for abstraction in contrast to the undisciplined and emotional Indian . . ." (Krishna 2006: 101). Britain's "orderly
mind," then, naturalized the subjugation of the "undisciplined and emotional
Indian" (Krishna 2006: 101).

For China, British imperialism created "arrogance" as a national identity later internalized by the Chinese themselves. Lydia H. Liu (2004: 30)
demonstrates the "terror of intersubjective communication" when the
British empire negotiated with the Qing dynasty after the first Opium War
(1842). In formulating the Treaty of Tianjin, Britain objected to the
Chinese characterization of the British as "*yi*" because, they complained,
it meant "barbarian." In fixing "*yi*" to mean "barbarian" only, the British
disregarded the word's variety in Chinese usage that included, among others,
a geographic designator of cultural status. For example, one of China's
legendary kings was identified as "*yi*" since he came, like the British, from
the eastern seas. The British also failed to appreciate the nuance of "*yi*"
in Confucian discourse. For example, the Manchu rulers of the Qing
dynasty also qualified as "*yi*" since they were non-Han. But they drew on
Confucian precepts of "*de*" (virtue) to emphasize the right to inherit the
Mandate of Heaven through benevolent governance. The British, in contrast, sought to punish Qing China for the "disrespect" they showed in
calling them "barbarians."

In this way, the British stamped a binary logic of Self vs Other onto
the Chinese. With the defeat of the Qing dynasty, the British initiated a
series of "unequal treaties" to ensure their "equal" status in China. Other
European powers quickly followed suit and unequal treaties pocked
China's political landscape for the next century. Not surprisingly, as Liu
documents, popular lingo in China later denigrated all Europeans as
"ghosts" or "devils."

A contemporary version of such intellectual imperialism comes from
Alastair Iain Johnston (1995). Ming China, he contends, exercised a
"strategic culture" much like the *realpolitik* practiced in the West, whenever territorial disputes erupted. Moreover, this "*parabellum* paradigm" dominated despite centuries of inculcation in a Confucian–Mencian paradigm
that emphasized accommodation, enculturation, and co-optation toward all
non-Han, non-Confucian peoples. Johnston's implications are clear: Self vs
Other transcends culture, time, and space. Nowhere does he explain, however, how or why both paradigms remained, particularly since Johnston
(1995: 253) dismisses the Confucian–Mencian paradigm as a "linguistic cus-
tom" only. Without accounting for the persistence of these two paradigms
to *co-habit* in Chinese thought and practice, Johnston's argument must
rest on Orientalist stereotypes that the Chinese were either very good at
fooling people (including themselves) or they were really automatons of
violence who turned to "strategic thinking" whenever the need arose.

The colonizing Self denies any intimacy with the Other despite constructing
the latter. In 1998, Iran's former president, Mohamed Khatami, quoted
Toqueville on CNN. He sought to show common philosophical roots to
the Iranian and American republican revolutions (Khatami 1998). Instead,

he outraged the editors of *The New Republic* (*The New Republic* 1998). They could not accept that an Arab and an Islamic cleric like Khatami could draw on an iconic source of American democracy to account for Iran's revolution.

As Salman Sayyid (2006) notes, this rejection exposed the "contingent nature" of "Westernese." That is, the vision of unity (hegemony) in all language, thought, and discourse through the guise of traditional Western Enlightenment values like Reason, History, and Science was, when pressed, for members only. Only those deemed "Western" (i.e., heirs to the Anglo-American tradition of republicanism) could qualify by default. In contrast, those deemed "non-Western" or worse, "anti-Western," must earn their admission by demonstrating fidelity to the West. "Thus," writes Sayyid (2006: 10), "Khatami's use of Tocqueville is not the source of delight that Tocqueville is being 'universalised', instead rather horror at the way the Khatami interview seeks to rupture the [Plato-to-NATO] sequence to which Tocqueville belonged . . . Rather than engage with Khatami, the editors resort to claiming ownership of Tocqueville." Under such conditions, Sayyid (2006: 14) concludes, "the subaltern can only mimic."

This colonial logic ultimately damns the colonizer. Rey Chow's explanation merits quoting at length:

> What I am suggesting is a mode of understanding the native in which the native's existence – that is, an existence before becoming 'native' – precedes the arrival of the colonizer. Contrary to the model of Western hegemony in which the colonizer is seen as a primary, active 'gaze' subjugating the native as passive 'object', I want to argue that it is actually the colonizer who feels looked at by the native's gaze. This gaze, which is neither a threat nor a retaliation, makes the colonizer 'conscious' of himself, leading to his need to turn this gaze around and look at himself, henceforth 'reflected' in the native-object. It is the self-reflection of the colonizer that produces the colonizer as subject (potent gaze, source of meaning and action) and the native as his image . . . Hegel's story of human 'self-consciousness' is then not what he supposed it to be – a story about Western Man's highest achievement – but a story about the disturbing effect of Western Man's encounter with those others that Hegel considered primitive. Western Man henceforth became 'self-conscious', that is, uneasy and uncomfortable, in his 'own' environment.
>
> (Chow 2003: 342–343)

Put differently, the "master" looks in the mirror and is horrified. As drawn from the gaze of the "slave," this "master" is necessarily brutal, false, all-too-human, acting on whim and fancy and power. And he has nowhere to hide. The hollowness of his proclaimed ideals of Beauty, Truth, Perfection, Rationality, and Science, derived from the supposedly superior legacy of European Enlightenment, confronts him daily and intimately as the "slave" serves his breakfast, polishes his boots, cradles his children, sleeps in his bed. For this reason, the master-colonizer cannot rest easily or comfortably.

In the case of Qing China, Britain asserted its hegemony but also exposed the fear and anxiety behind it:

> [T]he British attempted to contest their troubled self-image in the language of the other, be it *yi/barbarian*, *fan gui/foreign devil*, or any nonsense word that remotely suggested disrespect. Might we not glimpse in this obsession a rare moment of self-doubt within the imperial unconscious with regard to the mystified location of the "barbarian" and its relationship to the sovereign self? The sovereign subject is trying to root out the ghost of the "barbarian" from its own deep-seated uncertainty before it can become whole, positive, and real.
>
> (Liu 2004: 105)

Recognition of such "banal violence" within the Self is not just an existential dilemma. It seizes the Self forcefully, immediately, and physically as well. Note this excerpt from a 24 February 2008 article in the *New York Times Magazine* on military life in Iraq:

> "I hate this country!" [the young sergeant] shouted. Then he smiled and walked back into the hut. "He's on medication," Kearney said quietly to me. Then another soldier walked by and shouted, "Hey, I'm with you, sir!" and Kearney said to me, "Prozac. Serious P.T.S.D. from last tour." Another one popped out of the HQ cursing and muttering. "Medicated," Kearney said. "Last tour, if you didn't give him information, he'd burn down your house. He killed so many people. He's checked out."
>
> (Rubin 2008: 42)

Liberal internationalists must stay alert. As heirs to this colonial logic, they must pursue an unrelenting agenda of remaking Others into the image of the Self while forestalling internal anxieties and fears. Like the British with Qing China and colonial India, the Bush Administration needed to discipline the 9/11 terrorists not simply for attacking civilians on home soil but, as Bush announced, "to save civilization itself."

CONCLUSION

Whether driven by poverty, disease, conflict, and/or war, people desire a better life. For this reason, they are susceptible to the neoliberal imperium's dual strategy of hypermasculinized security based on hyperfeminized exploitation. It promises better conditions but also attracts insecurity of all kinds, not least those of the state, involving surveillance, militarization, and other technologies of violence. Like sex trafficking and other "desire industries," the "global war on terror" seeks to keep people "in place" by managing their desires through terror (e.g., criminalization, victimization, police raids). In this way, both racial and sexual inequities structure relations between rich and poor, North and South, men and women, adults and children, within as well as between countries. It is no coincidence that most of those targeted for the "desire industries" are considered "prostitutes of color," even if they may be ethnic Caucasians from Russia and Eastern Europe. They are also labeled "underclass" when many of these women are well-educated. Clients, meanwhile, are simply identified as "rich."

An older, naturalized understanding of colonialism and patriarchy operates here as well.[20] Nearly five centuries of Western colonialism and imperialism have left us with two, interrelated legacies: a militarized enrichment of the haves by the have-nots (see Johnson 2003) and a racialization-cum-sexualization of the Other (see Ashcroft, Griffiths, and Tiffin 1995). As Cynthia Enloe (1990) has noted, the US entertainment industry propped up Carmen Miranda as a symbol of US-Latin American relations precisely because she distracted attention from the unholy alliance between multinational corporations such as the United Fruit Company and the Central Intelligence Agency (CIA). The term "banana republic" cleverly referred to the desired commodity, the CIA-corporate manipulations of regional and local politics, and the lack of fortitude shown by local states under US hegemony. Today, neoliberal globalization has defused this potent symbol of Latin American humiliation and US hegemony into a highly successful clothing chain store. The politics of the market trumps the "original" branding of the Other, further consolidating the neoliberal world order.

The imperium, however, cannot exercise such desire and violence without mobilizing an underlying infrastructure of *intellectual* complicity. Such complicity must operate at various sites simultaneously to support, enhance, and make possible the rationalizations needed for empire. In the next two chapters, we discuss two processes of complicity and their connections: that is, (a) the production of specific knowledges to perpetuate (b) a subjectivity of fear and property applied to world politics. We begin with the production of knowledge in and about IR at its principal site of operation, the academy.

3 The House of IR

Sau giận vì duyên để mõm mòm   I rage against my fate – a fruit too ripe.
Tài tử văn nhân ai đó tá   Talented men of letters, where are you?
Thân này đã hẳn chịu già hom   Am I condemned to shrivel up and rot?
Hồ Xuân Hu'o'ng, "Confession" (circa 1810)[1]

The academy sustains the imperium not only intellectually but also practically. That is, the academy gives the imperium the rationale for its acts of power. Here, the House of IR serves both functions for the academy most effectively. By the House of IR, we refer to mainstream theories within the discipline of IR and the social relations that give them relative positions of power within the academy and world politics.

We begin with IR's foremost problematic: i.e., fencing off a majority of the world. Analogizing IR to a colonial household highlights its structural intimacy with capitalist-patriarchy, accounting for its hegemony in world politics. We conclude with an examination of the consequences of colonizing IR as an academic discipline, a source of knowledge production, and a field of practical politics. We find that gestures toward "fairness" and "representation" in the academy too often remain just that. The academy's complicity with power surfaces most prominently when cracks in academic policy, especially at tenure and promotion time, expose acts of racialized, sexualized, and class brutality by decisionmakers who are only following "rules and procedures."

THE ROLE OF THE ACADEMY

IR, we argue, operates like a colonial household. This House of IR shouts to the world: it's "I vs You!" Like the singular, patriarchal, and colonial household that stands for the colonial state, the field theorizes about itself from a position of imperial sovereignty. Staking out "civilization" in a space that's already crowded with local traditions of thinking, doing, and being yet proclaimed, in willful arrogance, as a "state of nature" plagued by fearful "anarchy" and its murderous power politics, the House of IR aims to stave off "disorder" by imposing "order." Directing Others with declarative statements, the House of IR assumes to know both the problem (i.e., "power for the few over the many") and its solution ("more power for the few over the many"). Such suffocation of Self and Other leaves a multi-generational legacy similar to the actual colonial household's. That is, erasures and violences that flip the household's original intent: order turns into disorder, repulsion into desire, purity into hybridity. In the House of IR, especially, another practice rules: the treatment of the academy's institutional power as an extension of political power, regardless of empire's devastations and/or secret indulgences.

IR HOUSEHOLD RELATIONS

Our understanding of the colonial household comes from Ann Laura Stoler (2002). Her study of colonial management in Indonesia and Indochina under Dutch and French rule, respectively, tracks the "genealogies of the intimate." She asks: how do racialized categories of identity emerge and become naturalized into the lexicon of colonial governance? Given the potent politics of categorizing identities, Stoler examines "the histories of their making, the exclusions they enabled, and violences they condoned" (Stoler 2002: 8).[2]

The House of IR exhibits a similar politics of exclusion and violence.[3] It clearly identifies who's "in," who's "out," and who's precariously "on the border." It also stratifies who's "upstairs" and who's "downstairs." This hierarchical division of space reflects the House's participation in and complicity with material relations of production and its uneven distribution of social wealth.

Inside the Household

Pater realism

As its "founding father," realism heads the House of IR.[4] Though labeled a peculiarly "American social science" (Hoffman 1995), realism claims an intellectual lineage that dates to ancient Greek history, especially that recorded by Thucydides (5 BC) (cf. Lebow and Strauss 1991; Garst 1989; Jansson 1997; Monten 2006).[5] Subsequently, realists have added luminaries of power politics like Machiavelli and Hobbes to their roster. But it was a generation of scholars from post-World War II Europe, Britain, and the US that gave realism its distinctive voice. Power, they asserted, reflects objective laws of calculated (sometimes amoral) self-interest for all states across time and space. John Herz, George F. Kennan, Walter Lippmann, and Hans J. Morgenthau each saw "political realism" as the cure to what they considered the fateful cause of war among nations: "legalism," "utopianism," and "idealism" (Keohane 1986: 9).

Abstract individualism pivots realism's understanding of the world. Primordial individual units (states) struggle in eternal competition over

resources that confer power and wealth. In this way, realists justify instrumental reasoning and behavior. But then how do realists explain the
existence of an interdependent international political economy in a world
of conflicting nation-states? Hegemonic stability theory comes to the rescue
(Kindleberger 1973). It posits a dominant state or hegemon that willingly
bears the asymmetrical cost of global leadership so the inter-state system
may survive peacefully and prosperously despite anarchy and competition.
Game theoretic models explain such cooperation under anarchy as a pris-
oner's dilemma. Still, these approaches preserve realism's basic premise in
abstract individualism. They place outside the realm of realist inquiry issues
like ideology, the social bases of state power, its practices, political struggles, and strategies for reproduction (Rupert 1995).

Yet realists openly accept their origin in the white colonial/imperial state.
They invoke and canonize Thucydides' *History of the Peloponnesian War*
as the genealogical text for IR. The book details Athens' struggle against
Sparta for hegemony in the ancient world, interpreted by realists as a
cautionary tale on the uses and abuses of state power. This teleological and
political move disciplines IR, in effect, by deciding who and what counts
in not just the study of world politics but also its practices through
statecraft. Accordingly, some are included, recognized, and legitimized
at the cost of the many. Realists constantly echo what they claim to be
Thucydides' key lesson in power: "The strong do what they can, the weak
suffer what they must." In this way, realists rationalize empire's brutal legacy,
turning it into an ideological and political commitment. Expect violence
and colonization, some realists trumpet, for it is integral to empire. And
empire, they add, is what international politics is all about. Conveniently
silenced is another reading of this text that tells of empire as a crisis not
only for world politics but the empire itself.[6]

Realism stems from another lineage, rarely acknowledged: i.e., the
global capitalist economy. It accounts for realism's birth into the world
and its growth, sustenance, and eventual dominance in the House of IR.
In turn, realism generates an ideational infrastructure for global capitalism's public, political face: the modern, capitalist state. What is all this
warring imperialism *for* if not more wealth and resources for national
elites? Global capitalism delivers what the white colonial/imperial state
seeds.

Mater liberalism

Liberalism naturally allies with realism. They share common roots in the
white colonial/imperial state and its relationship with global capitalism, albeit
with a conceptual division of labor. Whereas realism commands the House
of IR by focusing on the state ("power"), liberalism organizes, manages,
and reproduces it by emphasizing the market ("interest") (see Gilpin 1987).
Liberalism started out as a proud tradition of defiance against authority,
such as Martin Luther's fiery repudiation of Catholic Church hegemony
in sixteenth-century Europe. Since then, it has evolved into an ideological

instigator of "free trade," "open markets," "instrumental rationality," and other pillars of global capitalism (Polanyi 1944; Hirschman 1977).

Realism and liberalism work in tandem by drawing on the mirage of "politics" and "economics." Publicly, they convince "contemporary statesmen [like] the mercantilists of the seventeenth and eighteenth centuries [that] power is a necessary condition for plenty, and *vice versa*" (Keohane 1984: 22). Privately, realism–liberalism maintains an infrastructure of elite, bourgeois rule by seeming to care about democratic peace, prosperity, and freedom – but not really.[7] Realism–liberalism's abstract, ahistorical conceptions of the state, the market, and the individual are bound by particular cultural expressions (Western, white, male) that result from concrete political struggles (bourgeois, colonial). Yet both the "world" (materiality, structured inequalities) and "politics" (practices, discourse) disappear from world politics (Agathangelou 1997). Classical liberals like Kant, Locke, and Woodrow Wilson, for instance, advocated a legally-based "perpetual peace," "limited government," and a "league of nations" to forestall global warfare that, by extension, preserves the realist–liberal inter-state, commerce-based system, in principle, if not in form. Similarly, contemporary liberals like Hedley Bull (1966) and David Held (1995) talk of an "international society" or "cosmopolitan democracy," respectively, but without regard to the worldviews or participation of Others in these processes.

Today, liberalism reinvents itself into a new family of arguments labeled neoliberalism. Without losing the liberal logic of public vs private, individual vs collective, Self vs Other, neoliberalism professes good intentions for the masses while complying with elite demands for new ideas for and methods of preserving colonial–patriarchal–capitalist structures and their necessary subjectivities. Take the treatment of "third-world" women, for example. Liberal and standpoint feminists end up colluding morally and politically when they seek to "protect" brown women from brown men by helping them become more like "white" women.

Still, nothing is what it seems. As we see below, mater liberalism and daughter neoliberalism each has sought to convert Others with missionary zeal but ended up, instead, with hybrid progeny.

Caretaking daughters: neoliberalism, liberal feminism, and standpoint feminism

The good daughters of the House of IR exhibit wonderful caretaking traits. Neoliberals seem to have resolved the realist dilemma.[8] Economic "interdependence" (Keohane and Nye 2000) and its institutional preference for negotiation and continuity, they argue, account for "cooperation under anarchy" (Keohane 1984). That is, market relations raise the transaction costs of conflict. Indeed, neoliberalism sets the market as the arbiter of all social relations. It posits that corporate growth generates wealth, employment, and prosperity – all the necessary ingredients for social order, with limited government interference to boot. That these strategies also extend US interests, norms, and practices – i.e., a hegemonic regime (Stein 1984)

– is but a subsidiary consideration. Neoliberalism turns realism's hegemonic stability theory into a user-friendly manual for happy, consumer-based management.

Gender contestations within global capitalist crises push neoliberalism to update itself. For this reason, neoliberals find sister-solidarity with standpoint feminists (Keohane 1989). The latter propose that "strong" objectivity would pertain when the "standpoints" of various identities, especially those that have been excluded or marginalized (e.g., black women), are taken into account (Harding 1991). Of course, tensions strain any sibling relationship (Tickner 1997). But neoliberals partner comfortably with standpoint feminists by appropriating the latter for specific capitalist institutions and practices. For instance, neoliberals claim an interest in promoting a "network view that emphasizes how institutions could promote lateral co-operation among organized entities, states, or otherwise . . ." (Keohane 1989: 248). Standpoint feminism, as one neoliberal describes it, seems the perfect wife/mother/hostess: it offers a "conceptual" approach to IR that emphasizes "power as the ability to act in concert," allowing for "collaborat[ion] [in the face of] collective problems . . . [and] purposeful human action and subjectivity in creating new conditions of life . . . stressing connectedness, and obligations to other inhabitants of planet earth . . ." (Keohane 1989: 245–251).[9]

But where is gender analysis itself? Neoliberals and IR standpoint feminists tend to equate "gender" with "women" (Carpenter 2002). This conflation elides the role of men, masculinity, and patriarchy in the formation of gender in social relations of power. In defining gender normatively ("what is appropriate or useful, what is not"), they grant power to some agents – "good girls" (Weber 1994) – who can police or mediate capitalist relations for others.

Martha Nussbaum's "capabilities approach" offers one such example. Her focus on capabilities shifts governmental action from *what* individuals should think or do (which would amount to tyranny) to *how* they can accomplish a more fulfilling life.[10] Once society provides individuals with the basic infrastructure to *make choices*, Nussbaum assures us, "the stage is fully set" for an independent, well-informed, fulfilled life; the "choice is up to them," she asserts (Nussbaum 1999: 45). In particular, she proposes, the capabilities approach would free "third world" women of the "shackles" of their thousand-year old traditions and beliefs (Nussbaum 2000), as if these have nothing to do with contemporary relations and forces of power.

Nussbaum's logic echoes an earlier era of missionary authoritarianism. Insisting on the liberal norms of "personhood, autonomy, rights, dignity, self-respect" (Nussbaum 1999: 56) as a universal good, Nussbaum does not consider their *interactions* with other norms, values, practices, histories, and institutions. She refers to a group of feminists in China who reject Confucianism in favor of the liberal norm of human rights, thereby highlighting liberal feminism's international significance. "What is East and what is West?" she asks rhetorically (Nussbaum 1999: 9). Not once, though, does Nussbaum consider the possibility that liberal theorists could benefit from other philosophical traditions, including Confucianism.[11] Nor does Nussbaum acknowledge her own adherence to a thousand-year-old tradition: i.e., what she claims to be Aristotelian logic. Because Nussbaum sees "third-world traditions," particularly in their patriarchal form, as obstacles to the full realization of personhood through choice, she implicitly rationalizes their dismissal (to put it mildly) or extinction (to put it more harshly).

This "civilizing mission," Gayatri Spivak reminds us, is an old, colonial tale that does *not* bear retelling (Spivak 1999). Nussbaum never reflects on her privileged, masculinized position as a highly-educated, highly-paid white woman from the US talking to "poor women" in India or China subjected to "outdated patriarchies." Not only does she appropriate the knowledge of these women, which is passed on at great risk and acquired through lifetimes of physical, mental, and emotional labor, but she also makes them the object of her writing and politics. Still, Nussbaum pities them for not being "free" or "rich" enough to speak.[12]

Ambivalence bedevils this colonial logic. Stoler's tale of white women in the colonies could well substitute for the liberal, caretaking daughters of the House of IR: "Charged with guarding cultural norms, [these good daughters] were instrumental in promoting [the House of IR]. But it was partly at their own expense, for on this issue they were to be almost as closely policed as [the Other]" (Stoler 2002: 60). For this reason, while neoliberalism, liberal feminism, and standpoint feminism may find social and political emancipation appealing and a seeming basis for solidarity with the Other, they are bound, nonetheless, to the dictates of the House of IR.

In the House of IR, the Other refers to non-Western, non-white sources of knowledge, traditions, or worlds. These may be smuggled in as "servants" or "wards" of the House but otherwise not recognized as legitimate subjects, knowledges, and/or worlds in their own right. Such alienation does not allow the House to formalize connections between and among different producers of knowledge, although informal cross-fertilizations flourish even from the most unexpected sources. One "delegitimized ward" (D-ward), Asian capitalism, results from mater liberalism's consummation with the Confucian world-order during the nineteenth and twentieth centuries. The "delegitimized twins" (D-Twins), peripheral and transitional economies, come from neoliberalism's contestations and struggles with socialism in the late twentieth and early twenth-first centuries. The same applies to the "delegitimized terrorist" (D-Terrorist), al Qaeda, and its relations with neoliberalism, especially since the Soviet occupation of Afghanistan in the 1980s. Detailed descriptions of each follow below but we come by way of the legitimate heirs of the House of IR, beginning with neorealism.

Heir apparent: neorealism

Son #1 intrigues the most. Heir apparent to the House of IR, neorealism springs not from the union of realism and liberalism but an open affair between realism and its gold-digging neighbor, economics. Mistress of her own house but impatient with opportunistic ambitions, economics merges almost giddily with realism to produce neorealism. Waltz (1979), for instance, constructs the international system as a market and states as individual firms, magically accounting for "order"[13] without an "orderer"[14] in an international system that is posited, *a priori*, as anarchical. On this basis, Waltz infers that only great powers matter since they alone account for change and consequence in world politics.

Similarly, neorealists and their cousins, rational choicers, have stormed the House of IR. Like Jimmy Cagney's dying psycho gangster in *White Heat* (1949), they crow manically: "Look, Ma, I made it! Top of the world!" They find no contradiction in denying legitimacy and rights to others, be these involving intellectual debate,[15] hiring/promotion/grants,[16] or publications,[17] while failing to deliver on their own golden promises of, among others, "prediction," "law-like" regularities, and "causal explanations" (Green and Shapiro 1994).

Yet neorealists remain insecure. Their own zero-sum logic induces a paranoid worldview that treats Others as competition only for legitimacy and resources – in this case, in the House of IR. As Stoler notes for colonial governance in southeast Asia, "it was not the progeny of [cross-category] unions who were problematic but the possibility that they might be recognized as heirs to a European inheritance . . ." (Stoler 2002: 39). For this reason, tensions between neorealism and the other progeny of the House of IR remain severe.

On the borders, upstairs

Rebel sons: Marxism, Gramscian IPE, postmodern IR, constructivism–pragmatism

Rebel sons populate the House of IR. Marxists disrupted the household with their contentions of "*dependencia*" and "world systems" in the 1970s–1980s (Cardoso and Faletto 1979; Wallerstein 1974, 1980, 1989), Gramscians with their exposures of "hegemony" in the international political economy (IPE) in the 1980s–1990s (Cox 1987), postmodernists with their "third debate" from the 1980s (Lapid 1989), and now the twins constructivism–pragmatism with their "linguistic turn" (Onuf 1989; Wendt 1999; Fierke and Jorgenson 2001; *Millennium* 2002). These rebel sons challenge realism's standing as their paternal authority given mater liberalism's old "mentor," critical theory. Each rebel son strikingly resembles critical theory in voice and commitment (dialectical historical materialism for Marxists, counter-hegemony for Gramscians, anti-Eurocentrism for postmodernists, emancipatory language structures for constructivists and pragmatists). At the same time, they share with realism considerable similarity in form, such as an exclusive reliance on Western intellectual traditions, concepts, and methods.[18] Accordingly, ambivalence also torments these rebel sons of the House of IR. They prescribe emancipatory change, sometimes to the point of establishing their own households, yet they still seek approval from pater realism. Der Derian's and Shapiro's (1989) reader on

postmodernism in IR and Alexander Wendt's (1999) version of constructivism provide two such examples.[19]

Postmodernists in IR seek to de-center the "West." They challenge the
notion of a free, rational, and private individual by problematizing knowledge production as relations of power. These, in turn, are rooted in social
structures and institutions such as capitalist-patriarchy. Enlightenment
knowledge, IR postmodernists argue, follows a "partial" logic of inclusion
and exclusion such that one mode of knowledge defines itself in relation
to another within a hierarchical ordering. These do not conform to
autonomous objects of knowledge, as claimed by liberal empiricists;[20]
instead, they foreground the "divisive practices" of social life. "Our subjective sense as persons . . . is created by recognizable discursive practices
that simultaneously implicate us in power-relations. . . . In [their] concern
about subjectivity as subjugation, [postmodernists are] also the historian[s]
of power" (Gregory 1989: xxi).

Despite their critical, revolutionary interests, IR postmodernists end up
being as static and reformist as realists and liberals. In setting up local practices as independent of the global logic of exploitation, IR postmodernists
ultimately paralyze those very forces (local, multiple, marginal) that they
claim to recognize and support. IR postmodernists take this "offshore" criticality as a necessary criterion for non-hegemonic theorizing (Shapiro
1992: 49). In the ensuing vacuum, however, they ensure *de facto* power
(see Agathangelou and Ling 1997).

A second case of ambivalent rebellion comes from Wendt.[21] He recasts
realism into a "social" theory of the state. Its "ontological priority"[22]
gives the state a "body" (sovereignty) that is full of "life" (motivational
dispositions, national interests) and wrestling with four types of identity
(corporate, type, role, and collective), as well as two kinds of interest
(objective and subjective). Together, these properties infuse the state with
"desires, beliefs and intentionality" (1999: 197). Wendt's conceptual
innovativeness notwithstanding, he ultimately reinstates a realist premise:
the self-enclosed (read elitist, patriarchal), self-sufficient (read colonizing),
rational (read Western) state. Indeed, Wendt's theoretical framework
implicitly reproduces realism's dominant logic. It surfaces most clearly when
he jockeys for position within the House of IR. Against "anti-essentialists
. . . like Postmodernists," Wendt writes, he focuses on "social construction
at the level of the states system" (emphasis in the original, 1999: 198). But
"against thicker essentialists . . . like Neorealists and Neoliberals," Wendt
argues for "a minimalist vision" (1999: 198). Altogether, he concludes, this
"leaves a lot of room [in the House of IR] for constructivist theories of
international politics" (1999: 198).

Wendt gives little space, though, to theories that share an analytical base
in social construction such as postmodern theories of feminism and queer
theorizations. At best, Wendt rationalizes, they are redundant ("there are
structurally similar, non-feminist critiques of liberalism that come to many
of the same conclusions") as feminist analyses; at worst, feminist analyses
are ineffective, particularly when addressing issues that Wendt himself deems

important: "less clear [is] whether . . . gender has had a causal impact on Westphalian sovereignty" (1999: 296). Wendt does not show how feminist and non-feminist theorizing about IR may reach the "same" conclusions, nor does he explain why feminist approaches should be judged on gender's "causal impact" on sovereignty. This hegemonic and ahistorical collapsing of explanation with interest pretends that theory-building just happens. It is innocent of a past, cleared of present ambitions, and primed for future development. Yet, as we see here, none of the above could pertain or ever has.

Daughters deemed "fallen": postmodern theories of feminism and queer theorizations

Postmodern theories of feminism and queer theorizations stand out as the "fallen daughters" of the House. They have strayed from the household center and, consequently, dangle dangerously on its edges.[23] Yet postmodern theories of feminism and queer theorizations share with their "rebel brothers" a noble lineage in mater liberalism's early cross-fertilization with critical theory. The House disdains postmodern theories of feminism and queer theorizations precisely because they show that identity – specifically, gender, sexuality, and notions of desire – is not "natural" or "essential" but socially constructed to privilege a colonial, imperial, patriarchal, and heterosexist order.[24] Put differently, the House of IR marginalizes postmodern theories of feminism and queer theorizations for exposing its strategies of secret lusts and unrequited desires.

In *Faking It* (1999), Cynthia Weber retells the history of US-Caribbean relations through a queer lens. Weber begins with the well-established construction of the US as "straight hegemonic masculinity" to, for example, Cuba's "trophy mistress" status. But Castro's anti-capitalist, anti-US revolution in 1959 regendered Cuba from miss to mister "with a beard," no less, causing a castrating "midlife/hegemonic/masculinity identity crisis" (1999: 1). Subsequently, US foreign policy toward Cuba, specifically, and the Caribbean, generally, has sought to re-masculinize, re-phallicize America through various strategies (e.g., invasion of the Dominican Republic, bombing of Grenada, extraterritorial arrest of Manuel Noriega in Panama).

Aside from its vanity, Weber notes the utter futility of such nationalist "faking it." "[T]he American body politic," she writes, "never 'had' a phallus to lose" in the first place (Weber 1999: 131). America created for itself this hypermasculine need to display hegemony in the form of phallic power (military, economic, political) and now feels eternally committed to replacing phallic power or compensating for it somehow. More effective, Weber suggests, would be for American power to enter "a third space" that is "in between 'being' and 'having,' female and male, feminine and masculine" (Weber 1999: 131). In making this "queer claim," the US may achieve, ironically, its goal of a "hegemonic subjectivity" (Weber 1999: 132).

How the US would constitute this "third space" is beside the point here. What the rulers of the House cannot forgive are such exposés of skulking desires in the liberal–realist state. Its biggest desire, Weber suggests, is to project a public heterosexuality that wants to consume and be loved by Others even when the object of strategic desire, like Castro's Cuba, switches national gender identities. Calls for protecting the "national self-interest" take on a wholly different meaning from that of "objective," "rational" calculations of "ordered preferences" as propounded by liberals, realists, and their "good" progeny. Instead, war, occupation, and other strategies for "regime change" turn into *simulations*, rather than actual exertions, of power. Such put-ons of "fake" power seem all the more pathetic, Weber concludes, given their dildo-like artificiality and neediness.

Now we turn to the "downstairs," where the "servants" live, work, and produce for the House of IR.

On the borders, downstairs

Native informant servants: area studies and comparative politics experts

The House of IR treats those who labor in the fields of area studies and/or comparative politics as "servants." These "downstairs" members gather ethnographic, "thick descriptions" ("low politics") so that the "upstairs" members may theorize grandly about the world ("high politics"). Indeed, those upstairs depend on the ethnographic sustenance and services provided by those downstairs, especially during times of crisis (e.g., give us information: "who's in power in China?"). Yet the House of IR historically considers comparative politics (with area studies as one of its components) to contain a method only (for comparisons) and no substance (see Lijphart 1971).

As in any household, "servants" embody ambivalence. They are, after all, the domesticated Other. In interviews with former Indonesian domestics in Dutch colonial households, for example, Stoler (2002) finds a distinct lack of sentimentality for their former employers.[25] So, too, do the servants of the House of IR grate at their marginalized, exploited status. Instead of being treated as scholars and theorists in their own right, the House of IR treats them as "native informants" (Narayan 1997). And the minute they refuse to collaborate in such schemes, these "native informants" are exiled from the House of IR.[26]

"Upstairs" members of the House welcome this asymmetrical division of intellectual labor. It allows for so-called autonomous sites where there is no clear relation between, for example, identifications of the "global" and "First-World" either as theoretical frameworks or empirical cases. Glossed over are the implications of these theories on social relations. Reading "native works" tends to reproduce asymmetrical social relations, without interrogating the practices that exploit and oppress "natives" like women, people of color, workers, peasants, the environment. Exploitation and oppression continue through (a) the constant division of the world into those who are "developed" and need no more instruction, those who are "developing" and require further education, and those who are "underdeveloped" and warrant more external control and management, and (b) the production of ideas which explain and justify this division through the institutionalization of (Western, white, colonial) laws, rules, and ideas.

Native informants provide "order" for the House of IR. They discreetly let in the "illegitimate" offspring produced by House members and "unruly," "native" traditions like Confucianism or socialism. Progeny such as Asian capitalism and peripheral-transitional economies become household "wards" and, by extension, service the white colonial/imperial state and its global capitalist consort. In this way, the House of IR contains the challenge of these wards within a racialized, sexualized bourgeois hierarchy. Again, Stoler's (2002) findings for the colonial household on the outskirts of empire apply as well for the House of IR:

> Métissage represented not the dangers of foreign enemies at national borders but the more pressing affront for European nation-states, what the German philosopher Johann Gottlieb Fichte so aptly defined as the essence of the nation, its "interior frontiers" . . .
>
> (Stoler 2002: 79)

D-Son Asian capitalism and the D-Twins peripheral and transitional economies, respectively, exemplify this notion of an "interior frontier." Their politics may seem conservative, given their attempts to implement neoliberal economic development, but their epistemologies for doing so are not. In this sense, these delegitimized wards of the House of IR have more in common with their rebel brothers, marxism and postmodernism, than is usually recognized.

D-Ward: Asian capitalism

Asian capitalism results from mater liberalism forcing her attentions onto the Confucian world-order since the nineteenth century (Ling 2002b). Accordingly, Asian capitalism exhibits such *métis* features as: a Westphalian state grafted onto Confucian patriarchy, capitalist rationality wrapped in collective institution-building, and market development ordered through social hierarchy (Ling 2002a). Yet the House of IR has exiled Asian capitalism as exotica only, not worthy of theorizing – until the latter gained enough economic clout to bribe its admission. In the early 1990s, the Japanese government funded a World Bank report that lauded Asia's "miracle" economies with their state-led development as exemplars of liberal capitalism (World Bank 1993; Wade 1996; Berger and Beeson 1998). Asian capitalism seemed on its way to household legitimacy – until a regional financial crisis struck (1997–98).

We need not recount the crisis here. What's noteworthy for our purposes is the vehement denunciation of Asian Capitalism from the House of IR. Neorealists and neoliberals trotted out, without question or reflection, all the old colonial, racist stereotypes about Asian "cronies," "despots," and "mismanagement" (Ling 2002a). "The Western form of free-market capitalism," Alan Greenspan intoned, is the *only* model for the world to follow (Greenspan, quoted in Singh and Weisse 1999: 204). Thus the House of IR justified a return to the practices of the white colonial/imperial state with its global capitalist agents self-righteously "saving" Asian Capitalism by buying its bankrupt enterprises at firesale prices. As it appropriated major sections of Asia's markets, so too did the House abscond with regional ideas like an "Asian Monetary Fund," now re-lingoed into a "new global financial architecture" with a "social safety net" to prevent similar disasters in the future (Wade 2007).

Acceptance into the House of IR, once so hopeful, is forever dashed. At most, Asian capitalism may enter the House as a "ward," slipped inside by sympathetic but powerless native informants.

D-Twins: peripheral and transitional economies

Neoliberalism has been busy with socialism and other economic systems. With the fall of the Soviet empire and China's change of economic heart to a limited form of capitalism, neoliberals have sought to convert socialism and its economic cousins, but ended up cavorting with them instead, producing the twin progeny of peripheral and transitional economies. These exhibit an interesting mix of masculinized realist state politics (e.g., anti-terrorist campaigns through anti-Other, anti-immigrant policies in Russia, the former Soviet republics, and the Mediterranean states) and feminized neoliberal developmental policies (e.g., importation of female migrant laborers for sex and/or domestic work). As Agathangelou (2004b) shows, peripheral economies in the Mediterranean and European Union (EU),[27] at the behest of Core Economies in the European Union, have set up "security zones" against the very population that they import for cheap labor. Yet the House of IR continues to deny the discursive, normative, and theoretical distinctiveness of these economies, insisting on characterizing them as exemplary acolytes under Anglo-American-European tutelage.[28]

Three other "illicit" communities thrive outside the House of IR: i.e., critics of Orientalism, postcolonial IR, and worldism. None seeks acceptance into the House of IR. They are not motivated by an angry sense of robbed entitlement though each shares a clear lineage with members of the House. Rather, each intrinsically challenges, critiques, and engages with the House, and centralizes configurations of race, gender, sexuality, class, and nation. Together, they constitute successive generations of intimate alternatives to the House of IR.

Outside the house

Intimate Alternative #1: Critics of Orientalism

The critique of orientalism springs from a union between literary theory – true exotica for the House of IR – and two rebel sons, Marxism and postmodernism. Edward Said (1979), a scholar of European literature, drew on Gramsci and Foucault to understand and eventually coin the term, orientalism. It refers to strategies taken by Western Enlightenment leaders to construct the Self primarily by negating the Other. In this case, the Other comes from a geographically and culturally-demarcated "Orient" that . ranges from Turkey to Japan in latitude, and Mongolia to Australia in longitude. Said analyzed French, German, and British travelogues, speeches, scientific tracts, and religious documents, to detail how the "West" saw itself vis-à-vis the "Oriental Other." He concluded that a lopsided logo-centrism resulted with the Western Self monopolizing all the terms of value ("beauty," "truth," "perfection," "progress," "rationality") at the expense of the Oriental Other ("deformity," "evil," "incompletion," 'stagnation," "chaos"). More than enslaving the Other, the West emasculated it through a cultural/civilizational rape.

The West demonizes Islam today, Said charged, precisely because it has refused to serve as a "civilizational womb." Western renditions of "the Palestinian problem," for instance, typically dehistoricize and decontextu-alize the region's complex history into an essentialized identity politics where "Palestine" (by extension, "Islam") becomes equated with "terrorism" now stamped as "evil" (Said 1988). Israel, for instance, uses such Orientalist presumptions as a basis for state policy toward the Palestinians and their government.

Orientalism's very *raison d'être*, Said emphasized, was to rationalize violence in the colonial order through the state (see Mitchell 1991). What results, as demonstrated in Chapter One, is a reactive-parallel strategy of imperial politics by both colonizer and colonized. Each feels justified to do onto the Other what has been done to it in the past without regard to those who are violated and sacrificed in the process. The latest product of such angry, incestuous mirroring is the D-Terrorist, al Qaeda.

D-Terrorist: al Qaeda

al Qaeda sprouts from the House of IR's preoccupation with Islam since the end of World War II. Contrary to latter-day Orientalists who like to portray Islam as congenitally immune to "modernity" (Buruma and Margalit 2002), al Qaeda has learned deftly from neorealist–neoliberal prac-tices. Its first training came by crawling through the belly of the "Great Satan's" beast, the Central Intelligence Agency (CIA), to oust the Soviets from Afghanistan in the 1980s. Since then, al Qaeda has taken on neoliberal corporate strategies to effect a global approach to terrorism (Weber 2002).

Postcolonial IR aims to transform such rage and violence in world politics.

Intimate alternative #2: postcolonial IR

Orientalism cross-fertilized with the rebel twins, constructivism and pragmatism, has produced a generation of postcolonial theorizing applied specifically to IR. It combines the "world-making" and "multiperspectival" approaches of constructivism–pragmatism with an explicitly postcolonial agenda of rehistoricizing race, gender, class, and culture as integral to narrations of Self and Other. Whereas orientalism identifies a particular social construction of Western Self vis-à-vis its Oriental Other, postcolonial IR inquires into their structural and cultural intimacies. Worldism pushes this inquiry even further. It begins by re-articulating historical contestations, negotiations, conflicts, struggles and violences as social relations. Second, worldism interrogates the *status quo* production of subjects *via* race, class, sexuality, nationalism, religion, and so on. These are not simply stereotypes/narratives assigned to Self and Other but moreso enactments of social power. Third, worldism takes seriously the existence of multiple worlds, economies, and subjectivities. Girded by Marxist historical materialism inflected through postcolonial sensibilities, worldism constitutes a third alternative to the House of IR.

Intimate Alternative #3: Worldism

As Part II of this book details worldism, we refrain from doing so here. For now, we emphasize that worldism questions the House of IR: its foundations ("power and interest"), its borders ("in vs out"), the presumed identities and claims of its members ("legitimate vs illegitimate"), their normative values ("good vs bad"), and asymmetrical positionings ("up vs down"). Indeed, worldism challenges the very project of constructing IR as a "house" in the first place.

The academy rules in a manner similar to the House of IR. It appropriates the knowledge, resources, and labor of racialized, sexualized Others for its own benefit and pleasure while billing itself as a "marketplace of ideas." Others qualify as "innocent" children, wards, or servants at best, or "unteachable" barbarians at worst. In either case, Others must wait faithfully for their admittance, if ever, into both the academy and the House of IR.

WHAT'S WRONG WITH THIS HOUSE?

Social relations of power underwrite the House of IR. These account for IR as a discipline, a source of knowledge production, and a field of practical politics. Though hidden behind public positions, reforms, and standards that seem internationalist and fair in scope, colonial erasures, violences, and desires perpetuate parochial and discriminatory practices.

For this reason, the House valorizes IR Cosmo Man.[29] He serves as globalization's most logical and desirable embodiment while policing patriarchal borderings of race, gender, class, and culture in IR. Patriarchy's intellectual production is not new, as indicated by the quote from Hồ Xuân Hu'o'ng, an eighteenth-century feminist poet from Vietnam, at the beginning of this chapter. What is new about Cosmo Man in the House of IR, though, is that his version of world politics is imposed on all Others, regardless of race, gender, class, sexuality and nationality. In this way, the House of IR elides its own collusion with power under the guise of "objective" and "rational" knowledge production.

So, too, does the academy.

Disciplinary impact: collusion with power

The academy interacts with power ambivalently. It publicly welcomes "multicultural," "international" education while privately making it difficult to tenure and promote faculty, especially those of color and women, who challenge capitalist-patriarchy's version of Self and Other. In this way, the academy re-enacts those desires and abuses that shadow the colonial household.

Yet institutions of higher learning increasingly clamor for multicultural, international education.[30] Externally, the academy needs to satisfy globalization's demand for a more cosmopolitan, educated elite. Internally, the academy also needs to globalize to: (a) retain an increasingly multi-ethnic student body, especially those who can pay high tuition fees during times of constricting budget cuts,[31] (b) uphold its liberal reputation as a "marketplace of ideas," and (c) keep apace with managerial, financial, and technical trends arising in various parts of the world. These apparent contradictions allow the academy and its elites to use the intellectual labor of Others while denying them due credit or acknowledgement for it. This appropriation is not for cultural stakes only. It provides an intellectual justification for an unequal access to and distribution of wealth.

Not surprisingly, white males dominate our discipline. A July 2005 report from the American Political Science Association (APSA) on the advancement of women in the profession found that:

> [d]espite substantial gains at all academic ranks since the 1970s, women comprise only 24 percent of all full-time faculty in 2001, an increase of just 6 percent since 1991. The percentage of women assistant professors has stalled at about 35 percent over the past five years. Ironically, the overall increase in women political science faculty is largely due to steady growth in numbers of women at the full professor level. More and more women are now hired in part-time or non-tenure-track positions, while the percentage of men in these categories is declining.
> (APSA 2005)

Data on postgraduate enrollment in US academies mirror this initial scenario (NCES 2004). A relatively even spread of men and women not only enter the classroom but also graduate with higher degrees. In the social sciences, women accounted for 57 percent of all graduate enrollments in 1997 (Brandes *et al.* 2001: 325). As a general category, women received 49 percent of doctorates in the social sciences in 1993, with a steady increase for women of color.[32] The National Center for Education Statistics (NCES) projected this trend to continue until the end of the century (NCES 1997). Yet all male faculty enjoy an average 10 percent advantage in salary at both public and private institutions (Bellas 2002) while nearly half of all faculty appointments made at institutions of higher learning fall in the adjunct or other part-time category – with women as the majority recipients (AAUP 1993).[33] A recent study claims that institutions, more than discrimination, accounts for a gender gap in wages (Glenn 2008). Women tend to teach more at public, master's level institutions where teaching overtakes research and its funding possibilities. Still, this study could not explain why a gap of $3,200/year between male and female professors still persists at research universities. Nor do these data break down according to racial categories. Anecdotal evidence suggests, however, that the racial and gender disproportion found in the academy's "formal (tenure-track) sector" would spill over to its "informal (adjunct)" one.

Another recent study by Monroe, Ozyurt, Wrigley and Alexander (2008) indicates the entrenched nature of gendered problems in the academy. The authors argue that the situation of women "within the Academy, an entity somewhere between a medieval guild, Byzantine fiefdom, and corporate bureaucracy" (Monroe *et al.* 2008: 230), draws on the same political strategies and institutional power regimes as the neoliberal imperium to secure asymmetries and inequalities. The authors conclude the following after analyzing salary data and interviewing 80 female faculty at a large, research institution:

> Overt discrimination has largely given way to less obvious but still deeply entrenched inequities . . . Women attributed the persistence of gender inequality not to biology but to a professional environment in which university administrators care more about the appearance than the reality of gender equality and a professional culture based on a traditional, linear male model.
>
> (Monroe *et al.* 2008: 215)

At root, we argue, are the intersections of race with gender. These social relations and their problematic discursive frames remain assumed, rather than examined, in the academy. For example, one Asian-American female professor observed that,

> [i]f we act like the [passive] Singapore Girl, in the case of some professors, then they feel "she is [unequal to me]." If we don't act like the Singapore Girl, then [our] accomplishments must have derived from "a relationship with the chair" [or some other senior male].
>
> (quoted in Cho 1997: 209)

In either case, Cho concludes, an Asian-American woman – or any woman of color – has difficulty obtaining recognition for her *professional* achievements. This is so, we add, because she must function in a context – an institutional power base – like the House of IR, that is defined by similar logics of the white colonial/imperial state intimately aligned with global capitalism. As Stoler notes, "sexual control was more than a convenient metaphor for colonial domination. It was a fundamental class and racial marker implicated in a wider set of relations of power" (Stoler 2002: 45). Similarly, the academy has preserved its privileges with racialized, sexualized colonial management, buttressed by a process that deracinates and depoliticizes knowledge.

Knowledge production: deracination and depoliticization

Epistemic erasure, in short, is inflicted on the Other. In deracinating and depoliticizing knowledge, epistemic erasure psychologizes systemic pathologies while mystifying the exploitation and violence committed onto Others. Some Others, in turn, consent to internalize their own structural oppression in exchange for admission into the House not as a "servant" or "ward" but as an "honored guest." At the same time, another desire complex arises in the House of IR. It publicly seeks to do good ("spreading democracy") while privately yearning for adoration and respect from the Other, a desire that can never be satiated ("why do they hate us?").

In a volume self-consciously titled, *Global Voices: Dialogues in International Relations* (Rosenau 1993), four IR scholars (2 men, 2 women, all white) critically discuss the field. Each scholar deserves due credit, for his/her insights have contributed to our own understanding and evaluation of the House of IR. Nonetheless, one chapter by a postmodern feminist disturbs (Sylvester 1993). She seeks validly to introduce race and difference into the dialogue on IR but masks her privilege with a colonizing move. She writes *in the name* of a Zimbabwean woman rather than having an actual conversation with one. The chapter is written creatively in the form of a play with exchanges from various characters: i.e., Westfem and Tsitsi. Westfem represents a Western standpoint feminist; Tsitsi, a Zimbabwean woman. Throughout the play, Tsitsi speaks only in terms of her own particularities whereas Westfem pronounces on theory, history, and politics in a universal tone. At one point, Westfem even lectures Tsitsi about Zimbabwean men to which the latter submissively agrees. Indeed, Westfem speaks for all; Tsitsi only for herself, and not very well. In fact, Tsitsi admits as much.

> Westfem-self, I tell you, we women have been gagged by tradition and colonialism for so long that now it is difficult for us to insist on our own voices, ideologies, and statecrafts.
>
> (Sylvester 1993: 30)

Such epistemic, political, and personal erasure pervades the House of IR. The US academic self-righteously presents the woman of color as a victim of "third-world" patriarchy in need of "first-world" feminist rescue without questioning either her right or place to do so. No wonder many women of color, inside and outside the West, react to "feminism" as another form of "imperialism."

The House of IR benefits from such in-fighting. As noted earlier, those who live "upstairs" by theorizing about "high politics" take little account of those who labor "downstairs" with their data collecting for "low politics" – until some crisis in world politics demands specific, local knowledge. At that point, ethnographic "servants" must produce the information necessary for House members to plug into their established theories. They treat this information as data only, not subject to theorization or capable of overhauling existing frameworks.

Note, for example, recent revelations of torture and sexual abuse by American soldiers against Iraqi detainees in Abu Ghraib. Mainstream attention has localized the relations between US soldiers and Iraqi prisoners. Media pundits, military leaders, and psychological experts explain away the abuse as a psychological distortion rather than expressions of a larger socio-economic and political pathology: i.e., abuse of US power to secure hegemony for global capitalist-patriarchy. No one asks, for example, why certain identities ("minority," "them," "queer") are always the target of abuse, while others ("majority," "us," "heterosexual") perpetrate it? As Sherene Razack (2000, 2004) demonstrates in her analysis of similar abuses by and among Canadian peacekeepers in Somalia, colonial legacies of race, gender, sexuality, class, and nation spare no one – not even those fighting for "peace," "democracy," and "justice."

Scholars from outside the West sometimes internalize this epistemic erasure. The "insecurity" of states in the South, writes Mohammed Ayoob (1992), stems from internal, not external, sources. Their lack of "maturity" in state development renders them "weak, intruder, have-nots," eternally dependent on the North for economic and military assistance, producing a sense of "impotence" and "deprivation" that leads to a "perpetual state of schizophrenia" (1992: 71–91). In contrast, Ayoob characterizes states in the North as "developed," "mature," "rich," "powerful," "the center"; they are, in short, the "managers of the international system" (1992: 71–91).

Ambivalence suffuses such scholarship. Though motivated to "brea[k] the [knowledge] monopoly that control[s]" the international system (Ayoob 2002: 27), scholars like Ayoob nonetheless reproduce it. He proposes a "subaltern realism" to "supplement" or, at most "dent," IR. Yet this resorts to similar conventions of "timeless" and "universal" maxims by explaining "third-world states" in terms of their "essential" and "fundamental" nature. Ayoob aims to broaden IR with alternative perspectives, yet he remains lodged in classical, Western theoretical frames and supports his arguments with references to conventional readings of Hobbes. Most troubling is Ayoob's failure to address how imperial/colonial capitalism draws asymmetrically on mediations of "first-" and "third-world" states to achieve its vision and mission. Nor does he recognize the existence of each world within the other leading to a similar outcome for all.

One could argue that collective schizophrenia afflicts states in the "North" as much as those in the "South." David Held, for instance, asserts that democracy is not a "fixed notion." It could be "re-invented" and "cosmopolitanized" by "deepening democracy within nation-states and extending it across political borders," thereby better serving our globalized, contemporary world order.[34] Held's proposition seems reasonable until we remember capitalism's role in producing the nation-state. Among other things, the nation-state "unified [a] legal code that protected private property . . . This economic act was, of course, represented as the creation of a harmonious community of people with a common language and a coherent culture and worldview" (Ebert 1999: 393). Held seeks to reform globalization's new transnational institutions but neglects to query: why would the capitalist state and its advocates want to "deepen" democracy when they benefit daily from the exploitation of labor and other structural inequalities? Globalization may open new opportunities for some but it also entails for most a "struggle over structured inequality in the world economy" (Ebert 1999: 5).[35] Cosmopolitan democracy may aim for more equality and justice but it conveys, instead, an elite class position replete with bourgeois, patriarchal interests. Consequently, cosmopolitan democracy cannot recognize and support those that it claims to. The concept remains an elegant, if remote, ideal with which to tantalize the world but which never finds concrete expression. Still, many at the pinnacle of the capitalist world economy ask: why do they hate us?

Practical politics: practices of masculinity

With Cosmo Man in charge of IR both as a discipline and as a source of knowledge production, we return to the theme of Chapter One: i.e., contending bouts of hypermasculinity in world politics. Ostensibly, world politics involves hypermasculine jousts in politics (e.g., "terrorists" vs "infidels," "democratic regime change" vs "occupation"), economics (e.g., "developed" vs "developing," "structural adjustment reforms" vs "neo-colonialism"), and culture (e.g., "civilization" vs "hegemony"). In actuality, practices of masculinity erase historical alternatives to "democracy" or "Islam" or "development." These denials manifest themselves most glaringly in the current transnationalization of militarization.

Alternative movements for "democracy" (e.g., indigenous movements, Zapatistas), "Islam" (e.g., secular governance in Arab states), or "development" (e.g., World Social Forum) lose out in this masculinity game. They do not comply with the abstract individualism and self-aggrandizing power mongering that militarization and marketization demand. Similarly, global practices of masculinity ignore women's groups, peace organizations, labor unions, and other entities even though these daily impact world politics through conflict resolution, crisis prevention, food distribution, and other forms of collective action.

Technology becomes the only fixation in town, and cynicism pervades all. Perpetrators claim that they resort to violence on behalf of democracy and freedom but they kill, violate, and torture their own as much as the enemy. Razack dissects one hazing ritual among Canadian peacekeepers in Somalia, videotaped and later broadcast on Canadian television. "A black corporal had 'KKK' written on [his] shoulder . . . [while being] tied to a tree," sprinkled with flour, referred to as Michael Jackson's "secret," symbolically anally raped, and required to crawl on all fours (2000: 139). White soldiers torture their black brothers-in-arms by re-enacting colonial racism's iconic images of the Other. They brand the black recruit instead of lynching him, taunt him for not being white, feminize him as a sex toy, and compare him to an animal. Such acts of racialized, sexualized torture are neither new nor limited to institutions of incarceration "out there." Domestic prisons in the US exhibit similar abuses (Surkiewicz 2004; Agathangelou, Bassichis and Spira 2008). Militarization has arrived "in here."

CONCLUSION

The academy must recognize – and redress – its complicity in world politics. IR as taught in the academy reflects and validates the voices, visions, and actions of such elite "world-makers" as representatives of the state, civil society, the media, the corporate sector, and those in non-governmental organizations (NGOs) who support the neoliberal imperium, not to mention the academy itself. But there's another category of "world-makers" – and their contestations and struggles already affect the academy. These world-makers are not-so recognized, often illegalized and/or at the margins, and rarely heard from or seen as actors in world politics, such as the stateless (e.g., displaced persons, illegal migrants, refugees), the illicit (e.g., smugglers, prostitutes, drug traffickers, mafia gangs), and the informalized (e.g., the young, the poor, the illiterate, the feminized, and the "non-Westernized"). These groups affect world politics as much as, and sometimes more so than, their elite counterparts. Yet IR as a discipline – the academy as a whole – remains fixated on the former to the exclusion of the latter. 9/11 has demonstrated clearly that world politics cannot continue with "business as usual." It must come to a more worldly sense of world politics. This means engaging seriously with the idea that the world is multiple and that those "at the margins" directly relate with those "at the center of power." Linking world politics as a realm of practical politics with sources of knowledge production and a field of academic training and education demands that we begin with this recognition of the academy's complicity.

These changes, however, cannot come about without simultaneous redress of the neoliberal imperium's origins: i.e., its ontology of fear and property.

4   Ontology of fear and property

'Όταν βλέπεις το τέρας να
προσέρχεται προς εσένα και δεν
μπορείς πλέον να το αναγνωρίσεις
είναι επειδή αρχίζεις να γίνεσαι αυτό

When you see the monster
approaching and you cannot
recognize it, it is because you
are beginning to resemble it.
Manos Hatjidakis (2003)[1]

Manos Hatjidakis refers to a series of violent events that occurred in Athens, Greece in April 1985 when university students, anarchists, and other radicals were attacked during protests against an event organized by the new right (New Democracy). Hatjidakis, a famous writer and composer, criticizes the Greek authority's abuse of power but also points to the ways that we can all turn into monsters of violence without realizing it. This can happen not because we stop being afraid but because we become used to being fearful. In this way, we come to embody the social ontology of fear and property that maintains the imperium's practices, including the formation of IR theories.

Hobbesian fear and Lockean property have long partnered the worst speculations on human nature (competition, struggle, anarchy, murder) with Europe's Enlightenment ideals (progress, efficiency, perfection, freedom). Inducted by the Treaty of Westphalia (1648) as some claim,[2] constituting an "international society" for many (Linklater and Suganami 2006), mainstream IR heralds modernity by combining sovereignty and territoriality with trade and commerce to hedge against war and destruction.[3] Neoliberal globalization meshes fear and property into an ideology of market rationalism for the entire globe, buttressed by consumer choice as the foundation of individual happiness and democratic politics. These require policies of discipline, education, and reform to achieve the desired outcome.

This chapter will show that the social ontology of fear and property undermines its own goals of peace, cooperation, and community-building. Derived from the Hobbesian conjecture of a fearful State of Nature and Locke's defense of private property, this social ontology requires complicity in inter-state relations to attain "modernity." We note that iconic paean to nineteenth-century colonialism and imperialism in Rudyard Kipling's *The White Man's Burden* (1899). Though English, Kipling wrote the poem to urge the US to take up Spain's mantle as colonizer to the Philippines. Kipling's imperial visions countered vociferous criticism from within the liberal community including, among others, Mark Twain's. Yet these alternative voices lost out to America's desire, fanned by patriarchal elites like Presidents William S. McKinley and Theodore Roosevelt, as Twain put it, to "buy into [Europe's] Society of Sceptred Thieves."[4] Under this construct, all actors in the inter-state system must comply with standardized markers of "progress," even if it means a politics of erasure between Self and Other, regardless of context. That liberal politics allows dissenters to protest does not undermine or even dent such power plays.

This chapter refers to two recent examples of fear and property in world politics: i.e., neoliberal responses to (a) Asia's financial crisis (1997–98), and (b) US corporate corruption scandals (2001–2). In both cases, the neo-liberal Self is defined as a unified leader of "the global order" that must take charge to ensure peace, prosperity, and propriety. This logic prevails even when the Self is complicit with bankruptcy and corruption at the high-est echelons of government and economy. Now Others retaliate in kind, if not in method, as we see the rise of hyper-muscular regionalism in Asia and increased bombings and insurgencies in the Middle East. Such rounds of retaliatory violence can only lead to more of the same. We conclude with a call for an alternative paradigm of world politics.

Let us begin with the ontological underpinnings of the neoliberal imperium: Hobbesian fear and Lockean property.

HOBBES, LOCKE, & CO.

Fear, for Hobbes, was "natural." It inhered in the individual ("the passions") and the environment ("State of Nature") before the establishment of law and order by the state ("Leviathan"). From this primordial condition came secondary fears such as death from murder by one's enemies or through starvation. Both stemmed from the same cause: competition for scarce resources in the State of Nature. Given this equation of resources with survival and the constant insecurity that it induced, man's rationality com-pelled him to give up the absolute freedom of the State of Nature for the relative freedom of the Leviathan. Hobbes believed, then, that man must obey the Leviathan, that mythological figure, in order to be protected.

Locke argued for the same benefits from the state but with greater skepticism and nuance regarding absolute rule. Locke accepted Hobbes' premise of radical democracy in the State of Nature and that man's ability to reason led him into society. But Locke did not have faith that any state, especially with unchecked power, could rule *fairly*. It is necessary, Locke stressed, to safeguard the individual's rights against the state and only property could do so. For property results from the individual's labor; accordingly, it grants him a natural right over the product of that labor, whether it is land tilled for farming or the harvest from that farm. Locke emphasized: no one, including the state, can/should usurp the individual's rights over that property which he acquired or produced through the feat of his own hard work.

In both cases, Joshua Foa Dienstag (1996) reminds us, Hobbes and Locke sought to control "the passions." For Hobbes, the Leviathan allowed man's "rationality" to control his "animal appetites and aversions" (Hobbes, quoted in Crawford 2000: 120). Similarly, Locke defined labor as both mental and physical to fulfill the Christian life's highest ideal: that is, to "trai[n] for war, a war upon one's own 'lusts and vices'" (Dienstag 1996: 502). He seized upon education as the most direct instrument of inculcating the virtue of self-denial. Adam Smith (1776) took a more radical stance and coined capitalism's first slogan, "private vice, public virtue," assuming that the first would lead, invariably, to the second (though not necessarily the other way around).

Others have made similar observations about Hobbes and Locke. C.B. Macpherson and Leo Strauss find Hobbesian authoritarianism lurking within Locke's Christian asceticism to condone, ultimately, a "rapacious capitalism" (Dienstag 1996: 499). Carole Pateman (1988) dissected the Hobbesian notion of a "social contract" to reveal its anti-social nature given that women, despite their labor in both productive and reproductive senses, were packaged, along with "children and chattel," as men's property to bring into civil society.[5] For Uday Mehta (1997), the liberal tradition was always devoted to the bourgeois order. Classical liberalism moved easily from subordinating and exploiting certain internal subjects, like women and the underclass, to producing and subordinating external Others, like India, now labeled "inscrutable." As with the domestic underclass, writes Mehta, liberals utilized "strategies of exclusion" to exile these historical, cultural Others from the "adult," "civilized" world of the hard-working bourgeoisie, relegating them, instead, to the status of children who need education. Colonialism, in short, reframed the Hobbesian–Lockean tradition: Spare the rod, it preached, and spoil the civilization/worker/native/child.

Max Weber (1958) whitewashed the whole enterprise of colonialism by asserting that public and private virtues were coterminous, regardless of context, power inequalities, and methods of production. That is, the Western state is not pursuing any venal self-interest but acting on "rational" and "bureaucratic" impulses that are reflective of "the Protestant Ethic." He concluded that Others who followed a contrary ethic like that of Confucianism could not possibly reach the same level of capitalist development: "Confucian rationalism meant rational adjustment to the world; Puritan rationalism meant rational mastery of the world" (Weber 1951: xxix).

Albert O. Hirschman (1977) echoed this version of Western economic history. He documented how leading lights of commerce, trade, politics, and public opinion in industrializing Europe believed in their hearts and souls that capitalism tempered "the passions" with banal, calculated "interests." Francis Fukuyama (1989) updated this line to declare an end to History itself. The fall of the Soviet empire demonstrated that only one true path to development could unfold and that was Western Liberal Capitalism. Life would be more stable, prosperous, and peaceful, noted Fukuyama but with a hint of lament. No more would we have the heart-thumping, blood-curdling, saber-rattling battles of old for glory, territory, or ideas. We'd have, instead, capitalism's endless "accounting" and other such economic calculations.

Constructing an Other, then, served a vital function for the classical, liberal Self. The Other provided a convenient target not just for Europe's guns, ships, and trade but also a moral and physical landscape to project all those passions and desires not allowed at home by "rational" Protestantism. European colonialism and its seizure of alien lands, resources, and peoples could be justified as "education," if not "salvation." The Other simply could not qualify for "universal" principles of rights, laws, and sovereignty. They had none of what Europeans could identify as "civilization" or even "the individual": e.g., a Leviathan-like state ("this land is free!"), religious virtue through self-denial ("they have no morals"), codified laws to establish order ("they cannot govern themselves"), and most importantly, repression of "the passions" ("they're animals"). Postwar economic development in the twentieth century later rephrased these rationales by pinpointing "lacks" in the Other found to flourish in the Western, capitalist Self: e.g., "rationality," "impersonal decision-making," "specialization" (see Banuri 1990).

The neoliberal imperium amends these classical roots. It accepts the premise that the absence of a global Leviathan in world politics analogizes the interstate system to Hobbes' State of Nature. Strong, domestic Leviathans/states must make up the difference with sovereignty. Neoliberal IR extends this definition of sovereignty to other categories, such as, goods owned but not necessarily produced by corporations (legally defined as individuals), and ideas ("intellectual property") which are, again, owned by those who patent but not necessarily create them. But where classical liberalism claimed a self-deprecating banality, neoliberalism heralds an era of "democratic," if not "capitalist peace" (see Gartzke 2007). It contends that liberal capitalism raises the stakes for war, thereby discouraging it, due to investment's need to maintain uninterrupted, mutually-beneficial transactions. Indeed, such self-interested cooperation among states pertains even under conditions of international anarchy (Keohane 1984). Capitalist market practices, after all, produce all the fundaments of a democratic society: e.g., a "revolutionary" middle class, an active civil society, rational pursuit of individual interest that leads to self-censoring collective action and rule of law (Olson 1993; Held 1995). Neoliberal restructurings, as another venue for imperial-capitalism, embed democracy "in the depths of people's hearts and minds" (Sakamoto 1991: 122).

The transnational bourgeois order becomes multicultural and fun, if not downright hip. When the Soviet Union disbanded, for instance, neoliberals in the West celebrated with a series of television commercials that showed the former Communist bloc's dull, grey, uptight command economies finally "free" to pursue Western-style capitalism.[6] By implication, everyone *wants* to, not just should, be like the Western, Christian neoliberal Self. Note these advertising slogans from one of corporate capitalism's enduring icons, the Coca-Cola Company. A sample from the end of the Cold War in 1989 to the present conveys the easy, everyday allure promised by a bottle of Coke:

1990: "You Can't Beat the Real Thing"
2001: "Life is Good/Life Tastes Good"
2005: "Make it Real"
2006: "Welcome to the Coke side of life"
2007: "The Coke Side of Life"[7]

Still, neoliberalism retains its classical moorings by mystifying or denying its own desires or passions (Crawford 2000). Similarly, IR as an institution, set of theories and practices, posits that world politics is ruled by "rational," "objective" interests whose trajectories can be inferred formally, mathematically, and impartially (see King, Keohane, and Verba 1994). In this way, neoliberal IR preserves "pleasure" for the Self and "passion" for the cultural, historical, colonized Other, and the neoliberal imperium preserves classical colonial power even with "globalization's" new venues, formats, and seemingly radically different social relations (see Ling 2005).

Rudyard Kipling's "The White Man's Burden" encapsulates this classical ideal. Imperialism, it paenes, was not just for the Self but, more pressingly, for the Other.

"The White Man's Burden"

"The White Man's Burden," published in February 1899 in *McClure's Magazine*, exhorts the US to take over where Spain could no longer rule, the Philippines. (Often, the poem's subtitle is overlooked: "The United States and The Philippine Islands.") The poem demarcates clear boundaries between the American Self and its Filipino Other. The American Self, the poem argues, has an obligation to colonize, civilize, and enlighten its Filipino Other. After all, the American Self, like its British counterpart, gained its privileges through a naturally endowed superiority. The Filipinos were given no role other than to emulate, as best as possible, the Anglo-American Self. Accordingly, their relationship could only be unilateral, hierarchical, authoritative (if not authoritarian), and predictable. In a word: imperial.

The poem begins with a call (*Take up the White Man's burden – Send forth the best ye breed –*) for civilizational duty (*Fill full the mouth of Famine/And bid the sickness cease*). But beware, it warns, for noblesse oblige costs dearly. First comes resentment and ingratitude from your subjects (*Your new-caught, sullen peoples*). They don't know any better (*Half-devil and half-child*). Then you pay with blood, sweat, and tears (*Go make them with your living, And mark them with your dead*).[8] The entire endeavor seems hopeless sometimes (*Watch Sloth and heathen Folly/Bring all your hope to nought*). But your rewards, when they come, are transcendent. Empire gives its followers a rare manhood (*Come now, to search your manhood/Through all the thankless years*) that reflects *real* experience with and knowledge of the world (*Cold, edged with dear-bought wisdom*) that honors its soldiers for all time (*The judgment of your peers!*).

Theodore Roosevelt, then Vice-President and soon to be President, was so impressed with the poem that he sent a copy to his friend, Senator Henry

Cabot Lodge. It's "rather poor poetry," he commented, "but good sense from the expansion point of view."[9] Roosevelt was right. The poem served well for an expansionist US foreign policy. With its proximity to China and that mythical market, the Philippines beckoned as a much-needed antidote to economic downturns at the time. Colonialism was good for business, ruling elites agreed (see McClintock 1995).

The US won the Spanish-American War (1898) and paid Spain $20 million for the privilege of seizing its territories. (Upon hearing this, Mark Twain claimed that he "laughed until [his] sides ached." The US purchased territory that it could not possibly own, Twain pointed out, in order to take dominion over a people over whom it had no rights. This act is comparable, he cracked, to "an American heiress buying a Duke or an Earl."[10]) Before victory was assured, however, the US had promised the Filipinos their independence if they would aid the Americans by fighting the Spanish from within. The Treaty of Paris later reneged on this offer by ceding Spanish sovereignty over the Philippines, Puerto Rico, Guam, and Cuba to US control.

At home, outraged critics formed the Anti-Imperialist League. Its members, including Jane Adams, Andrew Carnegie, William James, and Mark Twain, among others, grew to 30,000 members, spanning 30 states.[11] Many expressed their disgust and dismay by lampooning Kipling's poem. Henry Labouchère penned his parody, "The Brown Man's Burden" (1899). Yes, Labouchère mocked, "Compel [the brown man] to be free" and if he dares to protest,

> Then, in the name of freedom,
> Don't hesitate to shoot.

Howard S. Taylor (1899) bemoaned the price that the poor man has to pay, in body and treasure, for the rich man's wars:

> With vigor on her borders
> And slow decay at home!

Let's not even go there, chastised E.A. Brininstool in "The White Woman's Burden" (1899). Until men recognize the burdens that women have to bear from morning 'til dusk, she retorted, they have nothing to complain about:

> If he had to mop up the kitchen,
> And dress the kids as well,
> And start the fire at 5 a.m.,
> He might of his "burden" tell.[12]

This liberal dissent, however, could not override the state's greater investment in fear and property. US imperialism continued unabated and, with it, an immediate complement: state violence. US troops brutally suppressed local Filipino resistance before marching triumphantly into Manila to declare America's sovereignty over the islands.

> Faced with a guerrilla struggle supported by the vast majority of the population, the U.S. military responded by resettling populations in concentration camps, burning down villages (Filipinos were sometimes forced to carry the petrol used in burning down their own homes), mass hangings and bayonetings of suspects, systematic raping of women and girls, and torture ... According to official statistics ... U.S. troops killed fifteen times as many Filipinos as they wounded. This lit [sic] with frequent reports by U.S. soldiers that wounded and captured Filipino combatants were summarily executed on the spot.[13]
>
> (*Monthly Review* 2003)

US troops also battled Muslim Filipinos, known as Morns, in the South. In 1906, the US military massacred 900 Morns, including women and children, by trapping them in a volcanic crater on the island of Jolo and bombarding them with bullets for days. President Theodore Roosevelt immediately wired General Leonard Wood, commander of the massacre: "I congratulate you and the officers and men of your command upon the brilliant feat of arms wherein you and they so well upheld the honor of the American flag."[14]

Today, the US continues to target the Muslims (Moro) in the Philippines' southern region of Mindanao. They are rumored to associate with other Islamic insurgency organizations like al Qaeda. The US has increased aid and military exercises, accordingly, with the Filipino government in Manila (Berrigan, Hartung and Heffel 2005). Another byproduct of America's decisive military victory in Iraq is that ruling elites in other parts of the world have stopped negotiating with local insurgent groups. They resort, instead, to military extremes like "shock and awe" (Klein 2005).

Echoes of Kipling still resound. The *Economist*, a key organ of neoliberal propagation, identifies a new round of "burdens" for the imperium.

NEOLIBERAL "BURDENS"

The *Economist* devoted a Special Report in its 14 August 2003 issue to the topic: "America and Empire."[15] Is America, it asked, as the world's only military and economic superpower, now also an empire? The magazine concluded with a resounding "No" for two reasons: (a) the natives (in Iraq and Afghanistan) don't like it ("please leave us to get on with our own affairs"), and (b) neither do Americans ("freedom is in their blood; it is integral to their sense of themselves").[16]

This version of history is selective at best. When do "natives" ever welcome an occupying power? And when does their lack of welcome ever stop an occupying force? The *Economist* acknowledged that white settlers in America's thirteen colonies rebelled against British rule ("Americans know that empires lack democratic legitimacy. Indeed, they once had a tea party to prove it") but failed to recognize that those settlers did the same to natives of the land they arrogantly de-populated as "the New World." Michael Hunt (1987) has demonstrated that American state-building was based historically on the annihilation, domination, and enslavement of the racialized, sexualized Other. Untold millions of native peoples, for example, were killed by a combination of wars, betrayals, dislocations, relocations, and germs (Churchill 1998). The savagery of the Morn massacre in the Philippines was but a small sample of how the US got to be where it is today. Other areas and peoples that were sacrificed at the altar of America's "manifest destiny" include Alaska, Guam, Haiti, Hawaii, Samoa, and Puerto Rico. For the *Economist* to erase this history with a facile gesture toward the rhetoric of American democracy, claiming that it's in "their blood," constitutes irony of the highest and most grotesque order.

The *Economist* is all-too predictable. As a vital member of the neo-liberal intellectual infrastructure, it has long participated in a colonial narrative of the all-conquering, globe-straddling (Western) capitalist ready to take (third-world) "virgin" economies and resources at will, making them "productive" in the image of the Self (Hooper 2001). In this Special Report, the *Economist* resorted to similar racist, sexist, and imperialist tropes. It began by claiming that "a surprising number have welcomed the new role" of America as an imperial power. It named Max Boot, an Englishman transplanted to New York initially as editorial features editor of *The Wall Street Journal*, and now Olin Senior Fellow in National Security Studies with the Council on Foreign Relations, a conservative think tank. The title of Boot's book, *The Savage Wars of Peace* (2002), was a line taken from "The White Man's Burden," to underscore his support of this nineteenth-century approach to world affairs. The book received the Best Book Award of 2002 from the *Washington Post*, *Christian Science Monitor*, and the *Los Angeles Times* and won the 2003 General Wallace M. Greene Jr. Award for the best nonfiction book pertaining to Marine Corps history. They lauded the book for presenting "[t]he U.S. imperial role in the Philippines . . . as a model for the kind of imperial role that Boot and other neoconservatives are now urging on the United States" (*Monthly Review* 2003).

The *Economist* cited others supporting US imperialism. Those giving it "a remarkably warm reception" included Robert Cooper, a British diplomat; Michael Ignatieff, former Director of Harvard's Center on Human Rights and, since 2006, a member of the Canadian parliament, now trying to become the next leader of the Liberal Party in Canada; and Niall Ferguson, a Scotsman transplanted to Harvard's History Department. Cooper has called for "a new kind of imperialism" modeled after the "post-modern European Union;" Ignatieff sees no alternative to imperialism if the rich and powerful seek to "save" the world from itself; and Ferguson gruffly reminds the US of its imperial obligations, much like those undertaken by the British empire, which "'though not without blemish', may have been the least bloody path to modernity for its subjects."[17] Nowhere in the Special Report were there any voices from people of color, women, or those outside the neoliberal mainstream. As for the Iraqi and Afghan people, the *Economist* derided them for having "teething troubles" when they refused to accept US occupation of their homes and their countries.

Neoliberal desire flames on violently. Just as the magazine colludes with the imperium by infantilizing whole societies and peoples in this manner, so too does it sexualize power, especially for the US: "In short, the empire now proclaimed in America's name is at best a dull duck, at worst a dead duck, unless it is to be a big strong drake that intends to throw its weight around for quite a while.[18] Noah Feldman, a senior advisor to the draft constitution in Iraq, clearly identifies with the latter. "Elections," he writes, "can seduce with the promise of release" (2004: 95). His explanation merits quoting at length:

> Elections hold out the hope of successful consummation, the seed of democracy implanted and the door opened for subsequent withdrawal. In this troubling vision the occupied people grip the occupier in an embrace both pleasurable and terrifying. In the imagined "successful" scenario, the occupier builds and leaves. When things go wrong, he (sic) cannot get out but is sucked into what American vernacular calls "the quagmire" – a situation from which he cannot extract himself, but in which he cannot remain without suffering unmanning damage.
> (Feldman 2004: 95)

To Feldman, then, elections point to different possibilities: the emergence of democracy, the embroilment of occupier and occupied in both "pleasing" and "terrifying" positions. Feldman's text brings to mind another famous, albeit fictional, narrative about imperial relations: *Madame Butterfly*. Lt. Pinkerton, the story's love-'em-and-leave-'em anti-hero, seems to serve as Feldman's model of "success" for contemporary US policy in Iraq and Afghanistan. Lt. Pinkerton, an American naval officer, not only failed to inform his Japanese mistress that he had a wife back home, but he also "graciously" adopted his son by her, to be raised "properly" in America with his American wife, after the mistress commits suicide. So, too, does Feldman suggest that America owes Iraq no more than the introduction of democracy and leave home with the progeny of a smaller vision of oneself (i.e., democratic America) and care less about the consequences (i.e., possible national suicide).

Feldman implies as much with his less-than-satisfactory scenario for locals when it comes to elections.

> From the perspective of the nation under occupation, elections seduce in a different sort of way. On one hand, they promise to give voice to the voiceless . . . In that same moment of self-creation . . . the nation being built can throw off the yoke of its occupier and declare its independence, thus breaking free of the humiliating status of being subordinated . . . On the other hand, people under nation building fear elections for the danger of what they may reveal. Fragmented results

may show that there is no nation there at all, just a collection of divergent interest groups who lack the common vision to make a government that will endure. The election of undemocratic forces is also to be feared.

(Feldman 2004: 95)

For the occupied, he suggests, elections and democracy may be a wet dream. The occupied could wake up in sweaty disillusion to find no love there, after all, just more anxieties about one's own uncontrollable, compelling urges.

The Iraq Study Group (ISG 2006) effectively agreed with this Pinkerton strategy for the US in Iraq.[19] Chaired by former US Secretary of State James Baker III and former Congressman Lee H. Hamilton, the ISG recommended that the US utilize a variety of steps, including involving Iraq's neighbors Syria and Iran, to facilitate a phased withdrawal from Iraq. "The United States should not make an open-ended commitment to keep large numbers of American troops deployed in Iraq," the ISG cautioned. Nonetheless, key sectors of the Iraqi polity, economy, and society should remain under US advisement. The US, the ISG suggested, should include "improvements to the Iraqi criminal justice system, the Iraqi oil sector, the US reconstruction efforts in Iraq, the US budget process, the training of US government personnel, and US intelligence capabilities." The US would withdraw its troops but retain control over key sectors of the country.

All this talk of an American empire, G. John Ikenberry insists, misses the point. The US, together with other "advanced democracies" in alliance with China and Russia, pioneers a "democratic political order that has no name or historical antecedent" and is "built on bargains, diffuse reciprocity, and an array of intergovernmental institutions and ad hoc working relationships" (Ikenberry 2004). This foundation in "cooperation and rules" has "limited and legitimated U.S. power." "When all is said and done," Ikenberry concludes, "Americans are less interested in ruling the world than they are in creating a world of rules."

At first glance, Ikenberry seems curiously naive. In asserting that rules constitute neutral standards, he seems to deny an obvious link between rules and the rule-maker. But if he is aware that power underwrites "a world of rules," then he is enacting both Hobbes and Locke by "acquiring" legitimacy through *his* rules to keep fear of Others at bay. The rule-maker, after all, has the final, authoritative word. These acts of power remain hidden because the very purpose of rules is to mystify power and its social relations. In this way, power remains naturalized, eternalized, and internalized. That various actors could "bargain" in so-called international institutions changes neither the unequal context in which they do so nor the unjust consequences that invariably result. The mere fact that most rules in dominant institutions govern the world without input from its majority populations – e.g., workers, women, and, especially, women of color – exposes the hollow self-interest that trumpets "cooperation," "rules," and "institutions" alone as any kind of "democratic political order."

Ikenberry (2004) reveals as much in a recent article on China and "the future of the West." How will "the postwar Western order," he asks, deal with "the drama" of China's rise in the existing global order? Ikenberry assures his *Foreign Affairs* readership that the uniquely "open, integrated, and rule-based" nature of the Western liberal order with its "wide and deep political foundations" will integrate China, not be disrupted by it – as long as China is "managed properly." "If the defining struggle is between China and a revived Western system," Ikenberry predicts, "the West will triumph." And the US, as author of this "unusually durable and expansive order," must "reinvest in the Western order, reinforcing the features of that order that encourage engagement, integration, and restraint."

The question remains. Why does Ikenberry, like so many in the neoliberal imperium, present China as somehow alien to or outside of "the Western system"? Has not China as a state been a "modern" entity for almost a century since its earliest inception as a republican revolution was inspired by Lincoln via Sun Yatsen, later re-made by Marx and Lenin via Mao?

Here, we discern the social relations of power between rules and rule-maker. Two such examples are the responses of neoliberal elites to cases of capitalist meltdown: (a) Asia's financial crisis (1997–98), and (b) America's corporate corruption scandals (2001–2).

"NEVER AGAIN!"

At the end of the twentieth century, Asia's "miracle" economies seemed on the verge of collapse. In 1997, a run on loans resulted with the IMF "rescuing" Thailand with $17 billion, Indonesia with almost $40 billion, and South Korea with $57 billion (Pollack 1997). A thirty-year dictatorship fell in Indonesia and riots and strikes erupted from Northeast to Southeast Asia. The region seemed mired in chaos economically and politically.

Neoliberal elites in the West crowed. There is only one economic model for the world to follow, intoned then Chairman of the US Federal Reserve, Alan Greenspan, to the Senate Foreign Relations Committee in February 1998, and that is "the Western form of free-market capitalism" (Sanger 1998: 1). The neoliberal, mainstream media denounced the Asian financial crisis for its "complacency, cronyism, and corruption" (Singh and Weisse 1999: 204) aided by a "culture of deceit" (Gibney 1998), among other factors. Editorialist Thomas Friedman of the *New York Times* claimed that Asian societies lacked the "software" (i.e., regulatory agencies, banking controls, transparency, bureaucratic professionalism, civil society) to match the "hardware" (i.e., relatively free markets, free trade, open capital flows) that advanced industrialization required (Friedman, quoted in Rao 1998: 1411). Another observer proselytized that Asians needed to strengthen certain values such as "directness" and "transparency" to counter their tendencies toward "circumspection" and "secrecy" (Rao 1998: 1411). *Time Magazine* likened the IMF to the "expeditionary forces" that America and other Western nations sent to an ailing Asia in the past (Lacayo 1997: 36).

Academics who previously had touted Asian institutions as a new model for late-modern capitalism now blamed these same institutions for being the problem (see Haggard 1999).[20]

"Never again" refrains throughout Asia today (Bello 2007). This slogan cautions against ever again subjecting the region to the West's neoliberal designs. Many regard those who precipitated the crisis – i.e., Western lenders – as "terrorists" (Bradsher 2007). In May 2000, the Association of Southeast Asian Nations (ASEAN) together with China, South Korea, and Japan formed the "Chiang Mai Initiative" (CMI) as part of the "ASEAN Plus 3" coalition.[21] It would allow member states to swap foreign currency reserves so no central bank could be raided on the scale of 1997–98.[22] Other measures for regional cooperation included surveillance and monitoring of capital flows along with personnel training that would facilitate this.

These strategies build on Malaysia's defiance of the IMF in 1998 by setting external capital controls to stem the crisis (see Nguyen 2003). Contrastingly, South Korea, the country that most complied with IMF conditionalities, now suffers from increased poverty (3 percent of the population in 1996 to 11.6 percent in 2006), greater social malaise (one of the highest suicide rates among developed countries), continued labor unrest due to massive layoffs, and unprecedented foreign ownership (up to 40 percent) within Korea's financial and industrial conglomerates or *chaebol* (Bello 2007).

Thailand, for example, is opting for a more inward-oriented, Buddhist-based Keynesianism called the "sufficiency economy" (*setakit pawpieng*) (Zuehlke 2008). Others turn to China, the world's fourth largest economy with huge credit reserves from the US economy, for political and economic leadership. Unexpected beneficiaries of the crisis have been the family-owned, patriarchally-controlled Chinese firms that network throughout the world but are most concentrated in East and Southeast Asia. These firms, more than others, were able to withstand the worst effects of the crisis by transferring capital to one another, on a fluid and emergency basis, due to their strong, personal ties cemented by clan, marital, or other kinship relations (Peng 2002). Most likely, these business networks will play an even stronger role in the region.

Still, these economies' plans for retributive growth depend on exploiting domestically marginalized groups like women. A 1 July 2007 labor law in South Korea, for instance, aims to regulate those workers, mostly women, "shed" into part-time status by *chaebol* reforms ordered by the IMF (Doucette 2007). Meant to promote part-time workers to full-time status after two years of employment at the same firm, the law has motivated, instead, the firing of women just before they qualify for such status; furthermore, their work can be outsourced to cheaper labor elsewhere (Ahn 2007). Women workers thus find themselves, once again, at the bottom of South Korea's developmental ladder (Han and Ling 1998; Truong 1999; Doucette 2007). For economies less industrialized than South Korea's, sex trafficking and sex tourism remain a compensatory source of profit-making. A $7–9.5 billion per year industry, human trafficking alone targets almost 200,000–225,000 women and children each year, mostly from Southeast Asia (International Organization for Migration 2000: 88).

THE ENRON EFFECT

Two months after 9/11, a series of corporate scandals rocked the US and the world. Instead of moral indictments, as experienced with Asia's financial crisis, neoliberals characterized the corporate corruption scandals as, simply, a case of "a few bad apples" (see Cavaluzzo 2004).

Enron, a "star" corporation and favorite of both Bush Administrations, collapsed from financial mismanagement through corporate looting. In quick succession came exposés of similar criminality by high-level, highly-paid chief executive officers (CEOs): e.g., $512 million at Global Crossing, more than $300 million at Tyco, over $300 million at Worldcom, $135 million (Canadian) at Nortel Networks Corporation. Thousands of workers lost their jobs, lifelong savings, and pension funds (Ling 2005).

Cries of "scandal," "misconduct," "crime," "wrong-doing," and "fraud" headlined the news but focused primarily on individuals and their personal failings. Where larger, institutional problems were recognized, these remained limited to specific problem areas: e.g., weaknesses in corporate governance, where practices may be legal but unethical; a "managers' capitalism" that subordinated workers' interests over the corporation's overall well-being; interlocking boards and networks that enabled yet camouflaged long-term conflicts of interest; the "tyranny" of shareholder values that distorted corporate production and growth; the prevalence of "absentee ownership" that divorced management from labor (Ling 2005). Neither did the government escape unscathed. Many accused the Bush Administration of "sleaze" and "stupidity" when it appointed sympathetic insiders to the Securities and Exchange Commission (SEC), the agency mandated to oversee the corruption cases. Certain politicians also came under fire for doing the corporate lobbyists' bidding by seeking deregulation at all costs. Alan Greenspan coined the terms "infectious greed" and "irrational exuberance" to account for this rash of corporate corruption. But only Walden Bello, a critical economist based in Bangkok and Manila, labeled the rash of corporate corruptions a "crisis" (Bello 2002).

The neoliberal media depicted the American corporate executive as a latter-day knight whose shining coat of armor laid tattered at his feet (*Businessweek* 2002) – but only temporarily. Individuals may have succumbed to greed and unscrupulousness but, unlike the degenerate, decadent "Orient," the US corporate sector did not function within a societal or cultural system that allowed such corruption to become the norm. The corruption scandals highlighted, instead, the inherent vitality and rightness of the American system and its business ethic. Clearly, better legislation was needed but the problem itself was contained, isolated, and idiosyncratic. A discussion on CNN's "Money Morning" on 2 December 2002, the first anniversary of Enron's collapse, reiterated this faith and optimism in the fundamentals of American corporate capitalism. "[T]he important lesson going forward is to make sure that that problem is staved and that people can count on the accounting transparency of our companies and our public accounting firms" (CNN 2002). After all, capitalism is all about dynamic change and destruction, with innovation as its promise and challenge. "[J]ust as crisis is in [capitalism's] nature," wrote Charles Leadbeater (2002) in the *New Statesman*, "so is adaptability . . . [From] bubbles, booms, busts and collapses [come] innovation, growth, creativity and vitality." Brian M. Carney (2002) of the *Wall Street Journal* declared: "Capitalism [can] fix itself [and so far] it's doing quite nicely [thank you]." He further thumped that the corporate scandals separated the "chaff" from the "wheat," allowing us to "marvel" at the "strengths" of the US corporate governance that "leav[es] the rest of the economy healthier," unlike Other industrial wannabes, like Europe and Japan, where "governments make every attempt to prop up their corporations – at a heavy economic cost" (Carney 2002). Peter T. Leeson (2002) of the *Chicago Sun Times* hymned that corporate America *can* redeem itself. The corporate scandals have returned America to its progressive, virtuous, and stoic *true* nature – that is, enlightened self-interest – thereby permitting "foreigners" to learn so that they, too, could progress. Capitalism's ability to "self-correct," Leeson thrilled, acts as a "great uniter" of different cultures, leading, of course, to world peace.

Indeed, the wars in Afghanistan and Iraq have redeemed the US corporate hero, allowing him to resurge bigger than ever. Mega-corporations like Halliburton (where Vice President Dick Cheney was CEO) received multi-billion dollar, "no bid" contracts even before the bombing stopped (*CBS News* 2003). As of this writing Halliburton remains the highest paid contractor for Iraq and Afghanistan, totaling almost $12 billion.[23] More generally, firms from the US and Western Europe dominate the privatization of military services and operations in the region. Compared to 135,000 US troops in Iraq as of June 2005, private contractors numbered nearly 155,000 in the same fields of operation at the same time (Calaguas 2006: 59).

Campaign contributions from the corporate sector helped. In 2001, even before the wars in Afghanistan and Iraq began, "ten prominent contracting firms expended over $32 million on US lobbying efforts and shelled out more than $12 million in political campaign contributions" (Calaguas 2006: 75). Halliburton led the pack with 95 percent of its $700,000 spent on Republicans; DynCorp followed suit with 72 percent of its $500,000 to the same (Calaguas 2006: 75). No wonder the Bush Administration lost little time in rehabilitating and revalorizing these corporations.

Businesses underscore hypermasculine whiteness as managerial wisdom. A 2006 study, for instance, finds that "leadership" is still defined in male terms only. In other words, when women exert "leadership," they are seen as "false men," but if they draw on typically feminine traits for management, they are judged "ineffective" (*Catalyst* 2007). The study does not differentiate race in its findings but as Richard L. Zweigenhaft and G. William Domhoff (1998) point out, the rules of corporate America still adhere to those set by upper-class, Christian, white males despite the entrance of women, Jews, blacks, Asians, Latinos, gays, lesbians, and trans peoples in the workforce.

CONCLUSION

Liberals secure a particular "world order" through Hobbesian fear and Lockean property. Who has property, who does not, and who uses fear to acquire, preserve, and/or expand property become crucial strategies in everyday interactions. Moreover, ideas about culture and subjects play crucially into these calculations. Being fearful and desiring property, then, become legitimized as a way of being. From Kipling's "White Man's Burden" to "crony capitalism" in Asia to the resurgent "white knight" of US/Western corporate capitalism, we see the neoliberal hegemony of fear and property in operation. Its path to "civilizing the world" with newer manifestations of Manifest Destiny is paved with the bodies of those who challenge and organize against such projects . . . Worthy of note is that Hobbes and Locke in the seventeenth century were articulating a process already underway a century before, when merchants ships inadvertently encountered cultures, societies, and peoples previously unknown to the European Self:

> When Vespucci speaks of a world he refers to the old notion of ecumene, of a portion of the Earth fit for human habitation. If he licitly designates the recently explored countries as a new world, it is because he intends to announce the effective finding of one of these other ecumenes.
>
> (O'Gorman 1961: 34)

Put differently, Vespucci did not consider the peoples of "the New World" as human; only Europe could make them so. In the 1500s, such anxiety about difference stemmed from Europe's peripheral location to the Islamic world. In "bursting the bounds within which Islam had confined it" (O'Gorman 1961: 90), Europe pushed its ontology of fear and property onto Others, transforming them into objects of and instruments for colonization, domination, exploitation, and humiliation. To justify these acts, Europe had to produce "texts of reason." Even when these seem to be about "dis-covery" (with emphasis on "covering") rather than fear and domination for profit, they nonetheless punctuated the terms of relations between Self and Other as alterity, thereby fixing the identities of both Self and Other as irreconcilably opposed. These texts, along with the newer ones discussed in previous chapters, make apparent that Eurocentrism (Amin 1989), qualified with newer forms of Manifest Destiny and their violences, still inform the neoliberal imperium.

The consequences of this ontology are grave. Redress requires another understanding of the world and our relations in it.

To wit, worldism.

Part II
In and of multiple worlds

5   Worldism

> *Mélange*, hotchpotch, a bit of this and a bit of that is *how newness enters the world*.
>
> Salman Rushdie, "In Good Faith" (1990, original emphasis)[1]

Let us now explain worldism. As suggested by Salman Rushdie above, worldism theorizes about how "a bit of this and a bit of that" builds "newness" into the world. It is this creative connection that we illustrate in this chapter. Toward this end, this chapter identifies worldism's main features and their intellectual precedents: i.e., constructivism, postmodernism, and postcolonial studies, along with Marxist and feminist contributions to history, philosophy, and revolutionary practice. We also chart how worldism differs from them in significant ways. To fully introduce worldism, this chapter continues into the next two, Chapters Six and Seven, by demonstrating, respectively, the role of fiction and poetry as methods for worldism and examples of worldist intervention into three sites of contemporary world politics: (a) the "Cyprus problem," (b) US–India–China "triangulation," and (c) the "global war on terror." Chapter Eight concludes the book by returning to those issues raised in Part I: the politics of erasure, neoliberal desire and violence, complicity in knowledge production, and the hegemonic ontology of fear and property. Chapter Eight also ends with a dramatic sequence. It features that classical Subaltern Man, Shakespeare's Othello, and what happens when he encounters a worldist approach to life.

First, let us answer: What is worldism?

MAIN ASPECTS

Worldism presents world politics as a site of multiple worlds. These refer to the various and contending ways of being, knowing, and relating that have been passed onto us from previous generations. Histories, languages, myths, and memories institutionalize and embody multiple worlds through simple daily acts like cooking and eating, singing and dancing, joking and playing but also through larger events like trade, development, conflict, and war. Worldism registers not only the "difference" that comes from multiple worlds (see Inayatullah and Blaney 2004) but also their entwinements. Selves and others reverberate,[2] producing multi- and trans-subjectivities that leave us legacies of reinforcement and conflict, reconstruction and critique, reconciliation and resistance. Such syncretic engagements belie seeming oppositions and contradictions among multiple worlds to reveal their underlying connections despite hegemony's violent erasures. On this basis, communities have opportunities to heal and recuperate so they can build for another day, for another generation.

Worldism as everyday life enacts self–other reverberations and syncretic engagements, especially by communities at the margins. Worldism as an analytical framework theorizes about them. Both types of worldist activity expose the problematic of empire in practice and logics. Building on the postcolonial notion that *all* parties make history, albeit with unequal access to power, worldism leads to an undeniable conclusion: our mutual embeddedness makes us mutually accountable. One cannot escape from the other. Mutual accountability brings with it duties and responsibilities, to be sure, but also possibilities: that is, (a) an internal dialectic of constant questioning to check and problematize hegemony, so that (b) we can expand our visions, strategies, and approaches beyond the narrow, hegemonic confines of realism/liberal internationalism, in order to (c) arrive at a more inclusive, conciliatory, and democratic world politics.

In brief, worldism consists of two simultaneous processes: descriptive and analytical. Worldism-as-description features the following: (a) *multi-* and *trans-subjectivities* that institutionalize the social and structural reverberations between selves and others; (b) the *agency* of all parties, despite inequities and injustices, to create, build, and articulate multiple worlds; (c) *syncretic engagements* that consolidate the entwinements of multiple worlds into concrete strategies for change, adjustment, adaptation, reformulation, and transformation; and (d) *community-building* that integrates and accretes these syncretic engagements despite denials of such efforts from hegemonic elites and their ideologies. Worldism-as-analysis draws on the struggles and learning undertaken in worldist daily life to emphasize: (a) *accountability* as a hallmark of worldist inquiry that ensures (b) an internal *criticality* to question, contest, and challenge hegemony, so that we may (c) arrive at *emancipatory reconstruction* even as we critique and resist.

The critical reader may interject: Couldn't "agency" and "accountability" in worldism be taken as a fancy way of blaming the victim? Are Jews, for example, responsible for the Holocaust; slaves for their enslavement; or any oppressed people for their oppression?

Worldism as a politics of multiple relations subsumes this liberal, individualist understanding of responsibility. Multiple relations produce a web of effects and consequences to any kind of decisions and/or set of practices. Accountability in worldism asks: Who's involved, under what conditions, and through which processes can we redress or transform the violence? What kinds of understanding are generated to account for these relations and/or to make them invisible? Without the painful concession that all of us, "abusers," "victims," and "innocent bystanders" alike, contribute to the production of hegemonic violence, whether it results in domestic abuse (see Adler and Ling 1995) or state violence (see Ling 1994), we may never realize how violence is conceived, generated, and sustained. By extension, we will never understand ways to end it. Instead, in our injuries and (self) alienation, we may reproduce time and again the same conditions of violence or hegemony that afflicted us in the past and which seems the only option for the present. Suspended political ideals, in this case, could also block us from action and change. Worldist agency and accountability compel us to face the complicities (including our own) that sustain violence in the making of history, so that we may, as Marx exhorted, change it.

Where do these ideas come from?, our reader may ask. Let us delineate the intellectual precedents to worldism.

INTELLECTUAL PRECEDENTS

Worldism draws on constructivism and postmodernism but also differs from them. Worldism shares with constructivism its emphasis on intersubjectivity, and with postmodernism its insights on asymmetrical difference: that is, the norms, institutions, practices, and behaviors that set up certain subjects and subjectivities as more privileged and protected than others. Power, then, cannot be reduced to an objectified, reified condition of who's "on top" or who "has more" but instead results from agents contributing to macro-political structures like ideology, organization, and capitalist relations. Power redefined in these terms stems from an intersubjective consensus within a context of material conditions and relations. The crux here lies in the *framing*. Since narration as a process is never complete, the story can always change.[3]

However, worldism departs from constructivism by asking: What *kinds* of intersubjectivity are constructed, by whom, and for what purpose, and how do theories of subjectivity restructure the world "otherwise"? And is this how we want the world to be? Not probing into the social relations of intersubjectivity, according to worldism, effectively erases the power politics of meaning, including the political economy behind such constructions.

And unlike postmodernism, worldism distinguishes power from the resistance it induces. Contra Foucault (1994), we differentiate between the colonizer and colonized in their experiences of colonial power (see Stoler 2002) and the entwinements that follow, both reinforcing and conflicting complicity (see Ling 2002b). Not doing so implicitly reinforces the imperialist assertion that "this is the way the world is": that is, it is not open to alternative concepts, discourses, strategies, or ways of being. These gaps in constructivism and postmodernism return us to the conventional treatment of power as domination, pure and simple. Ronen Palan (2000), for instance, finds a strain of conservative realism in Alexander Wendt's "naturalist" version of constructivism, primarily because he claims to offer a method only, and not an interpretation, of politics. Wendt (2005) himself admits as much. For similar reasons, Samir Amin (2004) calls postmodernism an "ideological accessory" to elite, bourgeois interests just as Aijaz Ahmad (1992) considers post-structuralist theories serve as alibis for imperialism. Both postmodernism and poststructuralism value critique and deconstruction over political action, thereby keeping *de facto* power intact.

We note that although critical theories like postmodernism and constructivism open up spaces to think about shifting power politics, they fall short of transforming the very asymmetries they critique. Inattention to structural, material interest and lack of integrating the Other *analytically* – that is, as a substantive maker of the world – undermines their claims of emancipatory social theory. Ultimately, the Other becomes a repository of raw materials for hegemonic actors and sites in the North to process.

Worldism acknowledges a deep intellectual debt to postcolonial studies. Here, race, gender, sexuality, class, and nationality serve as analytics *and* substance in examinations of power relations. Postcolonial studies demystify empire's boast, like Kipling's "White Man's Burden," that the imperial Self makes the world for all Others. And that world is unidimensional (top-down state power), unilateral (center dominates periphery), and unilinear (past–present–future). Postcolonial studies record a more nuanced and multiple history by problematizing the ways colonial power is imposed on the colonized. That is, colonization involves more than a unilateral and mechanical domination of the subjugated by colonizers and their states. As documented by postcolonial studies, tensions and contradictions emerge from these relations (Said 1979; Spivak 1999), leading to adaptations and integrations between hegemonic selves and subaltern others. From this interaction, "colonizers" and "colonized" produced something together over the course of time that neither anticipated nor perhaps desired but which all learned to live with, and eventually called their own. Divides along lines of property, race, class, language, religion, and ideology did not disappear. They fused, rather, into hybrid, creole, or mélange cultures that, nonetheless, contested these categories constantly (Ashcroft, Griffiths, and Tiffin 1995; Lewis and Mills 2003).

In recognizing that colonizer and colonized mutually construct their subjectivities, postcolonial studies attribute to both the legacies of power that we face today. Note, for example, Britain's principal instrument of colonial and imperial power: the East India Company. Sudipta Sen (1998) shows that, contrary to claims that the British brought capitalism to India, the East India Company had to adjust to pre-existing market structures and political relations to gain access to the thriving trade already in place in northern India.[4] Only through this kind of entry could the East India Company later redirect the trade to its favor. L.H.M. Ling (2002b) traces how institutional elites in East Asia learned syncretically and "interstitially" between two world orders – the agrarian-based, cosmo-moral universe of Confucian governance and the Westphalian inter-state system of commerce and trade – to cumulate into what we know as Asian capitalism today. Walter Mignolo (2000) highlights the "gnosis" of thought and action, Self and Other, that comes from centuries of transgressing and reformulating the colonial boundaries that comprise Latin America.

Of course, those subjected to hegemony must accommodate others more than those who perpetrate it. Yet hegemony's very asymmetry highlights the resilience and creativity of the marginalized. Ordinary people can journey across subjectivities to engage syncretically with others, even under conditions of poverty and inequality, to rebuild, reconstruct, and reorganize communities. Cherrie Moraga and Gloria Anzaldua (1983) characterize their straddling of multiple worlds as life on the "borderlands." Typically, they point out, women of color from the South must bear the biggest burden of negotiating the multiple worlds of language, culture, class, and gender to survive white-majority society in the North despite systemic discrimination and obstacles. Still, they are able to exercise internal reserves of freedom, thought, and action to sort *through* hegemony, not simply surrender to it. Similarly, the indigenous populations of the Americas, Australia, and New Zealand have entered into treaties with their white majorities to retain aspects of indigenous ontologies by formalizing them in Western institutions (Shilliam 2008).

Another example comes from Ashis Nandy (1988). Gandhi's strategy of nonviolence, Nandy claims, engulfed Britain's imperial hypermasculinity within a more complex understanding of gender and power drawn from India's classical mythologies. Gandhi succeeded, Nandy argues, not by over-throwing the British empire with military might but by displacing it. A worldist perspective adds that Gandhi's success also came from ordinary people who were reconstituting their daily lives already under, in, through, and despite empire's desires and violences. Indeed, Gandhi himself embodied that reconstitution despite his call to Indians to return to a more "authentic" way of life, as exemplified by his use of the spinning wheel. For this reason, Gandhi could push for the syncretic efforts that seeded India's revolution and independence.

Relational agency extends to a method of inquiry as well. Edward Said (1994) initiated a contrapuntal method to decipher the interplays between center and periphery, colonizer and colonized, the seen and unseen, in the production of colonial/imperialist power relations. This contrapuntal approach, Geeta Chowdhry (2007: 105) elaborates, helps us to historicize "texts, institutions and practices [by] interrogating their sociality and materiality [and] the hierarchies and the power-knowledge nexus embedded in them." From this basis, in Said's words, we may recuperate a "non-coercive and non-dominating knowledge" (Said, quoted in Chowdhry 2007: 105).

Postcolonial-feminist studies extend contrapuntality to recognize the entwinements of gender/sexuality with race and other aspects of colonial power relations. These include "analyses of bio-politics, expansionist capitalism, and questions of neoliberal political economy [that] emphasize the gendered, sexual, and racial hierarchies/genealogies of colonial and post-colonial relations, epistemologies, representational techniques, territoriality, law, and policy-making" (Banerjee and Ling 2006: 13). Two common concerns bind these inquiries: (a) How do global structures like capital, the military-industrial complex, or imperialism integrate with local patriarchal relations despite seeming conflicts and contradictions between them, and (b) What do the outcomes mean for the marginalized, the exploited, and the subaltern[5] (see Shohat and Stam 1994; Alexander and Mohanty 1997; Chowdhry and Nair 2002; Ling 2002b; Rai 2003; Eisenstein 2004; Agathangelou 2004b, 2006; Alexander 2005; Franklin 2005; Banerjee 2006)?

Not one but multiple worlds inform postcolonial studies. Some reveal sources and kinds of power previously hidden, dismissed, or denied. "Subaltern mimicry" for Homi Bhabha (1994), for example, subverts the hegemonic convention that the colonizer is always separate from and superior to the colonized. Mimicry's artifice, he proposes, shocks the colonizer into accepting a possible parity with the colonized.[6] Center-periphery relations thus become exposed as more complex than mere expressions of power from the centered Self to the peripheralized Other (see Escobar 1995). Other studies show that peoples and cultures comply with one another constantly and intimately in their private lives, even when elites deny such interactions in their public pronouncements (see Todorov 1984). As Ann Stoler (2002) demonstrates, the "colonial" Self could not maintain the official fiction of superiority to and exclusion of the "native" Other as the latter daily serviced "whites" in their barracks, their offices, their homes, and their beds.

Postcolonial theorizations, however, serve as a point of departure only. They do not explain, for example, *why* and *how* it is possible to negotiate across multiple worlds but, instead, only that we do. Evidence ranges from anti-colonial struggles to revolutionary projects to everyday acts of learning and resistance, revealing the ontological and epistemological praxes that enable agents to wrench freedom from violence and liberation from annihilation. Clearly, different worldviews are involved. But postcolonial theorizations do not broach the politics of "what is" (i.e., socio-ontological visions and the nature of the subject within) or its interpretations. Relatedly, postcolonial studies do not probe into how individuals, communities, and societies enact the visions, beliefs, norms, or theories behind "knowing what is" (epistemology) and the ways to undertake such inquiry (methodology). These pertain especially when historical circumstances bring one ontological tradition into contact with another. Yet these encounters and entanglements fuel the very hybrid, creole, and mélange practices that postcolonial studies document so extensively.

Worldism makes explicit what postcolonial studies imply. That is, interactions among worldviews reframe significant areas of thought, action, and being, even when original, defining principles and concepts are retained. Worldism adds: How do we learn from these syncretic adaptations so we could devise strategies for less violent social relations? Worldism as a descriptive process provides clues to such possibilities. "How" and "why" constitute the central focus of worldism as an analytical project.

WORLDIST ONTOLOGY, EPISTEMOLOGY, METHODOLOGY

Worldism proposes a relationality of social ontologies. That is, worldism as everyday practice springs from the interactions among contending social ontologies and their legacies of reinforcement and conflict. Worldism orients us to the existence of multiple social ontologies that make possible a condition of being. Epistemologically, worldism focuses on the interpretive *processes* behind these formations, their interactions with and relations to one another, and the larger context that sustains them. From this epistemological orientation comes a relational-materialist methodology: i.e., social formations reflect a dialectics of relations and structures. For example, worldism asks: What are the ontological and epistemological presumptions that keep "desire industries" separate from considerations of "national security"? What are the "processes of creation" embedded in these contestations?[7] Such questions lead to others that begin to rupture dominant articulations in world politics that prohibit such queries in the first place: e.g., how do ruling elites define "desire industries" and "national security", and why, and how do these characterizations differ from or resemble what ordinary people experience in daily life, and what do the disparities or similarities reveal about power practices in the world political economy? Asking these questions foreground how relevant structures (capitalist/mixed economies), institutions (neoliberal/authoritarian), practices (hypermasculine/hyperfeminine), and social relations (race, gender/sexuality, class, nationality) bind "desire industries" with "national security." From these conjunctions, we come closer to identifying the material and epistemic productions that connect "desire industries" with "national security," despite public pronouncements to the contrary.

Poisies

The Greek concept of *poisies* characterizes worldism. In *poisies*, worlds emerge from constant interplays, both interpretive and material, between selves and others. They create ceaseless, multiple constructions of being and becoming that transform familiar boundaries – material, geographical, capital, cultural, spiritual – into unfamiliar reconstructions of "we."

Specifically, *poisies* refers to different realms of existence (social ontologies) as inter-subjectively shared communal practices and languages. These mobilize specific subjectivities to enable collectively-formed social practices and constructs. The Greek verb *poieo* means "to make." It refers to all kinds of purposive activities. More than the instrumental definition of "to make" found in English, *poieo* connotes the deployment of one's power (*ergon*) that stems from the sets of relations and skills needed to realize this purpose, including the different systems of and contexts for interpreting those relations and skills. For instance, when Odysseus sought to escape from the island of Calypso, he "made" a raft. But he was not just making a particular raft. He was also drawing on a larger vision, purpose, and path of social relations that motivated the making of this particular raft for a life journey. The suffix "*sis*" to *poie-sis* always indicates an active, dynamic force or purposive activity that enables various kinds of social relations, subjectivities, and things.

Poisies, then, not only describes the world; it also articulates the world. In so doing, *poisies* shapes the world. As Pindar notes, *logos* is "the living word which is the power of life" that is also a "vision of reason" (Pindar, quoted in Detienne 1996: 48). *Poiesis* in worldism draws on this notion of the *ergon* of articulation to disrupt hegemony from discursive or epistemic regimes (Parry 1971: 20). In referring to relations drawn from speech, deliberations, contestations, and negotiations, *poiesis* delineates (a) the drama of theoretical imaginations, fantasies, and other kinds of linguistic significations and their social relations, (b) directions of change, but not in teleological terms, to render the world less violent, (c) the physical/material embodiments that structure our worlds, and (d) the possibilities that can emerge from contestations among social ontologies and their contingent power relations (Agathangelou forthcoming).

Worldism in the world

Other traditions also contribute to our understanding of worldism.[8] For example, Buddhism's *pratītyasamutpāda* ("co-dependent arising") and the Confucian notion of *ren* ("humaneness," "sociality") present similar worldviews of multiple and trans-subjectivities (although they do not use such terms).[9] Both believe that the self reverberates with others to transform into entirely new ways of seeing, doing, and being. Like *poiesis*, *pratītyasamutpāda* defines life as a coming together of elemental forces, both material and spiritual, across time and space. It is only through these interactions or reverberations that consciousness can be realized or awakened. Confucian *ren* turns this reverberative gaze to communal affairs. The *Analects* defines *ren* as the ability "to love *all* men" and to recognize that true knowledge requires the attempt "to know *all* men" (*Analects*, quoted in Hwa 1969: 191, original emphases), meaning that knowledge should be broad-based, non-discriminatory, and diverse. Usually translated as "universal virtue," "benevolence," "golden rule," "love," or "compassion" (Hwa 1969: 195), *ren* has taken on an authoritarian connotation given Confucianism's history of hegemony. The word's etymology, however, suggests a radically different inception. Composed of two characters, each referring to "person," *ren* literally and figuratively denotes community: that is, a society of two or more persons. "Only through sociality does a man become a man," writes Hwa Yol Jung (1969: 194) on *ren*. Like *poiesis* and *pratītyasamutpāda*, subjectivity in *ren* comes through social, communal efforts:

> *Ren* is the encompassing way of man [sic] in the world. It refers to the way of everyday action of man in relation to others in his life-world. What stands out in *ren* is the idea that sociality is the primary index of man's existence and as such it entails morality and is regarded as the highest moral norm attainable by man. *Ren* epitomizes the human life-world as the very structure of both sociality and values.
>
> (Hwa 1969: 195)

These philosophies tell a different story of the world. They enable us to think alternatively about the world(s) we live in and their dominant social relations. Nonetheless, we do not take *poiesis*, *pratītyasamutpāda*, or *ren* as set and fixed, evolved from millennia of "orthodoxy" despite internal debates, contestations, and reformulations (see Chow, Ng, and Henderson 1999). Rather, we draw on their defining elements and integrate them with contemporary insights derived from Marxist, postcolonial, and feminist studies and practice to contest hegemonic assertions about modernity, ontology, subjectivity, and world history. We do so, moreover, without presuming that the only way to negotiate across contending social ontologies is by projecting one's fantasies and desires onto others. Instead, worldism prioritizes a different locus of enunciation and existence that does not impose European Enlightenment's understandings of "modernity" with its contingent systems of organization: that is, the Westphalian inter-state system and its teleological understanding of development and change.

Making sense of multiple worlds has long preoccupied those outside "the West." Ravni Thakur and Chung Tan (1998) compare responses to European Enlightenment in India and China. Local elites, they note, were both enchanted and disenchanted with the West. Indians and Chinese embraced European Enlightenment's integration of liberal humanism with scientific methods as a means to "free" their respective societies from the superstitions, backwardness, poverty, and other societal "ills," as defined by Western "modernity." But Indian and Chinese elites were also savvy, as Tagore put it, to European Enlightenment's "demon of barbarity [that] has given up all pretence and has emerged with unconcealed fangs, ready to tear up humanity in an orgy of devastation" (Thakur and Tan 1998: 94).[10] Chinese reformer Liang Qichao (1873–1929) developed a theory of "three civilizations" wherein the West, India, and China would each learn from the strengths and weaknesses of the others to integrate into a new, stronger civilizational ethos for the future. Western civilization, Liang argued, subjugated humanity to machines; India's civilization suffered from the opposite by succumbing to spirituality; and Chinese civilization cannot go forwards or backwards but must adjust to circumstances as they change (Thakur and Tan 1998). Later revolutionaries like Gandhi, Nehru, and Mao built on these early attempts at civilizational entwinement to decolonize and nationalize India and China.

Japanese elites from the late nineteenth to early twentieth centuries grappled with similar issues but ended up imperializing their route to nation-building. Nishida Kitaro, for example, developed the concept of a "world-historical world" (*sekaishiteki sekai*) or a "world-of-worlds" (*sekaiteki sekai*) that resembles our notion of worldism. In Nishida's "world-of-worlds," individual nations would synthesize historically through a dialectics of culture into, eventually, a homogeneous entity (Goto-Jones 2005). Nishida's ideas, however, later served Japanese colonialism and imperialism in the 1930s–1940s through the East Asia Co-Prosperity Sphere, even though Nishida himself abhorred imperialism and colonialism. Christopher Goto-Jones (2005) believes Nishida inadvertently compromised his ideas by his method of presentation and choice of audience. Seeking to be heard, Nishida wrote to and for state elites. What he didn't count on was how easily these same elites absorbed his ideas for their own purposes.

The atomic devastations of Hiroshima and Nagasaki in August 1945 ended Japan's attempt to enter the West's imperialist club. "Civilization" as an operational concept for policy disappeared from world politics[11] until, half a century later, the theme was picked up again – this time, by a privileged member of the West: Harvard's Samuel P. Huntington (1993, 1996). The issue of "civilization" once more rose to the top of the agenda for academics and policymakers alike – and with the usual consequences.

From "clash of civilizations" to "dialectics of world order"

"The most important conflicts of the future," Huntington (1993: 25) declared, "will occur along . . . cultural fault lines." These divide into eight major "civilizations": Western, Confucian, Japanese, Islamic, Hindu, Slavic-Orthodox, Latin American and "possibly" African. Indeed, increasing intra-regional trade only serves to cement a "common culture" for some (e.g., European Union [EU], North American Free Trade Agreement [NAFTA], Greater China) at the expense of those that emerge from different or "unique" civilizations like Japan. Politics and economics, Huntington warned, cannot erase civilizational, especially religious, legacies. "A person can be half-French and half-Arab and simultaneously even a citizen of two countries. It is more difficult to be half-Catholic and half-Muslim" (Huntington 1993: 27). Huntington advised the West against two civilizations, in particular: Confucian and Islamic. They defy Western norms, goals, and aspirations; accordingly, the West must ally with more "compatible" civilizational partners to fend off the cultural assaults from Confucianism and Islam.

Huntington's *real* "clash of civilizations," however, cuts closer to home. Less concerned with fancy civilizations "out there," his argument centers more on whites vs non-whites "in here." Huntington asserted, for example, that Americans "react far more negatively to Japanese investment than to larger investments from Canada and European countries" (Huntington 1993: 26). Huntington developed this theme more apocryphally in a subsequent book on America's "national identity" (Huntington 2004). In it, he elaborated upon a "worst-case" scenario, first outlined in *Clash of Civilizations*: i.e., Hispanics would overtake the White House because "large segments of the American public blame the severe weakening of the United States on the narrow Western orientation of WASP elites" (Huntington 1996: 316). China, Japan, and "most of Islam," now combat an "Aryan alliance" of the US, Europe, Russia, and India in a third world war. Benefiting from this holocaust would be "those Latin American countries which sat out the war" and Africa "which has little to offer the rebuilding of Europe [other than to] disgorge hordes of socially mobilized people to prey on the remains" (Huntington 1996: 315–316). The Latino population in the US has yet to acquire the kind of political power Huntington sweats over but, one wonders, how he feels about Barack Obama becoming the first African-American President of the United States?

Regardless of Huntington's personal politics, some state leaders have seized upon his "clash of civilizations" to justify their own policies. In particular, many have used this argument to target populations they have deemed "unruly": e.g., "ethnic cleansing" against Serbs or Croats in Bosnia-Herzegovina, "*jihad*" against the "infidel" by radical Islamic communities, and "regime change" in Iraq and Afghanistan. As mentioned earlier, the Bush Administration extended Huntington's "clash" to the very preservation of civilization itself in the "global war on terror." Unlike Nishida, Huntington intended his ideas for imperialist policymakers and state elites (see Huntington 2004).

Contradictions, however, riddle this argument. Huntington never defined "civilization" or how he came to eight, exclusive ones in the world. Doing so would require him to acknowledge that civilizations, especially world religions, have borrowed syncretically from one another throughout history despite retaining distinctive characteristics (see Bernal 1987; Gilroy 1993). Huntington is equally unreflective about America and Americans. In asserting that "all" Americans would prefer Canadian or European investments to those from Japan (or other parts of the "non-white" world), Huntington makes two assumptions: (a) all Americans identify with privileged, white males like himself, and (b) all white males, especially the privileged ones, agree with his preferences. Neither assumption holds up to scrutiny. Why would Americans of Asian, Hispanic, or African descent, men and women alike and from all classes, prefer investments from privileged, white males from Canada or Europe over all "Others"? Nor do all white males agree on Huntington's insistence on "hypermasculine whiteness" (see Hall 2008). Huntington cites the EU, NAFTA, and "Greater China" as paragons of a transnationalized "common culture" but fails to recognize the cultural, religious, ethnic, and class contestations that roil within these regions. One may not be "half-Catholic" and "half-Muslim" on a formal basis, as Huntington (1993: 27) points out, but Muslims and Catholics intermingle informally throughout the world, like Confucians and Muslims in China or Christians and Muslims throughout the globe, due to inter-marriage and cultural assimilation over centuries. In brief, Huntington sets arbitrary thresholds to civilizations, cultures, religions, and peoples when they are, in actuality, organic legacies that grow, change, absorb, learn, and mutate over time.

In his response to Huntington, Hayward R. Alker Jr (1995) applied a dialectical–historical method.

> "Dialectics" connotes a whole series of ideas especially appropriate to civilizational relationships. It suggests relatively discontinuous transformations of multi-layered, differently paced, contradictory and synthetic developments. Domination, suppressive intolerance, subsumptive succession, limited accommodation, and mutually-stimulating co-existence are possible in such cases . . . [T]he word "dialectics" also connotes interpenetrating and contradictory generative practices, as well as dissociative dispersals, or assimilative, inclusive, and creative syntheses.
>
> (Alker 1995: 534)

In "coordinating" Huntington with three grander intellectual precedents on civilization drawn from F.W. Hegel, Arnold Toynbee, and Fernand Braudel-Immanual Wallerstein, Alker found the following resonances as well as discordances: e.g., a "late-modern" Hegelian *telos* for human development yet a denial of such for certain civilizations, like the Confucian and Islamic, that Huntington deems too reactionary for or incapable of managing; a Toynbeean concern with the destiny of Western civilization but Huntington's refusal to probe into "the interactive and inner-active development of a world-civilization" (Alker 1995: 546) that most intrigued Toynbee; and sharing a sense of "social time" or *longue durée* with the world-system perspective of Braudel/Wallerstein but without Huntington's recognition of what they considered to be the "material . . . conception of ecological-technological-economic-cultural civilization" (Alker 1995: 555). From this, Alker showed that Huntington offers only a slice of understanding "civilizations" in the West. Alker concluded that he preferred the "conceptions of our common, multi-layered history," even though "incomplete and uneven," to Huntington's singular story of humankind (Alker 1995: 560).

Alker's own, collaborative project on the "dialectics of world orders" (DWO) offers an alternative to Huntington's "clash of civilizations."[12] Reflecting the dialectical–historical method outlined above, this project expressly finds world politics consisting of over-layered, multiple "world orders" whose mutual penetrations produce nodes of cooperation as well as conflict. The project defines world orders as:

> geographically-linked socio-historical entities, identifiable on the basis of patterned regularities discernable among international or world actors, involving their conscious and unconscious relationships with each other and/or with their social and natural environments . . . World Order boundaries do not have to be absolute and mutually exclusive, so we expect to find overlapping and even interpenetrating orders, and smaller, possibly regional orders within more encompassing, truly global world orders.
>
> (Alker, quoted in Amin 2008: 1)

The DWO project takes us far into theorizing about another kind of world politics. Hermeneutically, it comes close to meeting the intellectual horizon of postcolonial-feminist studies. That is, where the DWO project seeks to shift our discipline's attention from Huntington's state-centric, nativist, and gendered vision of international relations to a more nuanced, expansive, de-centered, and dynamic one, so too do postcolonial-feminist studies focus on worlds as their analytical premise. Only, the DWO project remains anchored to an "inside" and "above" position, revealing its Western-centric and elitist limitations,[13] whereas postcolonial-feminist studies expressly seek to voice world politics from "inside" and "above" as well as "outside" and "below." For this reason, the DWO project has not been able to disengage from treating "world orders" as simply larger units of, for example, "empires" (see Amin 2008).

Our conception of worldism learns *poietically* from these intellectual and historical endeavors. Worldism aims not to fuse "civilizations," however defined, like the early modernizers in India and China. Instead, worldism stresses the open-ended power *relations* among multiple worlds and what these produce. The reinforcements and conflicts that come with these entwinements underscore that "development" is not merely about those problems identified by neoliberal modernity for the international community (e.g., terrorism, immigration, in/security, poverty). Rather, worldism stresses that "development" involves ontological contestations. In raising questions at the level of syncretic formations, worldism asks: How do we shift the terms of discourse from "what you (marginalized peoples) need to do to develop" to "how can we learn from your struggles with modernity to realize a common vision of development?" Decision-making cannot take place, like in Nishida's time, or as Huntington would like, behind closed doors and among certain privileged characters. Our vision of worldist accountability at the nexus of multiple relations inheres with a criticality that continuously destabilizes and thereby perforates hegemony. We recognize that such criticality will incur its share of rejection and retribution from institutional elites ranging from those in the EU to China who have aligned themselves with the capital-owning classes of the neoliberal imperium. But learning from the DWO project – and Huntington and Nishida before it – we do not theorize worldism from or for elites only. Worldism as a descriptive process explicitly draws on the syncretic strategies, both ontological and practical, that are utilized by ordinary people on a daily basis to live with hegemony in ways that they best know and can. Accordingly, worldism as an analytical project theorizes from both "outside"/"below" and "inside"/"above," thereby acknowledging that our worlds are already first and foremost global. Worldism tracks, for example, how macro-political structures like the transnationalization of insecurity directly affect as well as reflect micro-personal treatments of the body (e.g., war, torture, sex, and death) and relations of intimacy (e.g., domestic and racial violence) (Razack 2004). To transform hegemony by building alternative understandings of "us," worldism helps us redirect micro-personal energies, visions, voices, and actions back to the collective, macro-political structure. Through *poisies*, worldism radically democratizes world politics.

What's a worldist methodology then?, our critical reader continues. We answer: relational materialism.

Relational materialism

Worldism posits that trans-subjective relating and imagining *materialize* as well. We call this a methodology of relational materialism. It grants that people interact with what they know and seek to know; accordingly, they actively participate in (re)producing it. Like Marx's image of man making History by digging his hoe into the earth, relational materialism recognizes a division of labor in the making of histories: e.g., some dig earth, others hunt deer, still others cook and carry children on their backs. From these different occupational and socio-structural relations, communities construct contending perspectives on history and how it is produced.

The positionality of the inquirer, then, intimately accounts for the phenomenon under examination. This positionality generally reflects, though it is never reducible to, social relations that stem from a particular material context. Similar to a constructivist, a relational-materialist cannot stand apart from what is observed. However, a relational-materialist differs from a "pure constructivist" by not collapsing the definition of knowledge and its production into one process. In other words, a relational-materialist approach recognizes the impact of physical and material specificities such as race, class, gender, and sexuality on the production of knowledge and its political implications From these sources of dissonance or contradiction, the relational-materialist distinguishes between how life is lived for certain populations (e.g., Iraqis under military occupation) and its idealization through norms, values, and institutions for others (e.g., democratization through regime change under the Bush Administration).

From these spaces of disjuncture, relational materialism interrogates the invisible, the unsaid, and the silenced. In foregrounding the "concealed operations of power and the socio-economic relations connecting the myriad details and representations of our lives" (Ebert 1999: 7), relational materialism exposes the pitfalls of empire's seductions under neoliberalism: i.e., promises of satiating desire in exchange for passivity on violence. Note, for example, Turkey's experience as a "peripheral" state. With EU membership dangled as a lure, Turkey aims to "Westernize" (i.e., neoliberalize) even while the EU continues to label it as "not European enough." Critiques emerge from these dilemmas; more profoundly, so do strategies for change. These expose the politics of power and its differential effects on different communities, including the exploitation of particular local knowledges (e.g., herbal cures), their globalization, contingent institutions, practices, and ideologies (e.g., intellectual property rights).

Our critical reader may persist: What does worldism look like? Even if one accepts that worldist processes unfold daily, how does one *know* it – especially given the entrenched nature of realist/liberal internationalist thinking, doing, and being in our scholarly and popular imaginations? Without demonstrating how worlds and subjectivities reverberate, worldism remains an abstract exercise only.

In response, we turn to fiction and poetry. These illustrate the alternative visions and practices in worldism and how they operate.

6   Alternative visions and practices
Fiction and poetry

假作真時真亦假，　Truth becomes fiction when the fiction's true;
無為有處有還無。　Real becomes not-real where the unreal's real.[1]
Cao Xueqin, *Story of the Stone* (circa 1750s)

Fiction and poetry enact worldism in three ways. Already mentioned is that fiction and poetry give voice to all classes and hues of subjectivity on a simple, daily basis, without requiring certain thresholds of wealth or technology. Second, fiction and poetry provide the most direct means of illustrating the multi-layered, mutually-penetrative, dynamic interactions among contending ways of thinking, being, living, and relating. As suggested by the quote above, our world is not set in stone. The possibilities are there even when "truth" and "reality" seem to be the only options available. We argue, similarly, that by drawing on fiction and poetry, we can shake us loose from the familiar and the conventional to consider the supposedly unthinkable and impossible. Third, fiction and poetry, as sites of linguistic engagement, instantiate the worldist commitment to democratizing social relations and generating alternatives for community-building through syncretic engagements. Unlike other art forms, fiction and poetry, especially when orated, rely on a symbiotic collaboration between the artist (author or poet), the medium (story or poem), and the audience. Fiction and poetry, as we articulate them through worldism's relational ontology, create the possibility for a common meaning that binds a community. In Chapter Eight, we demonstrate this symbiotic collaboration with a play.

In this chapter, we begin with one of the most famous novels in the Chinese language: *Dream of the Red Chamber* or *Honglou meng* (*circa* 1750s). An exemplary fictive account of travel and transformation across multiple worlds, *Honglou meng* affirms that worldism is neither new nor unique. Next, we proceed to poetry as a method for worldist contestation, disruption, and articulation. Poetry-as-method problematizes the conventional, hegemonic construction of Self vs Other and reminds us that it is but one of many narratives of social relations. This contextualization yields two realizations: (a) power suffuses social relations, and (b) we have options to disrupt hegemony for better and more just alternatives. We cite several contemporary poems in Greek as examples of poetry as socio-ontologic epistemes and method. We end this chapter with a fiction of our own. It retells the story of "modernity" and "development" from a worldist perspective.

JOURNEYS IN, THROUGH, AND ACROSS MULTIPLE WORLDS

Buddhist enlightenment and *Honglou Meng*

Honglou meng portrays worldism of a kind. Actualizing the principle of *poisies* through the Buddhist notion of *pratītyasamutpāda* (in Sanskrit) or *yuanqi* (in Chinese), meaning "co-dependent arising," the novel demonstrates trans-subjectivity in motion by bringing together something identifiable yet constantly subject to change. I-Hsien Wu (2006: 10) writes that *Honglou meng* exemplifies a journey, a process, that "embrac[es] and confront[s] the multiple aspects of life." In particular, the novel shows the interplay between worlds (e.g., mythic and human) that induces journeys of multi- and trans-subjectivity. Agency exists in all types and from all sources (e.g., an inanimate object like a stone can gain consciousness through despair and become transformed into a boy by two immortals). Crossing worlds literally in these journeys, *Honglou meng* reflects simultaneous engagements with the past, present, and future (e.g., cycles of debt repayment in the human world for a kindness bestowed in the mythic world and vice versa). These underscore the worldist message that communities continue despite the fact that life is often like a dream, sometimes nightmarishly so. Operating constantly within the novel are the dialectics of critical questioning ("what is reality, what is illusion?"). These call for a sense of accountability within the novel ("who's responsible for what?") as well as between the reader and the novel ("what is the novel teaching me, what do I learn from it?"). These processes capture what Wu (2006: 267) finds to be the novel's overarching message: acts of writing and re-writing, like worldist agency and syncretic engagement, render "the narrative [e.g., hegemony] always in flux, even when . . . written on stone . . ."

The novel itself embodies a multiplicity of worlds. Unlike the conventional Western book written by a single author at a single time with a single title, *Honglou meng* represents an ongoing, collective enterprise. Constituting its own field, "red studies" (*hongxue*) span 250 years since when the novel was first circulated as a manuscript. *Honglou meng* (*Dream of the Red Chamber*) is the most widely used title but the novel bears others as well: *Shitou ji* (*The Story of the Stone*), *Qingseng lu* (*The Tale of Brother Amor*), *Fengyue baojian* (*Mirror for the Romantic*), and *Jinling shi'er chai* (*The Twelve Beauties of Jinling*). It is generally acknowledged that Cao Xueqin (circa 1715–63), the impoverished scion of a fallen aristocratic family, penned the first 80 chapters. It is also generally known that family and friends frequently commented on and revised the material as Cao showed it to them. After Cao's death, a committee of devotees led by Gao E (circa 1738–1815) further collated, edited, and wrote the novel, adding 40 chapters of their own. In fact, the author never kept a single, whole manuscript. No less than 11 versions of his manuscript existed in his lifetime, each in varying degrees of completion with the story slightly changed or a lot depending on the copy.[2]

Different political regimes have treated the novel differently (Wu 2006). Confucian commentators of the late Qing period, for example, appreciated the hero's eccentricity (e.g., his fondness for girls and femininity, his dislike of studying, his difficult relationship with his father) but felt compelled to domesticate him with orthodox, Confucian values (e.g., discarding the feminine, studying hard, embracing patriarchy). From the early Republican era in the 1910s until the Maoist period in the 1970s, Chinese scholars historicized the novel, respectively, as allegorical political history, personal and family history, and Marxian social history. Since the 1980s, attention has focused primarily on the composition of the text: e.g., the problematics of writing, the fictionality of the story, the novel's dialectical method. More recently, some are returning to the novel's religious meanings given its Buddhist philosophy and imagery (see Wang 1987).

Multiplicity is structured within the novel as well. It introduces four levels of narrative at the outset, each linked to the other, requiring the reader to traverse from one frame to the other to get the full story. There is (a) a General Narrator inviting the reader to enter his fictional world which (b) recalls a conversation between Stone and the General Narrator about (c) a prior conversation Stone had with a Daoist deity, Vanitas (*kong kong dao ren*), about (d) the story that becomes *Honglou meng*.

In the preface to this "main" story, Stone recounts two additional conversations in reverse chronological order: (i) one between Stone and two visiting immortals, a Buddhist monk and a Daoist priest, that centers on (ii) Stone's prior story of how it/he became Stone in the first place. The story goes like this: when the goddess Nuwa sought to "repair the sky and salvage the world" (*butian jishi*), she selected 36,501 stones of which she rejected one – Stone. This singular rejection causes Stone to lament so loudly and pitifully (*bei hao*) that he, in the process, gains consciousness (*linxing yitong*). His cries attract the attention of a Buddhist monk and a Daoist priest who are visiting nearby. They approach the hapless stone. Meanwhile, Stone overhears the two immortals talk about the human world, coined as "red dust" (*hongchen*) in Chinese Buddhist terminology to convey the messy, wanton, and ultimately disillusioning nature of human affairs.[3]

Curiosity strikes. Stone beseeches them to transport him to the human world. "I am an obtuse thing (*chunwu*)," Stone begs, whose heart "dearly admires (*xinqie muzhi*) . . . the glory and splendor of the human world" (*renshijian rongyao fanhua*) (Wu 2006: 233). They grant his wish but duly caution him that "[i]n the end all just amounts to a dream (*daotou yimeng*), and [everything] revert[s] to emptiness (*mengjing guikong*)" (Wu 2006: 233). Stone insists on his wish and he is transformed. The immortals turn him into a small piece of jade that appears in the mouth of a newborn babe, appropriately named Baoyu ("precious jade"), the novel's central character.

This dialogue between Stone and the two immortals demonstrates world-ist trans-subjectivity in action. It brings together two opposing languages: one of "knowledge" and the other of "desire for experience" (Wu 2006: 233). From this conjunction emerges the action needed for transformation. Stone's participation in the process "stresses the creation of human tragedy by the subtle interaction between cosmic design and individual choice [accentuating] the importance of agency" which, in this case, "bring[s] Stone from the mythic to the human world" (Wu 2006: 233).

Given the dialectics that ferment within, nothing stays fixed and the journey is never complete. For example, the novel's juxtaposition of Stone's exterior materiality (his physical "obtuseness") with his interior spirituality (his "consciousness") suggests the existence of each in the other, thereby denoting the dynamic, transitory nature of both. The immortals judge Stone accordingly that it/he "has assumed the form of a treasure [but] does not yet possess real wonder . . . Only when Stone returns from [his journey to the human world] does it complete its transformation, not in [physical] form, but in spirituality" (Wu 2006: 234).

The novel underscores that with trans-subjectivity comes intimacy. And with intimacy, we gain three insights: (a) one is always connected with others; (b) one is always responsible to others; accordingly, (c) we have the potential to heal, recover, and reconstruct together. These intimacies pertain even when opposites seem to prevail. Transcending time and space, across the human and mythic worlds, *Honglou meng* binds subjects and events in a karmic chain of continuous, nested relations. For instance, Baoyu loves his cousin, Daiyu, but is tricked into marrying Baochai, another cousin. Daiyu dies from a broken heart. This triangular relationship between Baoyu, Daiyu, and Baochai is repeated in a sub-*rosa* triangle between Baoyu and lower-ranked women (*qie*) in his household, Skybright, and Aroma. Each *qie* resembles her respective "double" in her relationship with Baoyu. For instance, Skybright (Daiyu's "double") is accused of having an affair with Baoyu, though she never did, and later dies after being exiled from the household. Similarly, Aroma (Baochai's "double") does have physical relations with Baoyu but is rewarded for doing so. These women, in turn, have similar complementarities with another pair of *qie*, Fivey and Musk. And the permutations go on.

At the same time, the novel questions the whole category of "opposites," "affinities," and "complementarities." Baoyu has a cousin, for example, also named Baoyu. The cousin's surname is Zhen, a pun for the word "real"; our hero's is Jia, a pun for "fake." Juxtaposed thus, they seem to contradict each other (although Zhen Baoyu started out as eccentric as Jia Baoyu but later reformed to orthodox ways). Zhen ("real") Baoyu is depicted as a paragon of virtue who studies hard for the imperial exams. Our hero, Jia ("fake") Baoyu (an alter ego for Cao Xueqin, the "real" author) seeks only to have fun. Although Jia ("fake") Baoyu eventually emulates Zhen ("real") Baoyu by studying hard and ranking high in the imperial exams, he reverts to his "real" nature by giving it all up to become a roaming, penniless monk. Which is the "real" Baoyu, then? Perhaps, the novel suggests, there is no "real" or "fake" Baoyu but, rather, the realness and fakeness of either Baoyu arises from their relationship. And if so, does "realness" or "fakeness" have anything to do with the over- all story?

Reality and illusion, the novel implies, are as deceptive as any pair of dichotomies: e.g., prosperity and decline, union and separation, orthodoxy and eccentricity, love and lust. On this last score, *Honglou meng* is especially prolific and nuanced. "Love cannot live without lust, as the novel repeatedly warns the reader," writes Wu (2006: 90). Based on the Buddhist notion of "enlightenment through feelings" (*qingwu*), *Honglou meng* has Baoyu adventuring with various female and male characters. Specifically, the novel details a wide spectrum of female personas and sexuality, ranging from the delicate Daiyu to the powerful Xifeng to the nurturing Baochai, each smart and beautiful in her own way, voicing herself through dialogues, arguments, jokes, lamentations, songs, poetry, theater, and so on.

The novel also explores a panoply of human sexuality. Take, for example, the siblings Qin Zhong and his sister, Qin Keqing, both cousins to Baoyu. The novel does not detail but hints strongly that Baoyu romps sexually with both the brother and the sister at separate times. These sexual ventures, along with several passages of homoerotic lust and play in Baoyu's "school house," emphasize the complementarities of sexuality even in supposedly opposite forms and acts. Indeed, the adventures them- selves perform complementarity: (a) they transgress those borders made "acceptable" by orthodox social relations while (b) reconciling difference *with* relations, masculinity *with* femininity, heterosexuality *with* homo- sexuality. The novel thus gives us passion, joy, lust, and play in all its flavors and tastes, shades and coloring.[4]

Of particular interest is Baoyu's relationship with Daiyu. Their love grounds Baoyu's swirling emotional life but remains unrequited since Daiyu dies young; indeed, at the very moment Baoyu marries Baochai. The novel describes in poetic detail that liminal tenderness between Baoyu and Daiyu when, no longer children, they begin to sense adult feelings for each other and yet have no wherewithal to consummate them. Transpiring primarily in Baoyu's special playground called the Prospect Garden (*daguan yuan*), symbolizing youthful ideal, purity, and poetry, they reveal their feelings for each other by reciting lines from the famous fourteenth-century romantic drama, *The Story of the Western Wing* (*Xixiang ji*).[5] When Daiyu mur- murs, "each day in a drowsy waking dream of love" (*meiri jiaqing sishui hunhun*), Baoyu is seized by "a sudden yearning for the speaker" for he understands to whom she is directing the quote and why (Wu 2006: 124). This doomed love haunts *Honglou meng*. But the novel reminds us, do not mourn too long for life cycles through dreams.

Buddhist Enlightenment through awakening is the novel's purpose and goal. It is why so many journeys are undertaken. Once Stone completes his tour of the human world, he returns to the mythic one from which he originated. Now he is an enlightened Stone, retelling his tale to Vanitas. At each level of engagement, an opportunity for enlightenment emerges: e.g., between the General Narrator and Stone, Vanitas and Stone, Stone and the two immortals in the mythic world, Baoyu/Stone and the other characters in the human world, then between Stone and Vanitas the second time around in the mythic world. This comes through the hermeneutic act of telling and re-telling, writing and re-writing. Both the General Narrator and Vanitas, for example, transform from being an "obtuse" reader/listener to an "ideal" one as they gain enlightenment through their exchanges with Stone. Interrupting Stone now and then for clarification or explanation, they add commentaries of their own, editing and re-authoring the story even as it is told to them.

These journeys are life- and mind-transforming but none leaves behind one discrete or bordered world for another. Instead, each world dynamically interacts with others to co-produce not only themselves but also the larger context. For example, Stone's mythic world reverberates with the human world to account for his experiences with and transformations in each. Similarly, the Prospect Garden serves as a mini mythic world for Baoyu and his friends when compared to the "dirty," "real" grown-up world of the Jia household (Yu 1978). Thus *Honglou meng* simultaneously juggles four, interactive, and mutually-penetrating worlds – i.e., the grand mythic world that oversees all, the human world of "red dust," the all-too-human Jia household, and the mini utopia of the Prospect Garden. Each world is nested within the other; each balances the other, each interacts with the other. Relations in the mythic world affect those in the human world, just as relations in the human world perpetuate those in the mythic world. Like Stone/Baoyu, certain characters in the human world resonate with alter egos in the mythic world: e.g., Baoyu's female cousin-in-law, Keqing, is a carnal sister to the fairy Disenchantment (*jinghuan xianzi*); his beautiful and competent sister-in-law, Xifeng, could be a human counterpart to the goddess Nuwa;[6] his young love, Daiyu, is a spirit known as the Crimson Pearl Flower (*jiangzhu cao*) who first encountered Baoyu in the mythic world as his previous incarnation, Divine Luminescent Stone-in-Waiting (*shenyin shizhe*). He gave Crimson Pearl Flower the opportunity to gain consciousness (that is, to attain speech, thought, and feelings) by watering her with dew (*ganlu guangai*) every day. For this reason, Baoyu and Daiyu are destined to be star-crossed lovers in the human world. Crimson Pearl Flower had vowed that should she ever become reincarnated as a human being, she would repay his kindness with a "debt of tears" (*huan lei*).

This brief rendition of *Honglou meng* cannot do it justice. It serves only to highlight those aspects of the novel that help us illustrate world-ism. These include multi- and trans-subjectivities reverberating through the agency of all parties concerned, including a stone and a flower, not to mention mortals and immortals. Their interactions provoke syncretic engagements in communities regardless of the form or world they happen to inhabit. Life imitates art in the case of *Honglou meng* as these very processes worked in the construction of the novel itself. Cao Xueqin may have started the novel but it is also the product of family and friends. And the making of *Honglou meng* as a community of "red studies" continues over time as contending political regimes interpret it differently, each contributing to the novel's multiple roles and identity in society, culture, and history.

The stories within *Honglou meng* also demonstrate worldism. Stone's multiple personas and their respective journeys – as a stone, as the jade in Baoyu's mouth, as Baoyu himself, perhaps even as the General Narrator – all instantiate multi- and trans-subjectivity in action and the abiding intimacies that syncretic engagements compel. At the same time, the novel conveys worldist commitments to criticality and accountability as it questions supposedly fundamental categories like "reality" and "illusion," "love" and "lust," "heterosexuality" and "homosexuality." Such questioning does not leave a vacuum, as may seem of the Buddhist notion of "emptiness" or "detachment." Rather, it is a space rich with ambivalence and liminality, like the relationship between Baoyu and Daiyu, whose love transcends worlds yet remains forever unrequited. From this "middle space" of liminality, we find affinities and complementarities that bind even supposedly die-hard opposites. These connections offer a wealth of possibilities for reconciliation, rehabilitation, and reconstruction.

Honglou meng seems a fanciful tale. No "center" appears in this sprawling epic; therefore, no order or predictability or finality. Although one author (Cao) existed, many also had a hand in writing the novel (family, friends, a committee under the editorship of Gao E). And at least 11 manuscripts have been transmitted and transcribed, some long after the original author's death. The novel covers over 400 characters, each clustering around distinctive personas, subjectivities, sexualities, and types of social relations, some traversing the "mythical" to the "human," and back again. A dizzying array of venues is presented: e.g., dreams, fables, conversations-within-conversations-within-conversations, poetry, songs, and plays. Characters relate to one another reverberatively, contrapuntally, rotationally, oppositionally, complementarily, and iteratively.

Yet *Honglou meng* serves as an apt analogy for world politics. Like the Jia household, world politics aims to impose orthodoxy (an imperium) onto all others. And, as with the novel, world politics cannot sustain this mission given the multiple worlds that stir within, each with its own set of multiple, complex, and reflexive social relations, requiring journeys of multi- and trans-subjectivities for all concerned. Protagonists in the novel seek enlightenment continuously but there is no guarantee they will find it. In and of itself, one could interpret from the novel, this realization constitutes a kind of enlightenment. Perhaps what's important lies in the journey(s), rather than any single point of departure or arrival.

Our worldist reading offers an additional insight for both the novel and world politics. That is, multiple worlds generate alternative visions of what's possible despite all the conflicts and contestations that might apply. Acknowledging and valuing these multiple worlds will help us actualize social relations – and by extension, politics – that are open-ended, engaging, and less violent. We are not damned to unending cycles of hegemonic violence and fear.

In his poem, "Ithaca," Kavafis contributes to the practice and idea of journey(s) as a politics of life. His poetics draw attention to the ongoing and multiple processes of "Ithaca": struggles, violence, learning, joys, and above all co-enrichment.

The "Ithakas" of struggle, location, and social relations

Ιθάκη (*Ithaca*)

Σα βγεις στον πηγαιμό για την Ιθάκη,	As you set out for Ithaca
να εύχεσαι νάναι μακρύς ο δρόμος,	hope your road is a long one,
γεμάτος περιπέτειες, γεμάτος γνώσεις.	full of adventure, full of discovery.
Τους Λαιστρυγόνας και τους Κύκλωπας,	Laistrygonians, Cyclops,
τον θυμωμένο Ποσειδώνα μη φοβάσαι,	angry Poseidon – don't be afraid of them:
τέτοια στον δρόμο σου ποτέ σου δεν θα βρεις,	you'll never find things like that on your way
αν μεν' η σκέψις σου υψηλή, αν εκλεκτή	as long as you keep your thoughts raised high,
συγκίνησις το πνεύμα και το σώμα σου αγγίζει.	as long as a rare excitement stirs your spirit and your body.
Τους Λαιστρυγόνας και τους Κύκλωπας,	Laistrygonians, Cyclops,
τον άγριο Ποσειδώνα δεν θα συναντήσεις,	wild Poseidon – you won't encounter them
αν δεν τους κουβαλείς μες στην ψυχή σου,	unless you bring them along inside your soul,
αν η ψυχή σου δεν τους στήνει εμπρός σου.	unless your soul sets them up in front of you
Η Ιθάκη σ'έδωσε τ' ωραίο ταξίδι.	Ithaca gave you the marvelous journey.
Χωρίς αυτήν δεν θάβγαινες στον δρόμο.	Without her you wouldn't have set out.
Άλλα δεν έχει να σου δώσει πια.	She has nothing left to give you now.
Κι αν πτωχική την βρεις, η Ιθάκη δε σε γέλασε.	And if you find her poor, Ithaca won't have fooled you.
Έτσι σοφός που έγινες, με τόση πείρα,	Wise as you will have become, so full of experience,
ήδη θα το κατάλαβες οι Ιθάκες τι σημαίνουν.	You'll have understood by then what these Ithakas mean

– Κωνσταντίνος Π. Καβάφης (Kavafis 1911)

We read Kavafis to say that life entails conjoined, multiple journeys. The communal life of multiple worlds, Kavafis suggests, gives us both the materiality of the body and the creativity of the spirit. Thus, we are social from the very beginning. Our development is already entwined with a community that is itself an agglomeration of selves and communities. Accountability and life signify each other: i.e., one *means* the other. Kavafis draws on *poisies* here to articulate that the community and the self are created simultaneously and dialectically. The community gives birth to a self that finds itself in an ongoing struggle with its environments, including its fellow co-makers, through struggles in growth, crises, and transformations.

We are not alone, in short, and could never be. Kavafis urges us to "not be afraid" of the struggle and violence of "Laistrygonias, Cyclops, and Poseidon" for these are produced by a particular socio-ontology that abstracts our multiple worlds into Self/Other binaries, denying the multiple socio-ontologies that are integral to our lives, both material and spiritual, communal and individual. Extending this insight to the neoliberal imperium, we add that it alone benefits from such fears by preventing people from harvesting their own energies and creativity for more productive, sustainable, and freer lives. Instead, neoliberal desires engross our multiple relations, whether of mind and body, self and other, gods and humans, reducing us to manufactured fears and their violent consequences.

But we will encounter these fears, Kavafis cautions, if "we bring them inside our soul" and "set them up in front of us." Kavafis urges us, instead, to cherish the wisdom and experiences acquired along the way. These enable the voyager to recognize the enduring meaning of the "Ithakas" of struggle, location, and entwined social relations.

We need to negotiate these social relations, Kavafis suggests. Here, Kavafis reflects worldism's disruption of what Plato called *poitike*. That is, the pressure to abstract and codify multiple social relations into a one-size-fits-all, "the world is flat" rendition of our lives (see Friedman 2005). Worldism's multiply entwined structures and relations enforce, instead, a critical questioning of fundamental categories: e.g., who benefits from what, when, under what conditions, who says I am what and why? Such questioning shifts the seemingly immovable walls erected by dominant power relations. These not only block but also erase from consideration the multiplicities that already exist. "Ithaca" as a socio-ontological critique disrupts this hegemonic demand for a specific, "naturalized" Ithaca, as though it springs fully-grown from Zeus's head. In re-centering other perspectives and ways of being excised by the imperium, we discover that formalized rituals of "tolerance" and "peace" like treaties, truces, and peacekeeping, for instance, cannot suffice for they exact too high a price in simply sup-pressing and not transforming the violence.

Kavafis articulates that collaborative growth and enrichment requires a constant shifting of our activities and ways of thinking. In questioning the conventional, "flat" narrative of the isolated sojourner, Kavafis invites us to compose new ones so we may reach further, soar higher, and, eventu-ally, love more profoundly. Only with such widening and deepening vistas could we heal, enabling us to leave behind the fears and suspicions, the monsters and talismen, the saints and devils of our provincial origins.

This worldist "reading" of world politics is not merely an intellectual tool. It is itself an epistemology of interpreting, recognizing, and organiz-ing our times, our worlds, and the social relations within them. Worldist readings beget a "dialectical constellation" (Agathangelou *forthcoming*) within whose subjects and communities are not mere academic constructions but historical agents who socially co-produce the meaning of their world(s), their social relations, and themselves. In worldism, social ontologies are involved even in mundane, daily acts like dressing (e.g., does the occasion require a "modern," "Western" outfit or a "traditional," ethnic one? How would those gathered respond to a combination of the two?) or holding a town meeting (e.g., should convenors deploy all the languages used by the community: a combination of local dialects with the national *lingua franca*, which could be the colonizer's tongue, or impose one form of speech?) or setting up a commercial enterprise (e.g., should it accommodate religious *and* consumer needs?). In this sense, worldism points to the limits of Europe's Enlightenment model of "modernity." Worldism redefines it by refusing to place third-world communities, for instance, "outside modernity" or "impervious to history" (Fukuyama 2002: 30). Rather, worldism situates them centrally with other communities, however labeled. Their contrapuntal interactions, worldism emphasizes, account for current structures and relations in global development.

Worldism also recasts our understanding of "community." Though it may cohere along lines of state/village/family or language/religion/memory, no community totalizes into a monolith. It is always in and of multiple worlds: fluid, dynamic, permeable, and ever evolving. The mission of any imperium, not least the neoliberal one, is to divide-and-rule by delegitimizing worldist visions even while benefiting from them, as we see in processes of "globalization." But worldism allows us to recognize the "gaps" and tensions that exist within hegemonic social orders; it exhorts us, indeed, to recognize that violence typically reproduces itself due to the nested nature of social relations, their binding structures, and mutual embeddedness, even when "opposites" seem to prevail: e.g., Bush and bin Ladin, "desire industries" and "national security," "Self" and "Other." These syncretic junctures offer a rich resource for reconstruction and rehabilitation so that less violent relations could emerge. The first impetus for change, however, usually arises from a crisis. From it comes an opening for conceiving alternatives.

Poetry, as we theorize it here, gives us the probative space to do so. As a site and a formation, poetry allows us to articulate a political "web of subjects" (Agathangelou 2006) that differs from the conventional, narcissistic version narrated in capitalism, modernity, and contemporary world politics. Because poetry as an epistemology of socio-ontologies is predicated on the notion that multiple worlds inform our present in all its prismatic possibilities, worldism begins to dissolve the conceptual fortresses of the familiar and the entrenched, enticing visions of the new and the transformational to come into view.

ART OF POETRY AS POLITICS

[O]ur history (or our histories) is not totally accessible to historians. Their methodology restricts them to the role of colonial chronicle. Our chronicle is behind the dates, behind known facts: *we are Words behind writing*. Only poetic knowledge, fictional knowledge, literary knowledge, in short, artistic knowledge can discover us, understand us, and bring us, evanescent, back to the resuscitation of consciousness.

(Jean Bernabé, quoted in Mignolo 2000: 245, original emphasis)

Art offers one means of countering the "colonial chronicle." It can challenge and disrupt the dominant norm that the world needs incessant capitalist exploitations and violences, that the state is first and foremost sovereign, and that hypermasculine whiteness must be in charge. In so doing, art shifts the burden of what needs to be done (e.g., "development") from those at the margins (e.g., "third-world states") to where it belongs, the imperium. It is the center, after all, that secures the profits needed for systemic reproduction through brutalities likes racism, sexism, hetero-sexism, and war.

But contrary to what is suggested by the quote above, art is not pristine. Nor is it ideal or devoid of its own politics. Art does not simply "discover" or "understand" us, "bringing" us to "consciousness." Instead, we stress, art serves as a site of struggle and labor, like any other productive enterprise. Its value lies in *what* artistic knowledge conveys and *how*. For this reason, juxtaposing "artistic works" with the "colonial chronicle" highlights the social relations that make both possible and keep each in asymmetrical rela-tions with the other. These gaps in power and knowledge production need to be addressed to stem the historic violence of hegemonic world politics. On this basis, we may identify possibilities for healing and rebuilding.

Poetry-as-method points to trans-subjective, multiply-produced modes of relating and imagining. We are asked to refrain, for the moment, from fixing identity into one thing and not the other: that is, to suspend the hegemonic designation of any ontological starting point. Shifting to this probative space helps us to recognize (a) the multiplicity of worlds, (b) the processes through which subjects (re)produce themselves and their worlds in a delicate tapestry of asymmetrical social relations, and (c) possible ways of reconfiguring these processes so selves and others can forge new, less violent, and transformative relations.

The *ergon* of poetry

Poetry, according to Gaston Bachelard, is impudent. It breaks into "the dead formula of a system" with its "dictatorship of the mind" (Bachelard, quoted in Gaudin 1987: xxi), jarring the imagination to produce new images, relationships, and possibilities for action. Bachelard emphasizes that lan-guage *acts* by bearing a world within: "For Bachelard," writes Colette Gaudin (1987: xxi), "poetic language works, not as a revelation of past conflicts or traumas, but as a reconciling force which at the same time effectuates and enlarges subjective life." Poetry intrudes upon perception (the status quo) to "reverse the real and the figurative poles" of meaning to open new vistas of thought and vision (Gaudin 1987: xlii). In this way, past connects with present, solitude with communication, "reconciling the world and the subject" (Gaudin 1987: xxxv). Such reverie comes not easily. It is earned through disciplined reading, writing, and thinking. There can be no "lazy dreamer" (Gaudin 1987: xxviii). Imagination frees us of ourselves and the known so we can enter an experimental, exploratory trip to otherness (Gaudin 1987: 16).

Worldism inverts Bachelard's formulation. From finding the material in the poetic, worldism discovers the poetic in materiality, particularly divisions of labor configured by race, gender, sexuality, class, nation-state, and culture. "These conditions and dimensions make up the *echos-monde*," according to Nevzat Soguk (2006: 385), "the echoes of the world that urgently need to be 'sensed', 'cited', and registered across the world." For example, the neoliberal world economy does not just structure the world according to certain interests, products, and markets. It also *imagines* the world in particular ways (see Agathangelou and Killian 2006). Marx first theorized about capitalism's imagination as "commodity fetishism" and "alienation." We emphasize capitalism's overall worldview, particularly its latest neoliberal variant (see Cameron and Palan 2004). In exposing neoliberalism's nightmare scenario of excess built on fear, greed, and violence, worldism helps us realize that we don't have to accept, share, or participate in this vision. There's a choice. Through poetic articulation and practice, worldism registers the variety of visions that contest this project. And through syncretic negotiations, worldism signals a multitude of approaches to life, living, and being. From these processes, we can identify more viable and sustainable relations to deal with different structural constraints.

Roland Bleiker (2000) and others (Costantinou 2000; Sylvester 2001; Soguk 2006; Rajaram 2006) apply these insights to world politics. They see poetry as a source and means of "critical history memory." Like Glissant, these theorists treat poetry's *echos-monde* as a means to prevent hegemony by "stretching the boundaries of our minds" (Bleiker 2000: 281). Worldism adds that this intervention prohibits hegemony's saturation of multiple socio-ontologies and the contestations among them.

Soguk elaborates with a reference to the Israeli-Palestinian conflict:

> [O]ntopoetics reveals in its imposed tempos, postures, and rhythms the work of the occupation in Israel–Palestine. The massive interventions in the land fold into sweeping interventions on bodies, creating unique ontopoetical conditionality both for the Palestinians and the Israelis. Visible and invisible conditioners – from walls, ditches, tunnels, and barbed wires to checkpoints, lines, work permits (given or denied), residency documents (issued yet subject to revocation), and bus routes mapping perfectly to locations of suicide bombings reveal the concurrent political rhythms and tempos imposed on the land and the bodies.
>
> (Soguk 2006: 384)

This lineage of violence connects Palestinians and Israelis. It includes the various conditions that resist and contribute to such violence at the same time: e.g., "checkpoints," "lines," "work permits," "residency documents." Worldism extends this inquiry by recognizing the contending social ontologies that operate behind these struggles and their acts of violence, conditioning, and contestations.

Still, the critical reader may ask, how much is our identity dependent on those stories that we cannot control or change? In response, we paraphrase Robert Cox (1986): all stories are "for someone" and "for some purpose." If these change, so do the stories. But we need more than an "aesthetic turn" in world politics. Poetry serves as a *method* or site of labor for transforming and reconstructing our worlds.

Wait!, our critical reader could interject again, isn't poetry exactly the opposite of what worldists claim to want, to radically democratize social relations? Isn't poetry elitist by nature? Wouldn't something else, like film, enable more democratic engagement and participation? After all, film reaches more people than poetry.

Film-making requires technology not yet readily available to the masses.[7] Whereas, poetry – whether in the form of folktales or songs or simple ditties – has expressed human needs, goals, aspirations, and desires from ancient to present times (see Nepali 2003; Arons 2004). Contrary to popular misimpressions of fiction and poetry as an elitist pastime, both can articulate a *demos* that is substantively democratic. Unlike a filmmaker or even a painter, a poet or singer or storyteller doesn't need a lot of materials or capital or technology to produce a narrative. The purpose of using fiction/poetry as a method, moreover, is not to reach a common end-goal – i.e., a unified interpretation – but to engage in a process of public deliberation where we identify spaces of contestation – such as asymmetrical power relations and why these exist – to forge connections and solidarities. From this process of speaking with, listening to, critiquing, and collectively engaging with others, we begin to account for the multiple worlds that people come from, live by, and die for.

Fiction and poetry, in short, serve as sites of contestation over power. Telling stories through narrative or poetic form not only provides voice but it also demonstrates the variety and scope of voices that exist, thereby curbing the hegemony of a singular, "flat" narrative. In the process, we not only alter our original stories but also produce new ones together with others. No mere reflection of postmodern polyvalence, this method shows that poetry and fiction can help us *critically* politicize social ontologies, their contingent relations, and aesthetic subjectivities. These bear power implications for the imperium's privileging of Self over all Others. Excavating the silences, lulls, and gaps between these voices does not signal an end to understanding but a beginning of negotiations across them. We can suspend, if only for the moment, the pressures of power to foreclose social relations in their multiple registers. In so doing, we are no longer subject to narrowly-punctuated social relations that support some interests at the expense of the many due to presumptions that fear and property dictate human existence.

Let us see, then, how a worldist approach turns poetry and fiction into a daily practice of political critique. The following excerpts make explicit the contestations, tensions, and disjunctures that entwine selves with others, loosening the rigid borders that alienate us from visions of what's possible and sustainable.

Contesting/disrupting the "liberal" world order

For Tsiolis (1997), the critical-political poem offers a way out of the injustices and inequities that produce the "pained self" ("I did X" or "I thought Y") by generating a transformative vision of what to strive for in the world ("the world is like Z"). He cites Kiki Dimoulas's poem, "Unexpectations."[8] In it, Dimoulas sees a picture of a soldier, long dead. Yet she infuses new life into the bereaved by challenging the fiction and practice of erecting boundaries of all sorts – physical, emotional, national, cultural, religious. The bereaved thus finds a larger, more embracing community than the isolating sovereignty of grief.

Εμένα έχει χρόνια να πατήσει	It's been years since any thief
κλέπτης το πόδι του στο σπίτι	Set foot in my house
ούτε για καφέ.	Even for coffee.
Επίτηδες αφήνω ξεκλείδωτο το	I deliberately leave the pot
μπρίκι	unlocked.

For Vrasidas Karalis, Dimoulas's poetry "transubstantiates": "the universe becomes world once again, agony becomes longing, absence appears as time redemption."[9] We read Dimoulas's poetry as a deconstruction of dominant narratives of social relations while simultaneously reconstructing with language another vision, another sensibility. Her world has experienced the dissolution of postwar humanity and finds itself, literally, at a dead end. She intervenes in this insecure landscape with a creative, dynamic re-envisioning of a "new" world: "through astonishment and surprise . . . her lines suggest the stability of a world that eyes can't see, but which becomes whole through its imaginary reconstruction within the poem as an organic whole."[10] Neither time nor love nor the dead soldier is lost. Rather, all maintain "a continuous and active presence. Through her lines, personal time is born anew and is accomplished forever as collective experience and prismatic image."[11] In this way, Dimoulas fuses social ontology with politics and aesthetics (Agathangelou 2004b; Agathangelou and Killian 2006).

Through poetry, words and memories and whispered dreams can be recuperated. And this process returns to our collective consciousness the possibility of change. We can perceive worlds other than the one espoused by the neoliberal imperium. The pain of death and absence mobilizes connections previously thought not possible. Stories of the everyday and ordinary challenge master fables and mirages, opening another window through which we can contemplate ourselves as well as others (Darby 2004). Realization of pain, injustice, and terror may motivate this way of being but it calls us, also, to remember humanity's ability to heal and rebuild amidst chaos, disorder, and insecurity. Such ordinary living may not promise the perfect dream; it recognizes, instead, the urgency of being present here, now, in this world, collectively and critically.

Contesting/disrupting borders: transformative socio-onto-poetics

Dimoulas also shows how we can see social relations in a new light. She compels us to face honestly the material structures that lead to unequal social relations. In her poem, "A Minute's Licence," she recalls a burglary at a neighbor's house. She proffers another response to the sense of threat, fear, and violation that burglaries typically induce:

Όσο δε ζείς να μ' αγαπάς.	Love me as long as you don't live.
Ναί ναί μου φτάνει το αδύνατον.	Yes yes the impossible's enough for me.
Κ' άλλοτε αγαπήθηκα απο αυτόν.	Once I was loved by that.
Όσο δε ζείς να μ' αγαπάς.	Love me as long as you don't live.
Διότι νέα σου δεν έχω.	For I've no news of you.
Και αλίμονο αν δεν δώσει σημεία	And heaven forbid that the absurd
ζωής το παράλογο.	should show no signs of life.

With the door/pot unlocked, Dimoulas re-positions Self (homeowner) and Other (thief). The thief-Other becomes a guest, not an intruder. The terror of boundary violation transforms, instead, into a social exchange (*"for coffee"*). Relatedly, Dimoulas urges us to shift the faultlines of hegemonic narratives by inquiring into the thief-Other – why he robs – as well as about the homeowner-Self – why can we afford the luxury of not locating our lives at the stakes of danger? Even if we do rob, say, through "innovative" accounting practices, why are we rarely caught, sentenced, and imprisoned by law and order? These questions highlight how the Self is not just any "self." It has a profile which is racialized, gendered, and classed (i.e., this subject can avoid dangerous methods) and it is always in a relationship with the "other" who also has a profile that is gendered, raced, and classed. This relationship depends on practices of violence and complicity to create and sustain the "self" in asymmetrical relations to the "other." But the question is: Is this relationship sustainable?

Let us now share another story. It tells of multiple journeys "out there" and "in here," for fulfillment and against estrangement.

CONDITIONING ESTRANGEMENT

There once was a young man from the Punjab. He was from a relatively well-off farmer's family. He worked and studied hard, eventually becoming an agricultural field officer for his county. He inspected crops and irrigation and such, often stopping by to chat with local farmers about their problems. He drew on these conversations to help them integrate their own experiences and wisdom with the technology available for agricultural production. His innovations proved so successful that his friends and neighbors, backed by the local farmers' association, put him up for a much-prized scholarship to study Development in a first-world Metropole. One fine Spring day, coming home from the fields, our young man saw the letter from the Ministry sitting neatly on his desk. With trembling hands, he carefully sliced open the crisp, white envelope with a pocket penknife . . . and jumped up and down with joy. Hurrah! He got the scholarship!! His life's dream has come true!

Soon after arriving at the Metropole, however, our young man began to question himself. Does he have "the right stuff," he wondered, to "make it"? "I am not well-prepared," he admitted sadly. His professors expounded in a language that he understood but could not *comprehend*. What they talked about seemed unconnected to his experiences in the fields of the Punjab. He seemed to be constantly scratching his head. They talked about "valid inferences" and "real facts" and "random sample surveys" when he knew the farmers of the Punjab didn't think or act that way, nor would they ever, no matter how many training sessions the Ministry held. And how could he ever conduct a random sample survey when Punjabis don't talk to strangers, especially about the most intimate aspects of their lives? Yet both he and his professors were supposedly seeking the same goal, Development.

Especially disconcerting was one professor, originally from Delhi. He spoke the language of Development fluently and elegantly, just like the other professors. Unfortunately, he wasn't much help to our young man. "Study harder," was all the advice this professor dispensed. Apparently, that was how he made it. Now he returns "home" occasionally to "consult," making large commissions, driving a shiny new car, and enjoying all the perks of an "expert."

"I come from the Third World, after all," our young man rationalized. "Of course I'd have to work hard! How else could I expect to catch up?" With this new insight, our hero redoubled his efforts to speak and think just like his professors.

One day, he attended a lecture given by a compatriot: a woman professor from Mumbai. Her topic was not the usual like "Autoregressive Appromixation in Nonstandard Situations" or "Water Conservation and Irrigation." Instead, she talked about "The Politics of Race and Gender in Global Trade."

During the lecture, it was quite clear to our young man that the woman professor did not speak the same language or use the same concepts as his other professors. In fact, she violated all sorts of rules of proper thought and conduct in the academy. She opened the lecture with a rhetorical question: "What's all this buying and selling in the world economy *for*?" She answered with a dramatic flourish: "Sex, sex, and more sex!" The young man, like the rest of the audience, was shocked into silence.

He went up to her after the lecture.

"Don't you think you were rather irreverent in your lecture?" he asked her.

"If I were," she responded unexpectedly, "what's the problem with that?"

"Well," he offered tentatively, "don't you think you're offending your audience?" For some reason, he felt uncharacteristically aggressive towards this small woman in a *sari*. She was at *his* Center, after all, in the heart of *his* Metropole. He decided to come to the point: "Don't you think you should be more respectful?"

"Why?" she asked maddeningly.

"Well . . ." he didn't know what to say.

"Do you feel you have to defer to your professors all the time?" she asked in turn.

"Yes."

"Why?"

"They're my professors!"

"Don't you feel you have anything to say to them?"

"Yes, but . . ." he hesitated. Suddenly, he needed to confess: "I feel as though I don't have the language to speak."

"Is it just the language itself?"

"No . . ." the young man wanted to clarify the matter even for himself. His words tumbled out, one over the other: "It's not that I haven't – or can't – master their language. It's that their language doesn't allow me to express who I am, what I'm about, the struggles I have in dealing with their world here, and mine there, and now my world in theirs here, and their world in mine there."

"When you bring your experiences into the classroom," she probed, "how do your professors respond?"

"They generally ignore it," he had to concede.

"Don't you think this is a problem," she queried, "especially when you're talking about development in your own country?"

"I guess . . ."

That night, lying awake in his dormitory bed, the young man tried to forget this conversation but couldn't.

"What am I *doing*?" he cried.

IMPLICATIONS

Denying multiple worlds can lead to the violence of self-estrangement. Confusion, anger, and pain are compounded. Despite his best efforts and intentions, our young man begins to shrink from someone full of ambition, confidence, and energy to one shadowed by doubt and anxiety. He feels he has to work harder just to stay in place. This objectification stems from what the professors deem to be the "best" or "most important" for Development. The Metropole knows best. It centralizes and hierarchizes itself even if it means defeating the very purpose of Development by disenfranchising Others.

Our young man initially absorbs the Metropole's epistemes. When he meets the woman professor from Mumbai, he aims first to discipline her by questioning her credibility and legitimacy to contest academic conventions. She should submit to him, he calculates implicitly, just as he has submitted to his professors. He assumes intimacy ("shouldn't you be more respectful?"). They come from the same country, after all! But contrary to expectations, she deflects his act of hostility and aggression by questioning his own, debilitating sense of alienation. Thus exposed, he enters into a crisis. It compels him to acknowledge the choices he has made, raising questions that could lead him to reorganize his own practices.

Our story dramatizes the need for worldism. The young man's interactions with his professors, and later between him and his female compatriot, reveal the unspoken tenacity of the ontology of fear and property. But it is not the only ontological story in town. The very crisis experienced by our young man highlights just the opposite: i.e., many ontologies bounce and grate and converge with one another in our daily lives. To reconcile and integrate these multiple worlds – not to mention heal ourselves from the pain and violence of hegemonic world politics – we need to theorize about the multiple ontologies that impact our daily lives, and why some prevail while others are dismissed or denigrated. In our story, the *lack* of communication felt by the young man with his professors underscores the politics and violence of hegemonic erasure. Yet his success in the fields back home testifies to his agency. He can draw on it to engage syncretically with his female compatriot to build a new community for development. This solidarity would extend beyond coming from the same country or religion or language. He may realize that the woman professor, normally an object of conquest or desire or servitude, may have something to teach him about his own need for emancipation and its strategies. In so doing, our hero may embark on another journey, this time across subjectivities, including those within himself. His moral and intellectual crisis may proliferate into other kinds of estrangement but it also forces him to face his role in his own alienation. Only then could he raise questions as to who benefits from this kind of participation, this conditioning of estrangement?

We read these same processes in Dimoulas's poetry. They spotlight the multiplicity of subjectivity, whether spiritually, materially, or textually, depending on one's reverberations with others. Dimoulas's poetry empowers both speaker and listener through the telling of the tale, where the agency of articulation dislodges hegemony from its moorings, to point to cracks and possibilities for transformation. Her narratives critically engage with others – e.g., reframing a thief as a guest, vivifying death itself – to produce unanticipated, unexpected results that could free us from a life that is "nasty, brutish, lonely, poore, and short." With this liberation, we may begin to heal and reconstruct. Facing squarely and honestly the consequences of our actions yet with hope and joy and irreverence for the future, we are left no longer to those "impenetrable areas of silence where screams were lost" (Bernabé, quoted in Mignolo 2000: 246). Instead, we discover new resonances from our voices, our communities, our worlds.

Differences reconcile in worldism because of context. In *Honglou meng*, competitions for glory or sex, even if one granted the permanence of such categories, devolve into irrelevant skirmishes when compared to the grander, more profound vistas of, for example, "enlightenment through feelings." Of course, such competitions make up the tapestry of life. They are part of the human condition. But that's precisely the point in *Honglou meng*. Competitions for glory or treasure, like love and war, constitute only a *part* – and a tiny one at that – of the larger horizon of human experiences possible. Ultimately, as the immortals advised Stone, we revert to emptiness. But this "emptiness" is not empty. It is, instead, rich with ambivalence and liminality, like the unrequited yet never forgotten love between Baoyu and Daiyu. This "third space" offers opportunities for surprise, endurance, engagement, innovation, and reconciliation. And they are much-needed. As *Honglou meng* reminds us, we cannot transcend the impact of our actions whether in the human or mythic worlds. We are always held accountable, whether we like it or not. For this reason, as Kavafis and Dimoulas articulate, our lives are open-ended and always in motion, undergoing journeys. These are co-constituted sites of struggle, learning, and understanding. They invite a deeper transformation with others of the asymmetries and violence that course through our multiple-worlds.

In terms of world politics, these readings give us a clear message. We need not stay within the imperium's ontological confines of fear and property, desire and violence. Here worldism makes its contribution. Through multiple worlds, worldism draws on the connections, intimacies, learning, and strategies that *already* bind selves and others to affirm that no one can dominate or surrender only. Our worlds produce us as much as we produce them – historically, materially, ontologically.

Let us now explore similar possibilities of transformation in world politics by applying worldist principles to three contemporary sites: (a) the "Cyprus problem," (b) "triangulating" US, India, and China, and (c) the 9/11 Commission Report.

7 Worldist interventions in world politics

Senhores negociantes	Gentlemen merchants
Aproveita a ocasião	Take advantage of the occasion
Faz tamanha exploraçao	Exploiting greatly
Vendendo for a da conta	By selling off record
Oleo, açucar, arroz, feijão	Oil, sugar, rice, and beans
Lembra os filhos sofrendo	Remember the suffering children
Por favor sejam	Please be
Humano e justiceiro	Humane and just
Mas a maior que eu vejo	But mostly what I see
É a deshumanidade	Is a lack of humanity

Brazilian landless worker speaking of the droughts in the Northeast[1]

In this chapter, we examine how worldism can help with pressing problems in contemporary world politics. As the landless worker from Brazil states above, exploitation may be the way of the time but to be a human being means doing something about the world's plights, not just theorizing about them.

We begin with the "intractable Cyprus problem." Lasting nearly four decades (some say hundreds of years), Cyprus hosts the longest-running UN "peacekeeping" mission (1974–present).[2] Next, we turn to US attempts to "triangulate" relations with India and China whereby one state aims to check another by "playing" a third. We conclude with the event that opened this book: the 9/11 attacks on the World Trade Center, the Pentagon, and the White House. Specifically, we focus on the 9/11 Commission Report and its recommendations for preventing future terrorist attacks not only on US soil but also throughout the globe. These sites of world politics certainly do not exhaust the range or type of issues that need worldist attention. Each exemplifies, rather, the neoliberal binary of Self vs Other and how it infiltrates policy-making in the national, regional, international, and global domains. A worldist intervention suggests some possibilities of emancipation from this disabling condition toward an empowering one of multiple worlds.

CYPRUS

Ethnic conflict and the production of global power[3]

Hangi Yarısını?	Which of the Two Parts?
Yurdunu sevmeliymiş insan	They say that a man must love one's
Öyle diyor hep babam	country
Benim yurdum,	My country
İkiye bölünmüş ortasından	has been divided into two
Hangi yarısını sevmeli insan?	Which of the two parts must I love?

Neshe Yasin, *Which Half in Nicosia?* (1995)

Cyprus usually invokes the label of an "intractable" conflict due to "ethnic rivalries" (Joseph 1997). Its resolution, writes Michael (2006: 1), "has eluded third-party mediation for half a century."[4] In the 1990s, former UN Secretary-General Boutros-Boutros Ghali referred to Northern Cyprus as "one of the most highly militarized areas in the world" (Embassy of Cyprus 1995: 1).

Conventional analyses take as given the binary of Greek vs Turk in Cyprus. Greeks and Turks are cast as staking absolute claims on the island's political, educational, national, and economic identity. Greeks, representing 78 percent of the population, administer 60 percent of the island; Turks, who comprise 18 percent of the population, prevail on the other 40 percent. These analyses cite Greek Cypriots protesting Turkey's unlawful occupation of Northern Cyprus since its "invasion" in 1974. Similarly, Turks are quoted as saying that their only means of ending asymmetries between Greeks and Turks in economic and political power was by seizing territorial control. Conventional analyses usually conclude that while Greeks and Turks claim they are open to dialogue and negotiation, they have yet to find a way of doing so. Thus "stalemate" becomes the operative definition that filters through and encompasses all social relations in Cyprus.

A worldist approach

Worldism ruptures these hegemonic understandings of the island and the conflict. In highlighting the existence of socio-ontologies besides neoliberal globalization, we see that the idea of "Cyprus" and its "ethnic conflict" stem from social relations already embedded in an historical and social environment. What worldism reveals in Cyprus are interlocking regimes of Ottoman and British (neo)colonialism/hetero-imperial-patriarchy. These contend for power in Cyprus, demonstrating the "incompleteness" of the neoliberal imperium. That is, the imperium remains permeable even when seeking to consolidate a regional identity that is "white European," particularly through "truth" discourses and practices that affect the island's socio-economic relations and mainstream understandings of sovereignty and nationhood. Through worldism, we see that different social relations thrive at the interstices of these interlocking "white" and "white but not quite"[5] imperialist regimes, as manifested by the island's multiple worlds (e.g., "mixed" villages, unions, other grass-roots movements, leftist political legacies). These contestations reveal the discursive and practical "gaps" – interregna, so to speak – that perforate the "international" social order, indicating latent sources for transformative, emancipatory strategies and practices for Cyprus. Not dependent on the notion of an evolutionary/ teleological project and its constituent self, these strategies and practices point to, instead, the web of social relations and their subjects that are always relational, fluid, and changeable, depending on the context.

Affinities and complementarities: discursive hooks between mutual negation and liberal internationalism

Building on the notion of "affinities and complementarities," worldism points to two master narratives at work in Cyprus. These emerged especially after World War II when the US along with Europe moved to develop a globally-racialized class structure (i.e., European and white) for international capital to organize itself. Much of this consolidation depended on narratives that would articulate this "reality" and suffocate alternative socio-ontologies, conditions, and relations that would disable its production. Locally and regionally, a discourse of mutual negation rationalizes a "fatal incompatibility" between Greeks and Turks on the island. In this discourse, Greeks label Turks as "*barbaros*,"[6] "the scourge of God," and "anti-Christian." In turn, this discourse has Turks portraying Greeks as "ingrates," "murderers," and "traitors."[7] Turkish hegemony also proselytizes that non-Muslims (i.e., the Greeks) are second-rate subjects. As the *kafir* (the unbeliever), Greeks remain forever the outsider. Regional powers, Greece and Turkey, support this discourse of mutual negation given their respective ties to the two communities.

Internationally, the discourse of liberal internationalism prevails in mediating organizations like the UN. It presumes that liberal internationalist norms, institutions, and practices will "free" Cyprus from this conflict. Just the opposite, however, results. A worldist analysis shows that liberal internationalism tends to reinscribe, rather than mitigate, those very state-based politics that incarcerate Cypriot social relations: e.g., local self-determination, territorial sovereignty, human rights, and a hypermasculine/hyperfeminine competition as part of this order at any cost.[8]

Relational materialism at work: disrupting local, regional, and international complicities

Specific interests motivate these discourses. Ruling elites in each of the four communities involved – Greek Cypriots in the south, Turkish Cypriots in the north, Greeks in Greece, and Turks in Turkey – benefit from the island's segregation, albeit differentially. Since 1974, the island's economy has been divided into two lucrative sectors, with each local community trading most with its respective regional sponsor.[9] As of the early 1990s (the latest data available), Greek-Cypriot trade amounted to approximately 15 percent of the island's imports and 20 percent of its exports, with more than 50 percent of its trade with the EU (especially the UK) and the Middle East receiving 20 percent of exports (Wilson 1992, 1994). Today, Turkey supplies 55 percent of imports in the north and absorbs 48 percent of its exports (Hodges 2007). Greece and Turkey benefit strategically, also, from a divided Cyprus. For Greece, Cyprus enables its economic and political expansion in a pan-Hellenic entity (Kalyonc and Yucel 2005). For Turkey, the Turkish Republic of Northern Cyprus (TRNC) provides a valuable seaport and military outpost. Other than the 1974 war, Turkey and Greece have nearly come to blows over Cyprus in 1964, 1967, 1976 and 1996 (Rumelili 2003).

The US also preserves a powerful role in the region. During the Cold War, Greece and Turkey feared that the (former) Soviet Union sought to expand into the Mediterranean (see Agathangelou 1997). Consequently, they aligned local and regional interests with US military power in the region. The US, in turn, ensured a stable investment environment for capital formation (see Annual Report 1994; Droushiotis 1996). The US interest in Turkey has intensified, also, since the two Gulf Wars; consequently, US responses to the Cyprus problem have tilted towards Turkey.

Producing "Cyprus as stalemate"

Mutual negation and liberal internationalism reify, institutionalize, and professionalize "stalemate" in Cyprus. First, the discourse of mutual negation marginalizes the many communities that now comprise Cyprus and could have a role in constructing alternative social orders and their relations on the island. These include longstanding communities like the Armenians, Latins, Arabs, and new, migrant ones from Turkey, Eastern Europe, the former Soviet Union, and several Asian countries. Second, mutual negation and liberal internationalism "hook" into each other to entrench Cypriot social relations in violence, hierarchy, and asymmetry. For instance, former UN Secretary-General Boutros-Boutros Ghali pursued a peace initiative in Cyprus in 1992. But it generated more suspicion from both sides, leading to greater alienation in each (Bolukbasi 1995). Similarly, both the UN and EU intervened with the Annan Plan[10] in November 2002, followed by the Hague summit in March 2003, and referenda from January–April 2004.[11] None of these initiatives succeeded in shifting social relations in Cyprus. "Stalemate" seemed inevitable.

A worldist perspective explains why but not with the usual reasons. Contrary to conventional presumptions of a "fatal incompatibility" between Greeks and Turks on the island, accounting for the "stalemate," worldism urges us to look at the socio-ontologies behind the discourses and their "hooks." From this perspective, we see that capitalist modernity seeps into all social relations, making itself apparent in the ways Cypriots think about and articulate their political positions. The two dominant discourses may hook into each other but they also contradict each other in significant ways. For instance, liberal internationalism demands a unified state following the rules of the liberal social order whereas mutual negation pushes for a unified state and/or a bi-zonal, bi-communal federal state based on local self-determination.

The UN's and the EU's ontological priority in capitalist modernity, for example, defined citizenship as a "dependable," "manly" subject of development and politics. He is the Western, white, hetero-patriarchal male intent on conquering and accumulating property. Struggles or subjects that do not comply with this "international" social order of "peace," and the property relations that constitute it, are obliterated and/or absorbed. Indeed, the Annan doctrine reflected the neoliberal ontology of fear and property by calling for more "hands on" interventions for a bi-lateral, bi-zonal federation, thereby eroding a sense of national sovereignty among Cypriots.

Additionally, capitalist modernity seeks to recuperate and/or violently extract any other ontologies that might challenge or differ from the neo-liberal one. As Albert *et al.* (2008: 36) note, the "establishment of strict borders between different social orders as well as between a specific order and its potential alternatives" aims to exterminate those ontologies that do not fixate on the Other as "enemy." Reflective of different social relations and orders, these other ontologies disrupt the notion that a social order can exist only if all other practices and voices are extinguished. Possibilities in transforming the stalemate in Cyprus necessarily come from pointing to these alternatives. We consider some below.

Worldist intervention: movements, praxis, and thinking in the interregnum[12]

Contesting socio-ontologies: possibilities for radicalizing politics

As noted above, Cyprus is not merely a site of practical and/or political conflict; it swirls also with socio-ontological struggles. These persist because sites like Cyprus were never fully absorbed into the West's patriarchal-colonial empire. Indeed, the hegemonic ontology that marks Cyprus as a "stalemate" reflects more accurately a remnant event, a social relation, from the Great Game's "Eastern Question," later changed into newer dynamics by the Cold War and today, by the neoliberal imperium.[13] Recognizing this gap or "interregnum" in ontological contestations helps us realize that subjectivities and social relations, like those encompassed by "the state," are never static, to be used as instruments only for hege-monic control. Rather, their very relational and contingently changing nature allows one to "suspend judgment" about subjectivity. This "web of social subjects" opens up political and discursive space to allow multiple communities like those in Cyprus to intersect intersubjectively as well as materially, beyond neoliberal interests.

Today, many Cypriots are working to shift their social relations in ways that disrupt the discourses of mutual negation and/or liberal internation-alism.[14] They forge solidarities through bi-communal movements, working class movements, and women's movements, offering a basis for alternative political action, social relations and, indeed, a different understanding of the static, rugged individual/community/state competing in a world order of fear and property. These social movements challenge, albeit contradictorily sometimes, the hegemony of geopolitical discourses and practices by highlighting the multiplicity of roles, identities, and subjectivities that comprise daily life in Cyprus – e.g., those coming from mothers, wives, daughters, workers, teachers, students, as well as "Greeks" and "Turks," locals and migrants – to shift attention away from intransigent binaries like "Greeks" vs "Turks."

Multiple journeys: engaging in alternative projects

Cooperation and lively exchanges in Cyprus are not new. Many entwinements and movements back and forth in the Mediterranean have located Cyprus at the hub of economic, social, and political enrichment, and activity with surrounding communities. Such *"istorin"* (i.e., histories) disrupt the dominant methods that mainstream scholars and policymakers imposed in advance by inscribing ethnocentric imperial ideas on the geographical spaces of the island.[15] Since the 1990s, social relations in Cyprus have flourished at many different sites including grass-roots ones. These challenge the seductive and powerfully enabling strategy of "benign" neo-colonialism as neoliberal capitalism.

Even in Nicosia, capital of Cyprus, implicit cooperation prevails in managing the city's sewage system. Such cooperation is evident as well in the city's commercial and residential areas (Hadjri 2008). Since the 1990s, Greek and Turkish Cypriots have organized bi-communal events under the auspices of the US, the UN, and more recently, the EU. Bi-communal events and festivals have been held also between trade unionists, teachers, youths, artists, and athletes. Greek and Turkish Cypriot workers alike retain membership in the All-Cyprus Trade Union Forum, for example (Batchell 2004). And Cyprus has always had "mixed" villages where inhabitants speak each other's languages, shop at the same stores, eat the same kind of food, work together, and intermarry.[16]

Worldism also inquires into another world rarely discussed in Cyprus: i.e., patriarchy. Elites from both the north and the south typically frame state and nation-building in terms of the proud, racialized patriarch's protection of his privatized household from conquest, rape, and pillage by the Other. They assume that women and other feminized subjects (e.g., masses, workers, urbanites/farmers) "naturally" follow their rulers, always masculine subjects, and their men with unspoken, uncritical, and inexhaustible support (Anthias and Ayres 1983; Anthias 1989; Cockburn 2004).

Today, patriarchy can no longer make such assumptions. Women and other feminized subjects are a growing factor in Cypriot life despite serious social, religious, and structural obstacles.[17] A gap in wages and access to political and economic resources still exists,[18] but Cypriot women remain central to their respective societies and economies (Pavlou 2005). First, the entry of the Republic of Cyprus into the EU in 2004 enables many activists to work towards a new comprehensive legal framework to guarantee equal pay for equal work, non-discrimination in employment and job training, and equal rights to social security, maternity benefits, and parental leave. Second, the informal sector accounts for a relatively high level of employment for women (59 percent in 2002) given demands for "flexible" (part-time and/or temporary) workers, sometimes as undocumented or illegal domestics (Labour Force Survey 2004). State statistics do not include, either, women's uncompensated labor in their own households (INEK 2007).

A multi-racial, transnational coalition may be arising in Cyprus. It stems from a new proletariat class comprised primarily of domestic, sex, and other workers from countries of the former Soviet Union, Eastern Europe, Turkey, and many Asian countries such as Sri Lanka, China, the Philippines, and other parts of East and Southeast Asia. They work as nannies, sales-clerks, and often, as a means of last resort, prostitutes. This feminized proletariat has the potential of allying with counterpart groups in the EU, through the European Forum. Their numbers have been increasing in the past several years. In 2007, for instance, women across Europe accounted for slightly over 44 percent of all workers (European Commission 2008: 52).[19] Indeed, traditionally gendered jobs are experiencing dramatic increases due to the influx of female migrant workers in childcare, sex tourism, and arranged marriages (Trimikliniotis 2005). Solidarity between a Cypriot, migrant, and European feminized proletariat would expose and eventually transform the masculinized, elitist, racialized fiction that Greeks and Turks suffer from a "fatal incompatibility" and must subjugate themselves, in turn, to a world order of hypermasculine whiteness. A transnational coalition of feminized proletariat would reveal the actual collaboration *already in place* between Greek and Turkish elites despite the master narratives of mutual negation and liberal internationalism.

Indeed, the women's movement in Cyprus has been especially effective. In 1995, women in Cyprus mobilized Cypriot mothers to bring up their children with love and end the hundreds of wars and struggles that have taken place on the island (Hadjipavlou and Cockburn 2006). Multi-communal efforts by choirs, architects, doctors, academics, and youths continue, even as we write, to further connections and solidarities for less violent relations between the two communities (Oztoprak 2000; Calame and Charlesworth 2003; Anastasiou 2006).[20]

The "friendship" movement is also radically transforming Cypriot politics. The communist administration of President Dimitris Christofias, elected in 2008,[21] seems keen to form new coalitions across the two communities on issues like development and the formation of two politically equal polities (states) (Christofias 2008). This leads to interactions across local, regional, and global discourses and solidarities that make visible alternative movements in the interregnum including possibilities of a just and sustainable polity.

Radicalizing socio-ontologies: poetic possibilities of a just polity and way of life

Combined with a simultaneous push for a "civil society" in Cyprus by the EU and the US, these social movements are slowly eroding the master narrative of mutual negation in Cyprus. So, too, the binds of liberal internationalism are loosening. Social relations are forming along lines of regional, rather than national or ethnic, interests and goals. Now more than ever, linkages are possible across the multiple worlds of Cyprus regionally, nationally, racially, and across classes, genders, and sexualities.

Worldism readily admits that people can and will continue practices that lead to violence. But worldism's sensibility to multiple worlds provides us with alternative considerations of historically-sedimented, socio-ontic modalities of organizing social relations. That is, worldism shifts attention away from essentialized, reified structures that produce a unified, socio-political world order, state structures, and collective subjectivities whereby Cyprus, in this case, is rendered as not "fitting" within the current social order: e.g., Greeks and Turks are simply "barbaric" and/or "war-prone." Worldism reorients our attention to the multiplicity of social ontologies at play and their power politics. In the process, we discover that when the neoliberal imperium prioritizes one socio-ontological tradition at the expense of others, this hegemonic move not only marginalizes all other traditions but also radicalizes them.

A worldist approach asks: "Do we want to secure power for power's sake or do we want to live differently?" This question helps us transition from confrontation and its "negotiations" to alternative social relations and the syncretic engagements that may follow. Herein we discover, as suggested in *Honglou meng*, that affinities and complementarities bind even die-hard opposites. In Cyprus, newfound coalitions, alliances, and solidarities in civil society, aided by shifts in regional power, are making these affinities and complementarities more explicit. From a worldist perspective, Cypriots could transform the labels of "stalemate" or "an intractable conflict" and articulate Cyprus as site of "interregnum" and, consequently, a source of other possibilities *within* and *beyond* the Western imperialist project.

Put in IR terms, worldism shatters the mainstream illusion that only great powers matter (Waltz 1979). What the Cypriot conflict reveals is the central role of "small" states and "local" sites in enabling the neoliberal imperium to produce global power. Without the former, worldism stresses, the latter cannot function. And therein lies the potential for not just change but also transformation.

Even for those considered "great powers," worldism suggests alternative visions and practices.

"TRIANGULATING" US–INDIA–CHINA[22]

Mainstream analysts in the neoliberal imperium consider India and China to be tomorrow's hegemons. Given their Self vs Other binary, they view this development if not with alarm, then as an opportunity for strategic interaction based on "national self-interest" (Drezner 2007).[23] Many resort to a formula derived from Cold-War *realpolitik*: "triangulation." It borrows from a sports or game metaphor to convey international politics as a "field" where state actors "play." One state can retain or seek superiority by "playing" the other two against each other. From such calculi, the model holds, a balance of power can emerge in world politics for the benefit of all.

A typical example is John Garver's "The China–India–US Triangle: Strategic Relations in the Post-Cold War Era" (2002), published by the conservative think tank, National Bureau of Research (NBR).[24] Garver begins by asserting that "the US-led system of global power" dazzles all. It keeps China vying for US interest and India, US protection. (Along these lines, others in the neoliberal establishment like Fareed Zakaria [2006] urge closer relations between India and China. They share "[a] common language, a familiar world view and a growing fascination with each other . . . bringing together businessmen, nongovernmental activists, journalists and writers.") The US, according to Garver, remains indifferent to both India and China. An "India-China bloc," Garver (2002: 51) estimates, would be a ploy only, created simply to "induce the United States to pay more for Chinese and Indian abstention from such a combination." In particular, Garver (2002: 50) writes, cooperation with the US "would be a very big step toward the Chinese goal of being accepted as the peer of the United States as a global power."

Towards this end, Garver advises China to learn from Europe. If China is to fulfill its "historical destiny" as a global power, Garver states, the Chinese leadership must emulate that Teutonic icon of hypermasculine whiteness: "Iron Fist" Bismark.

> Unless China can produce a statesman closer to the caliber of Otto von Bismark, the *sine qua non* of whose diplomacy was to keep Russia, France, and Britain from uniting against Germany, the future may be gloomy, or to return to the narrower theme of this essay, alignments within the new post-Cold War Triangle may become rigid.
>
> (Garver 2002: 56)

Apparently, Garver does not believe that almost five millennia of Chinese history, culture, and politics could produce anyone comparable to the sterling qualities of the first Chancellor of Germany.

Banerjee and Ling (2006) note the hypermasculine whiteness behind "triangulation." It reflects a social order derived from the perspectives, experiences, and strategies of privileged, white males as interpreted by them. These include, for example, analogizing world politics to a game of chess, a pastime developed by and for aristocrats. They wonder:

> [W]ho gets to play at *whose* expense, and for *what*? That is, what's the *relationship* between the "players," the "pieces," the "chess board,"

the table on which the game is played, the room, the lights, and so on? Who *produced* what? Who cooks the food, for instance, and brings it to the players as they ponder moves for the game, who cuts the wood for the fireplace, who lights it? (Or, in an alternative scenario, who makes the fan to cool the players, the rattan chairs on which they sit, the silver tray from which they drink their gin and tonic?) . . . One could almost see the cigar smoke and smell the cognac fumes amid the gentlemanly laughter in Garver's posh, [neoliberal] club.

(Banerjee and Ling 2006: 10)

The point, Banerjee and Ling stress, is not whether Indians and Chinese can play chess. Indeed, the game is believed to have originated in India in the seventh century.[25] Rather, the "rules of the game" necessarily privilege the interests and strategies of those who transplanted chess to world politics: i.e., elite white males in hypermasculine competition with Others. Consequently, Banerjee and Ling conclude, participation in triangulation effectively places India and China in the position of the classical subaltern vis-à-vis the US as the ruling hegemon. They must constantly prove their national manhood, so to speak, to the white colonial master (like Asia's former "miracle" economies) or reject the game altogether (like the ill-fated non-alignment movement).[26] In either case, like the discourse of mutual negation in Cyprus, the triangulation model casts US–India–China relations as entrenched, insoluble, and "intractable."

A worldist approach

Worldism helps us get beyond such binaries, stifling even when applied to triangular relations. Given that triangulation reflects and sustains hyper-masculine whiteness, why would those who suffer from it comply? This question pertains especially to ruling elites in India and China, with their histories of anti-colonial, anti-imperialist struggle. Mainstream analysts like Garver presume that participation in the "Great Game" of triangulation salves egos, but history demonstrates that generations of Indians and Chinese have dealt with such seductions of empire before – and they have rejected them.

Worldism tells us why, without trapping us between empire and counter-empire. Alternative legacies of power, history, and culture, world-ism emphasizes, still live among us. For India and China, two millennia of interactions preceded the onset of Westphalian modernity.[27] Political capitals like Beijing and New Delhi, along with their economic satellites like Shanghai and Mumbai, may tune more attentively (at present) to the West and other centers of neoliberal power. But the borderland regions tell of a prior, grander story of trade and interaction than neoliberal glob-alization. Lasting nearly 20 centuries, the Southern Silk Road (fourth century BC–sixteenth century AD) registers a different set of sensitivities, concerns, and priorities. These reflect centuries of trade in horses, tea, sil-ver, and silk and the transmission of two of the world's major religions,

Buddhism and Islam. Linking south-central China (Yunnan, Sichuan) with neighbors in the Southeast (Vietnam, Burma) and South (Bangladesh, India), these borderlands embodied global trade in their time. Today, they brim again with possibilities for the future by layering the present onto the past.[28]

The "Kunming Initiative" (1999) is one example.[29] It aims to foster greater regional cooperation between four economically disparate and often politically contentious states: Bangladesh, China, India, and Myanmar (BCIM). This initiative has opened new routes connecting the Central Asian republics, China, and the Pakistani port of Gwadar, for example; it has revived old ones, as well, like the Chinese railway from Kunming to Kolkata. Official reasons for this initiative rehearse the neoliberal emphasis on globalization and trade, economics and national self-interest.[30] But these exchanges mean far more than that. They signal a renewed appreciation for another way of life richly populated by multiplicity and complexity, exchanges and flows, languages/religions/goods, despite clashes and conflicts. Yunnan alone, for instance, is home to 26 different minority groups, including Tibetans and the Dai, who are of Thai ethnicity. More profoundly, the Southern Silk Road facilitated dealings across cultural, linguistic, religious, and lifestyle differences without resort to hegemonic politics or conversion/discipline ultimatums. It was, in effect, what neoliberals today would call a "free" market.

Worldism re-centralizes these borderlands. It does so not just to restore these locations as historical sites but also to learn from them as a template for syncretic engagement. This recognition reorients current talk of "interlinkages" from neoliberal globalization's narrow focus on technology, trade, and finance to a more nuanced sense of conduits and circuits, adaptations and innovations, institutional and capacity-building that make our world politics today. "Borderlands" as a syncretic template integrates the political and the material, for instance, with the socio-cultural and the aesthetic, among others. In so doing, this template would rediscover and repair those archives of knowledge exiled or damaged by the politics of erasure. Worldism gives us then another mode of dealing with conflicts and contestations within dynamic, complex, and multiple sets of struggles and interactions (see Devahuti 2002; Tan 2002).

Worldist intervention: "borderlands"

From worldism comes four alternative ways of approaching US, India, China relations. Kavafis's cautions for finding "Ithaca" serve as a guideline:

Pluralizing the Self through journeys: a cosmopolitan perspective

Trade along the Silk Road enhanced a cosmopolitan outlook for masses and elites alike (see Weatherford 2004). Peoples, goods, ideas, religions, and lifestyles from Europe, Central Asia, the Middle East, China, Africa, and South Asia mixed openly and constantly. Buddhist pilgrims from India brought knowledge of math, astronomy, calendrical science, and medicine to the seventh century Tang court in China. Similarly, the subcontinent learned of key Chinese technologies like silk and sericulture, paper making and printing, use of the compass, and gunpowder. This juxtaposition of multiple worlds, and the mobility and fluidity that came with them, made an important political, not just commercial, impact: i.e., tolerance from ruling elites. Buddhist teachings on compassion and acceptance of non-organized diversity through "non-doing" (*wu wei*), for instance, helped the Emperor's court, dominated by Han Confucians, find a rationale to accommodate other ethnic and linguistic groups under their rule. Indeed, "silk diplomacy" was used often to solidify relations between Han Chinese and the Huns in AD 2 (Sen 2006).[31] Equally significant, Buddhism's integration with Confucianism helped to mitigate the authoritarian tendencies of the latter and the other-worldliness of the former to foster a new political activism tempered with compassion. For example, as governor of a local province, the renowned poet-official, Su Shi (AD 1037–1101), exercised both by convincing local wealthy families to donate funds for orphanages throughout his jurisdiction (Egan 1994);[32]

Acquiring wisdom and experience: women as shamans and benefactresses

Though patriarchy prevailed throughout, borderland societies granted significant venues for women's agency precisely because the environment was so mixed and fluid (Devahuti 2002). Women were seen as naturally shamanistic, given their general sensitivity to cultural mores and needs. Besides performing rituals of nature and other cathartic acts, shamans "look[ed] after the needs of individuals and families as well as of the tribe as a whole" (Devahuti 2002: 69). Women led in other realms as well, such as establishing a monastery or introducing sericulture to China's "hinterland" (Devahuti 2002). One could argue that valorizing women's "special" shamanistic ability entrenches, not reverses, hypermasculinity. But this recognition flouts a fundamental justification of hypermasculinity: i.e., it protects women and other feminized subjects even while exploiting them. When major decisions, such as life and death due to war or illness, or when and how to proceed on difficult travel across vast territories, rely on a female shaman's predictions, forecasts, or prayers, hypermasculinity's pretensions invariably crumble;

Widening and deepening vistas: *"Nizhong you wuo, wuozhong you ni"* ("I in you and you in me")

This rich mix in the borderlands inculcated a sensibility of multi-layeredness, intersectionality, and rotationality. For instance, the ancient kingdom of Khotan, now in Northwestern China, was, during the Silk Road era, "a most important centre of Buddhist learning and research, frequented for that purpose both by the Chinese and the Indians" (Devahuti 2002: 94). Khotan's past and present merit reconsideration contrapuntally, as Said would say, for it could become another center tomorrow. Similarly, Dunhuang, also in today's northwest China, provided a site for seventh century Indians and Chinese to meet, exchange, and flourish through Buddhism. These locations heightened the Buddhist notion of "*nizhong you wuo, wuozhong you ni*" ("I in you and you in me") where selves and others reverberate with one another to construct a mutual subjectivity (Tan 2002); and, finally,

Relationality of social ontologies: poetics of life

Worldist relationality in social ontologies crystallizes most explicitly in the poetics of life in the borderlands. Borderlands represent sites where goods and peoples mixed, after all, with religions and the arts. How the Tang Emperor Taizong came to initiate relations with India provides an apt illustration:

> The Tang Emperor Taizong . . . believed the dream in AD 64 of the Han emperor Ming (AD 57–75) that a golden deity was flying over the palace. He asked the courtiers to explain this dream and obtained the answer that it was a signal from the Buddha of India. The emperor, then, sent out a mission headed by Cai Yin to go to India to invite Buddhism to China.
>
> (Tan 2002: 132)

Not to be confused with an endorsement of astrologers or dream analysts, this anecdote conveys only that an alternative heuristic to understanding oneself as well as others can apply. It underscores that a very different kind of relationship prevailed between selves and others then, and can once again. A poetics of life leads us to recognize that certain inherited beliefs, like myths, fables, parables, and other collective memories, affect us as much as, perhaps more so than, the "rational" and "objective" concerns of the contemporary neoliberal imperium.

In sum, "borderlands," as a template for syncretic engagement, does not counter the binary of Self vs Other so much as sort through it. A cosmopolitan outlook places the logic of Self vs Other in a larger context: i.e., other options for interactions and negotiations are salient, available, and plausible. An analytical framework that grants agency to the Other, whether women or other marginalized subjects, also obsolesces colonial power relations expressed through hypermasculine whiteness or any other hegemonic claim to superiority. Racial divides dissipate when we interrogate their social constructions (what *is* "whiteness," after all?) based on structures of power where a small minority relies on the majority for labor, resources, and sustenance (what's the impact of hypermasculine whiteness on whites?) (see Hall 2008). The Buddhist notion of "I in you and you in me" teaches multi- and trans-subjectivity: i.e., the Self exists in the Other as much as the Other is in the Self. Reflecting Said's contrapuntal method and worldism's *poietic* reverberations, Buddhist mutuality highlights the dialectical criticality that inheres within social relations. In this framework, setting Self against Other would be tantamount to doing the same to oneself. The violence would not be contained "out there;" it would resound also "in here," given the systemic complicities of each. We see this happening as rival camps of hypermasculine competition compete against one another, like "white but not quite" Greek and Turkish Cypriots, Asian capitalists, or Muslim insurgents, who vow to avenge themselves against that ultimate source of hypermasculine whiteness: the West. More than ever, we need a poetics of life to help us place the neoliberal imperium in perspective. We can and should enjoy material comforts and pleasures but without being reduced to a contemporary version of the *poitike*: i.e., slavish, reactionary hypermasculinity, whether founded on whiteness or corporate virtue or any other identity assigned by the neoliberal imperium.

Let us now return to 9/11 and the events that opened this book.

9/11 COMMISSION REPORT

The 9/11 Commission Report continues to promote the binary of Self vs Other despite exhorting the US to "reach out, listen to, and work with other countries that can help" (The Report 2004: 367). Three features of the Report demonstrate this dichotomous logic:

1. The US Self has nothing to learn from the Terrorist Other. The American Self remains unchanged despite radical change all around. "[T]he American homeland," after all, "is the planet" (The Report 2004: 362);

2. But the Terrorist Other has everything to learn from the US Self. The Terrorist Other *needs* US (re)education because he is mired in incompetence, ignorance, and sheer lack of integrity. "The resentment of America and the West is deep, even among leaders of relatively successful Muslim states" (The Report 2004: 362). America-hating suicide bombers and global terrorism result. For this reason, "if the United States does not act aggressively to define itself in the Islamic world, the extremists will gladly do the job for us" (The Report 2004: 377);

3. Ultimately, it's Us vs Them. The Report cites the Terrorist Other to rationalize its own binary logic. al Qaeda, the Report claims, wants the US to "abandon the Middle East, convert to Islam, and end the immorality and godlessness of its society and culture" (The Report 2004: 51). And if the US "did not comply," the Report warns, "it would be at war with the Islamic nation, a nation that al Qaeda's leaders said 'desires death more than you desire life'" (The Report 2004: 52).

This treatment of Self vs Other can only escalate violence. For example, the Report calls for "coordination" among "leading coalition governments" to combat terrorism (The Report 2004: 379). In globalizing the "war on terror," the Report effectively sanctions a collective denial. That is, it forestalls asking questions such as: How did we get here? What's our role in creating such violence? Without this kind of internal interrogation, the coalition on the "global war on terror" will mean conquering and policing those Others whom the hypermasculine, neoliberal Self made in the first place. In turn, resistance from these Others will rigidify with outcomes already evident in daily news about insurgencies, bombings, torture, and deaths. So rules the neoliberal imperium.

Disrupting Self vs Other, conversion/discipline

A *poietic* intervention exposes these politics of erasure. Because worldism posits that identity/subjectivity emerges in conjunction with others through their social relations, malleability prevails. Consequently, one could risk listening to, communicating with, and learning from peoples who do not "fit" into those identities assigned by hypermasculine whiteness even when deeply fearful of and insecure about them. They are indeed always in relation to us. When we realize this, a process of engagement unfolds syncretically: i.e., struggles and collaborations at the interstices of Self and Other ensue. No "subaltern mimicry," these reflect, instead, a substantive integration or reconciliation of "difference" between selves and others (see Ling 2002b).

Again, we turn to Dimoulas for illustration. She questions what it means to be the "on the top" Self "protected" by barbed wires:

Ιδού *πως* σκοντάφτει σε μια σπιθαμή συρματόπλεγμα γύρω απο το χτήμα. Χαμηλό,	See how it catches on a stretch of barbed wire. Round the property. Low,
ήρεμο και όμως άν το καλοκοιτάξεις το καλοαισθανθείς διαιρεί την δική μου καλημέρα από του γείτονα	Tame and yet If you consider it carefully it divides My good-morning from the neighbor's
ολημερίς σύνορα φανατίζει σιωπηρά	All day long fanaticizing borders quietly
οπλίζοντας ξερόχορτα εναντίον των αδελφών τους.	Arming the weeds against their brothers.

In asking who's "in" and who's "out," Dimoulas demystifies the idea of Western freedom. Who is "free," in this case, and who is not? Aren't we all demarcated by barbed wires? If so, what of "self-protection"? If you look carefully, Dimoulas hints, you can distinguish her *"good-morning"* from her neighbor's. Such fanaticism (*"all day long"*) sets even Nature against itself (*"the weeds against their brothers"*). Nature – and those deemed "natural" – is conquered once again but for whose benefit, what purpose, and at what cost? Does this strategy preserve the Self or distort it, such that even Nature (*"the natural"*) wars against itself? Hierarchy, in short, undermines the very security that the Self seeks. Instead, as worldism suggests, we must *"untie"* ourselves from these rigidified boundaries that have their history in fear, ignorance, greed, and colonial power relations.

Dimoulas also cracks open the black box of "sovereignty" and other notions of "normalcy" and "legitimacy." Note this line in her poem, "Cartoon":

Ακόμη αυτά καπνίζεις;	Are you still smoking those?
Πάρε Κάμελ.	Try Camel.

If one were to smoke, she challenges, why not puff up "the best"? Dimoulas satirizes the brand *Camel*. It, like *Marlboro*, conjures up an image of the wild, open, rugged American West where Manifest Destiny subjugates all non-whites. But cigarettes ultimately ruin the smoker's health. Indeed, it is the seduction of such imagery – beauty, independence, power – that kills over time. Metaphorically and materially, neoliberal democracy (as embodied by the Marlboro Man) subverts our freedom and emancipation from necessity (illness, dependency, death). Who, then, conquers whom in the long-run? Who enjoys stability and longevity and who not? Who needs help and who gives it? In these scenarios, what is "normal" and "legitimate"? Worldism's focus on multiple social ontologies exposes the neoliberal Self's conceit and destructiveness in passing these discourses and practices as "truth." Instead, we must sort *through* these conjunctions of seduction and conflict that "clog" Self *and* Other to free ourselves of elite manipulation, exploitation, and coercion.

Continuing with the previous poem, Dimoulas punctures the mirage of "self-sufficiency":

Ἀς μη γελιόμαστε ὁμοιέ μου.	Let's not fool ourselves, my likeness.
Αὐταρκες είναι μονάχα το μάταιον.	Only the futile is self-sufficient.

Here, Dimoulas presents an ontology of mutual dependence and co-constitution. We all need one another, she stresses. Nothing proceeds unilaterally or unidimensionally. Such narcissism, even our own "*likeness*," merely mystifies power and its distortions. The Self needs the Other to survive; more profoundly, the Self cannot *be* without the Other. From this realization comes a necessary premise: we must work together because we cannot escape one another. We begin by asking: what do *we* want and why?

CONCLUSION

At each site of world politics, worldism shows us possibilities for transformations previously not considered. From the incarcerating binaries of Self vs Other (e.g., Greeks vs Turks in Cyprus, US vs India vs China, US vs al Qaeda), we find emancipation in a larger context provided by multiple worlds and their legacies of entwinement. Multi- and trans-subjectivities, for example, demystify sovereignty, enabling us to interrogate the relational-materialist forces underpinning "the state" and its agents, making "world politics" into what the neoliberal imperium claims it is.

Perforating this hegemony foregrounds the innovations, adaptations, and learning that are already underway in communities, achieved by people simply living their lives the best way they know how. Worldist inquiry deflates the neoliberal ultimatum of conversion and/or discipline. We realize, instead, that what the imperium seeks to dismiss, displace, or disappear *still* flourishes. That is, peoples and communities enact worldist visions and practices on a daily basis, and they have done so for a long time. Recognizing and appreciating this wealth of social ontologies provided by multiple worlds will give us the capacity to build towards a more inclusive, less violent and creative world politics.

In this way, worldism redefines "modernity" and "community." Recognizing the agency of all parties to co-produce our worlds places worldist inquiry at the nexus of multiple worlds and their legacies, in contrast to the conventional story of unidimensional, unilateral, and unilinear modernity. Instead, worldism throws these modernist presumptions into question: e.g., syncretic engagements occur even when prohibited by the state, as in the "mixed" villages of Cyprus where Greeks and Turks co-habit on a regular basis, another model of community-building on a global scale *before* the imposition of the Westphalian inter-state system, and multi- and trans-subjectivities that web us together even when a terrorist's bullet seems directed right at us. These examples demonstrate the fluidity, dynamism, and permeability of communities as they interact with others. Indeed, it is at these junctures of interacting social ontologies, where legacies of reinforcement and conflict emerge, that we detect the rich potential for reconstruction and transformation not just hatred and annihilation. The first impetus for change, as noted earlier, comes in the form of a crisis.

That's why we need the worldist notion of accountability. Unlike the UN and other institutions that are beholden to if not controlled by the neoliberal imperium, a worldist forum would recognize, legitimate, and hold accountable multiple voices, subjectivities, traditions, and discourses. More than a liberal gesture towards diversity, this worldist forum would provide a method of engaging across multiple worlds syncretically. Specifically, we draw on worldism's relational materialism to fashion a democratic process that is dialectical in method, historical in substance, and material in implementation.

The following questions would initiate this process:

- Who's accountable for what?
- How do we institutionalize critique and dissent, as well as reconciliation and reconstruction, in democratic deliberation? How do economic interests and other material considerations structure the discourse and practices of world politics?
- What kind of communities are we building, for whom, and why?
- Which agents contribute to what kind of impact on community-building? What inequities need redressing?
- How have we engaged with each other? Under what conditions? Why? How have we learned from each other? What are some moments of

syncretic connections and collaborations? How did these relations and processes emerge?

• Where do multi- and trans-subjectivities occur such that we can draw on them for syncretic engagement?

These questions help us to "suspend judgment" long enough to consider alternative ways of understanding the problem(s), if not to transform it (them). Clearing away the same old patterns of hatred, vengeance, and violence will allow us to co-constitute our worlds in accountable ways. Shifting paradigmatically from a binary of Self vs Other to the social relations among selves and others is crucial. This chapter offers three registers that indicate the ways peoples and societies have been living, working, and thriving on the "borderlands" for centuries. These suggest a different kind of thinking for a world politics that would allow for a more comprehensive process of deliberation and engagement, despite severe asymmetries and injustices. In this way, world politics may begin to shift from empire to multiple worlds.

8   A play on worlds

Here is my journey's end . . .
Othello, before fatally stabbing himself (Shakespeare, *Othello* 1603)[1]

Multiple worlds, in brief, *is* world politics. Ordinary folks throughout the globe deal with the entwinements and contestations of multiple worlds on a daily basis, in venues "high" and "low," "public" and "private," "inside" and "outside." Globalization intensifies our interactions with multiple worlds so that, more than ever, decisions are made within a matrix of contending social ontologies (e.g., "how do we engage with capitalist modernity to develop for the community, rather than the state or the corporation?"). Worldism helps by offering a vaster inventory of visions and practices, ways and means, than the narrow confines of neoliberal Self vs Other. Drawing most recently from five centuries of enforced contact through European colonialism and imperialism, worldism also accesses knowledges and strategies dating from before that, as evidenced by "borderlands" life along the ancient Silk Roads.

In globalizing world politics, worldism maximizes our freedom to "make a world with Others" (Wendy Brown, quoted in Bertsch 2002: 214). Worldism helps to break the vicious cycle of fear and violence seduced by neoliberal desire, thereby enabling a radical democratization of world politics. And it is radical because worldism involves recovery and reconstruction at the level of being, not just practice.

> Critical social ontologies require that we simultaneously disrupt and (re)construct: disrupt the dominant imaginaries that the (neo)liberal capitalist-neo-colonialism has created of itself and about itself and of us and about us, and (re)construct a throbbing living reality which accepts and articulates the existence and will of all in any of its expressions.
>
> (Agathangelou forthcoming)

Pragmatically, worldism offers the following guidelines:

1. **Multi- and Trans-Subjectivities Demystify Sovereignty.** Multi- and trans-subjectivities contest the neoliberal imperium's boundary-making that

keeps us, literally and figuratively, in place. In acknowledging the multiplicity and co-constituted nature of our worlds, multi- and trans-subjectivities demystify the hegemonic world order and its contingent sovereignties to rethink and reorganize the social (power) relations between selves and others;

2. **Democratizing Social Relations Perforates Hegemony.** Recognizing agency in all parties, despite differential access to power and resources, disrupts the imperium's presumption that only certain subjects have voice and impact on world politics. Democratizing agency helps us to imagine, identify, and develop alternative venues to connect and build communities, thereby perforating hegemony of its seeming invincibility;

3. **Syncretic Engagement Enables Innovation, Adaptation, and Learning.** Syncretic engagement extends beyond "subaltern mimicry" to challenge the very notions of "normalcy" (what is) and "legitimacy" (what ought to be). Specifically, syncretic engagement refers to processes and conditions that *become* normalized and legitimized, particularly when two hegemonic systems or traditions entwine despite asymmetries in power and resources. Syncretic engagements mobilize multi- and trans-subjectivities through innovations, adaptations, and learning to disrupt and transform, eventually, the hegemonic order that generated the crisis in the first place;

4. **Building Communities, Making History on a Daily Basis.** People build communities by living and working together on a daily basis, regardless of ideological and material obstacles. This act of everyday relations underscores the radical democracy within worldism as both a descriptive process and an analytical project; and,

5. **Accountability, Criticality, and Emancipatory Reconstruction Check Empire.** Worldism holds that selves and others cannot escape their mutual accountability given their mutual embeddedness. Accountability pertains even when the neoliberal imperium sets up the Self to control, discipline, and exclude Others. Their entwinement ensures an inherent criticality that questions "normalized" and "legitimized" categories like power and sovereignty, the state and empire. Indeed, accountability upheld by criticality ensures that recovery and emancipatory reconstruction takes place in light of critique and resistance.

SEDUCTIONS OF EMPIRE GIVEN WORLDISM

These guidelines compel new approaches to the seductions of empire. We proceed in reverse order: the hegemony of fear and property as a social ontology for world politics, neoliberal desire's dependence on and rationalization of violence, the academy's complicity with empire, and the politics of erasure in contemporary world politics.

Ontology of fear and property

Hobbes and Locke still figure centrally in today's hegemonic practices. For neoliberals, fear without legally-protected, private property would manifest in Locke's warning about unfettered state power ("where law ends, tyranny begins"); property without fear and uninhibited by moral or legal constraints would realize Hobbes's nightmare scenario of wanton desire satiated at will and in chaos ("warre of all against all"). Indeed, Hobbesian fear depends on Lockean private property for the Leviathan to take effect (otherwise, why not stay with the absolute freedom offered by the State of Nature?). Similarly, the Lockean right to property is premised on the Hobbesian fear to keep the State of Nature at bay (otherwise, why suffer a Leviathan?). The neoliberal imperium transforms this classical liberal tradition to have the Leviathan/imperium appropriate property anew each time and on a global basis – e.g., "new" land, "new" labor, "new" market shares – precisely to forestall fear of the local masses.

Worldism helps us (re)consider these neoliberal propositions by juxtaposing those dimensions of world politics previously kept apart. For example, note the relationship between economic development and national security. Agathangelou (2004b, 2006) examines how "economically-peripheral states" in the Mediterranean like Cyprus, Greece, and Turkey import migrant labor to comply with the neoliberal, competitive policies of the "economically-core states" in the EU. At the same time, these states justify an elaborate national security apparatus to keep out the migrants for seeming "dangerous" (i.e., terrorists). To regulate this migrant flow, Turkey serves as the EU's "security buffer zone" despite the country's own ambiguous status as not "European" yet. Other parts of the world also endure this development-security dualism. Mexicans, for instance, have migrated historically to the Western and Southwestern regions of the US to work in labor-intensive industries. Yet, the US government narrates a national security need to "patrol" these border regions while routinely being softer on the employers of "illegal" migrants than they are on the migrants themselves. Or, as noted in Chapter Two, Serbs and Croats somehow can overcome their "historical" enmity to collaborate on sex trafficking in the region. The ontology of fear and property creates such paradoxes throughout the globe: i.e., countering "development" with "security" even as capitalism binds both.

Worldism shows us how to learn *poietically*. That is, multiple worlds help us transform the hegemony of fear and property into the possibilities of engagement and syncretic development. These exist at "the margins" (e.g., grass-roots alliances and solidarities among women, unionists, youths), rarely reaching "mainstream" attention or validity given elite monopolies of institutional and discursive power. Only by voicing these syncretic ideas and agendas to engage the ruling orthodoxy could we devise a majority-based strategy toward a more democratic, participatory world politics. Still, those who bear the heaviest burden and greatest cost of hypermasculine competition (women, workers, colonized/subjugated peoples) cannot –

should not – shoulder the entire responsibility of convincing elites to think and act otherwise. Rather, let us focus on forging transnational alliances, both cultural and material, to make another world politics possible. One arena for action is the academy.

The House of IR

Worldism gives us other ways of knowing the world (epistemology) and being in it (ontology). In so doing, it provides a route to knowledge production not based on complicity with power. Mainstream IR, Steve Smith (2004) contends, perpetuates, even if unintentionally, the dichotomized world of Self vs Other that culminates into events like 9/11.[2] Smith urges IR scholars to heed an ethic of responsibility in their analyses and practices. He analogizes our production of concepts, theories, and methods in IR to the "singing" of Australian aborigines. They believe that, during "dream-time," they literally "sing their world into existence" (Smith 2004: 499). Not only does this ritual underscore agency in world-making, but it also carries an implicit note of caution:

> [IR scholars] sing our worlds into existence, yet rarely reflect on who wrote the words and the music, and virtually never listening out for, nor recognizing, voices of worlds other than our own until they occasionally force us into silence.
>
> (Smith 2004: 514)

To not hear these other voices, we suggest, reflects an elite privilege. After all, who can afford to not listen to others? This is particularly pressing when others have a different story to tell about themselves, their communities, and their world politics. In the telling, they sometimes recast the rules and roles of those who claim to speak for and from them, in ways previously considered "irrational." These interventions, like Hammad's poem on 9/11, reflect changing understandings and social relations created by transnationalized insecurities. We need a world politics, in other words, that respects and provides for the welfare of the world's majority, rather than the profit-making of its elite minority.

Herein lies worldism's most substantive contribution. It takes as a starting point that we need to hear and understand the music, the words, and the multiple voices that emerge from multiple worlds and sing them anew into existence. Worldism underscores another insight: neoliberal desire and violence, infused with race, gender/sexuality, class, and nationality, may initially scare us into a mournful silence but it invariably alchemizes, over time, into a righteous, murderous rage. Here, multiple worlds serve as both boon and bane. From them, we gain access to alternative visions, practices, and strategies to write and sing our own life-defining music. But multiple worlds can also be exploited to glorify "otherness" or "the past" to salve today's injustices and indignities, violence and pain. Empire succeeds in this case, turning violence into desire: e.g., "the Coke side of life."[3]

Neoliberal desire and violence

Worldism alerts us to the neoliberal twist in imperial desire. Neoliberalism reconfigures an imperial hierarchy of wealth and power into an ideology of equality and democracy. The siren song of glory, prosperity, and security transfixes us into organizing our lives to fulfill its goals without seeming imperialistic. Privilege, whether material, social, or moral, seems attainable by all for all. Dissent, particularly with regard to the inequities of privilege, is castigated as a politics of envy and sometimes violence by the few for the few. Note, for example, the US government's $700 billion bailout package for Wall Street in September 2008. Only when the economy's elites and their institutions needed money – which they mishandled – would George W. Bush's neoliberal government argue for and receive Leviathan-like sums to "rescue" the reprobates. At the same time, this bailout must ensue given the integral role of capital and credit in the US and world economies. Ordinary citizens are caught between a rock and a hard place – and must pay dearly for the privilege. They need the capital and credit to enable transactions in daily life (e.g., buying a house or a car, obtaining a loan for education or business), the "market" and its organizers argue, so they cannot afford for the financial sector to collapse. Hence tax dollars (including more loans from other countries since the US treasury is in deficit) must compensate for the billions gambled and lost on Wall Street even though ordinary citizens were neither the instigators nor beneficiaries of neoliberal excesses and corruption in the first place.

All find themselves succumbing further to the imperium. State control, if not terror, becomes a prerequisite to ensure a "better" job, a "freer" lifestyle, and an individualistic, no-questions-asked daily existence. Those from the working classes, people of color, women, and other marginalized populations comply as much as the leaders and managers of the imperium. A consumer-based politics emerges. It freezes politics into an end-state such as "democracy" or "Islam," rather than make visible the processes of social relations that distribute power and wealth in the world. Democratic voice and participation become exiled under the neoliberal imperium, even as it loudly proclaims the opposite.

"Desire industries" proliferate accordingly. Neoliberal individualism, competitiveness, and marketization combined with the structural inequities that perpetuate exploitation, poverty, desperation, and despair produce a global market for trafficking and evicting people from their communities. Desire industries rationalize three conflations: (a) products and people are interchangeable, (b) private consumption serves a public good, and (c) corporate efficiency requires the commodification and (re)colonization of "third-world" labor, generally, and women, specifically (Agathangelou 2002). These conflations normalize racism, sexism, and neocolonialism even as the agents of neoliberal globalization – e.g., multinational corporations, the media, and the developmental state – herald "consumption" as a guarantor of "freedom" and "democracy" (Firat and Dholakia 2000).

"Consumer citizenship" thus camouflages the violence at work, much like the neoliberal imperium's shiny, new malls and their advertising campaigns to "Define You" (see Yoto 2008).

Likewise, Bush and bin Ladin seek to define us. They fuse the logic of state violence with the desire of neoliberal capital to produce exclusionary practices of consumption as citizenship. Bush appeals to a Self/subjectivity that needs consumption to boost the economy even when it smolders in fire and destruction. bin Ladin's vision of the Islamic community excludes women and laborers as co-makers of their world in a political sense and yet requires their inclusion as "selfless others." Compliance with these versions of the patriarchal household, hunting, and other acts of hyper-masculinity may satisfy elite constructions of a national and transnational Self that is insulated and unified. But as this book demonstrates, violence to the Other also alienates and damages the Self. We need an emancipatory approach to world politics.

Worldism helps us begin by scrutinizing structures of privilege. Critical voices must ask: "Who benefits from, and who pays for, the sacrifices required by all this militarizing and globalizing in world politics, now further excused and extended by 'the global war on terror'?" This question explicitly links the public with the private, top with bottom, the material with the mercurial. Note, for example, the struggle of aboriginal communities worldwide to make land claims to states like Canada, Australia, and the US by exposing 500 years of on-going colonization (Smith 2005), the civil rights movements in North America to empower African-Americans and other racialized minorities to transform their communities despite the rampant racism against them (Dyson 2002), anti-imperialist movements in Latin America (Klein 2005), and recent popular protests around the globe at World Bank/IMF/WTO meetings as well as surging participation in the World Social Forum (WSF), held in protest against the World Economic Forum (WEF). Not just a rag-tag hippie movement, as some would dismiss it, the WSF signals the spread of alternative socioeconomic relations and practices undertaken by ordinary men and women on a daily basis.[3]

And governments are taking note. Like Malaysia during the Asian financial crisis, several countries in Latin America no longer feel compelled to abide by the neoliberal imperium's bromides for economic development. First Brazil and then Argentina repaid their IMF loans ahead of schedule to relieve themselves of international debt; now some countries in Latin America are forwarding the idea of their own bank to replace the IMF (AFP 2008). Thailand and Venezuela have identified, also, their own ideological program for development that differs significantly from the neoliberal one. "Is the IMF still relevant?" many now ask (Subramanian 2006). This question urges IR scholars and practitioners to take a more creative approach to world politics and its pressing issues. Indeed, current social movements have the potential to radicalize IR if critical scholars do not isolate themselves in ivory towers or institutions like the non-profit complex (Agathangelou and Spira 2007).

Politics of erasure

"Eu faço uma revolução, logo	"I make the revolution, therefore
existo."	I exist."

Glauber Rocha, *The Aesthetics of Hunger* (1965)

From worldism, we see that only one Self dominates world politics and it is neoliberal. This neoliberal, neoimperial Self does not recognize, value, or integrate Other worlds, subjectivities, and/or social ontologies even while benefiting from them. Many who have been seduced into this asymmetry now join those who seek to disrupt it. But they do so by retaliating in kind. Rocha's quote indicates what it takes to rid the violence that marks relations between colonizer and colonized. He suggests an ongoing struggle to validate the colonized. Currently, these struggles take place outside the forum of "international" organizations.

The UN and other Bretton Woods institutions continue to reflect "the West," particularly as it is interpreted by patriarchs and propertied males during their colonial heyday. These organizations may herald notions of "universality," "humanitarianism," and "democracy," but they still abide by the imperial ultimatum of conversion/discipline.

In a worldist world politics, erasure cannot continue. Recognizing multiple worlds and their entwined legacies puts aside, so to speak, the binary of Self vs Other as only one of many strategies available to deal with conflicts and contestations. And we need to realize these alternatives now. Despite their disparate power positions, Bush/America and bin Ladin/al Qaeda offer equally hypermasculinizing world politics, each camp with its asymmetries of race, gender, sexuality, class, and nationality branded on the bodies of ordinary people throughout the globe.

Worldism breaks this impasse by asking: What are the "affinities and complementarities" that bind even supposed die-hard opposites like Bush vs bin Ladin, US vs al Qaeda, Self vs Other? A dual inquiry must ensue: the US into its foreign policy greed in the Middle East (see Chomsky 2003); bin Ladin/al Qaeda/Taliban into their associations with "the enemy," whether through the CIA or the opium trade (see Robinson 2002).

In addition, worldism compels us to interrogate ourselves. Americans need to question, for example, why evil terrorists have "weapons of mass destruction" while the US government deploys "smart bombs," "daisy cutter" bombs, ten-ton bombs, and other instruments of death, usually unloaded on populations already devastated by poverty, disease, and despair (Egan 2002). Similarly, Muslims need to critique demagoguery disguised as spiritual leadership. Why is salvation gained only through death, especially for those fighting in the trenches but rarely involving the "masterminds"? How are the rewards distributed, not in heaven but this earthly life?

Neither camp can claim, in short, "I am innocent."

A PLAY ON WORLDS

We conclude with a play on worlds. As with fiction and poetry, a play enacts worldism's distinctive characteristic: i.e., it embodies what it claims to demonstrate. One must extend oneself to others, whether as an actor on stage or viewer in the audience, to vivify the play, thereby experiencing journeys of multi- and trans-subjectivities. This collaborative intimacy underscores the agency of all who participate in making the play possible: from playwright to crew to actors to audience. Their engagements not only give the play meaning by building a community that is dynamic, fluid, and cumulative – each performance changes in tenor, for instance, depending on the particular mix of actors and audience for a particular moment – but these performances also build on one another over time as actors and audiences gain greater insight into or give alternative interpretations to the roles, the plot, the message. And critics lurk in any audience, holding the playwright, the actors, and the play itself accountable with queries, challenges, and contestations. The experience of a play, especially a critical one, compels all who participate in it to hold themselves accountable with questions such as: What questions or issues does this play raise? How does it engage us to address prevailing problems? How do we draw on these insights to shape connections and solidarities with others to improve our lives, our communities, and our worlds with greater justice for all?

Still, we recognize that a play, like any artistic production, is not necessarily emancipatory in content or effect. As Augusto Boal (1985: 39) noted, "All of man's [sic] activities – including, of course, all the arts, especially theater – are political. And theater is the most perfect artistic form of coercion." When conventionally produced, theater can sublimate hegemony by having "the spectator delegat[e] power to the dramatic character so that the latter may act or think for him" (Boal 1985: 122). Such power transferals are most evident when the lead characters represent the gods, the aristocracy, or the ruling elite. In particular, Boal pointed to catharsis as an instrument of hegemony. Usually, catharsis is considered a positive act: it allows the individual (whether a person or an institution like a family, marriage, or the state) to heal by exorcising one's demons. But for Boal, the conservative nature of catharsis lies precisely in its function: i.e., returning the individual to its original state. In this sense, catharsis does not enable growth or enlightenment. It renders the individual content to stay where s/he started.

Boal proposed, instead, a "theater of the oppressed":

> [T]he spectator delegates no power to the character (or actor) either to act or to think in his place; on the contrary, he himself assumes the protagonic [sic] role, changes the dramatic action, tries out solutions, discusses plans for change – in short, trains himself for real action. In this case, perhaps the theater is not revolutionary in itself, but it is surely a rehearsal for the revolution. The liberated spectator, as a whole

person, launches into action. No matter that the action is fictional; what matters is that it is action!

(Boal 1985: 122)

Boal devised a series of experiments for his plays. A play with actors would begin. It would ask a particular question such as, "what should workers do about a ruthless, exploitative boss or a woman about an abusive husband?" The actors would proceed but the audience would be encouraged to intervene. Some members of the audience would direct the actors on how to play out a scene; others would act in the scene themselves. Various scenarios would be worked out in this fashion, leaving both actors and audience in deep discussion about each. From this basis, Boal believed, all participants would leave the theater with greater clarity about the issues, particularly as they are developed in solidarity with others given the collective nature of the process.

Worldism accords generally with Boal's theater of the oppressed. It highlights the agency of all to participate in the making of their multiple worlds through multi- and trans-subjectivities, forming a community of syncretic growth, learning, and co-transformation. But the theater of the oppressed suffers from one drawback. It retains the Self vs Other binary, now shifted to "oppressor" vs "oppressed" embodied in the "ruthless boss" vs "exploited worker" or "abusive husband" vs "victimized wife." Nonetheless, Boal's overall insights still apply, giving us a second take on emancipatory theater now informed by worldism. In our theater of multiple worlds, the "oppressed" critically engages with one another as well as the "oppressor," transforming all in the process. In particular, we ask: How do we draw on the "monsters" of fear and "illusions of power," made less scary in part by acknowledging others in the making of our worlds, to help us recognize "gaps" within hegemony so that alternative visions and practices can build towards less violent and brutal worlds? The goal lies not in the destination or arrival, but in the "wisdom" acquired along the way. Notions of Self vs Other become problematized and highlighted, in their place, are dynamic, mutual legacies of reinforcements and conflicts, resistance and reconstruction.

We have one more reason to conclude with a play. It allows us to engage the book's two parts. Part II presents worldism in response to our critiques of the neoliberal imperium in Part I, but some may perceive this as reproducing a binary of our own. A fictive venue like a play allows us to apply worldism to ourselves: that is, we have metaphoric elements of Parts I and II engage with each other to uncover the multiple worlds within empire and its own possibilities for transformation.

Shakespeare's *Othello*

Our play draws on Shakespeare's *Othello*. Usually, this play is presented as a tragic love story. A husband, Othello, succumbs to suspicions of adultery and kills his beloved wife, Desdemona. Othello's sergeant, Iago, precipitates this chain of events by whispering innuendos about Desdemona into Othello's unsuspecting ear. Iago resents Othello for promoting that "bookish theoric," Cassio, instead of himself, a worthier candidate to his mind.[4] Hence, Iago fingers Cassio as Desdemona's alleged lover when, in actuality, both Cassio and Desdemona are innocent and loyal to Othello to the end. Upon learning of Iago's treachery and his own displaced lethality ("*O fool! fool! fool!*"[5]), Othello fatally stabs himself.

Othello personifies the seductions of empire in form and content. To see the play as simply a love story erases its imperial politics. Othello is not only a Moor/Muslim but also an African, surrounded by Venetians who are all Christians and European. In not contextualizing the story, conventional treatments turn the deaths of Othello and Desdemona into individualized moments of *pathos*, as if neither of them had any other relationships or resources.

Note this judgment from the eminent Shakespearean scholar, A.C. Bradley (writing in 1904):

> I do not mean that Othello's race is a matter of no account. It has ... its importance in the play. [Race] makes a difference to our idea of him; it makes a difference to the action and catastrophe. But in regard to the essentials of his character it is not important; and if anyone had told Shakespeare that no Englishman would have acted like the Moor, and had congratulated him on the accuracy of his racial psychology, I am sure he would have laughed.
>
> (Bradley 1991: 177)

Publicly denying race (but privately allowing it) effectively delivers desire with violence in *Othello*. A subliminal interpretation emerges: i.e., a (black) Muslim man who murders a beautiful, virtuous Christian Venetian (white) woman from jealous rage *deserves* violence onto himself. No more an explicit demonstration of Self vs Other, with its tragic trajectory of conversion/ discipline, could we have, notwithstanding Shakespeare's poetic prose. This approach to *Othello* further eases *our* complicity with empire ("I'm scared so it's OK to kill") and the ontological assumptions that sanction such fear ("it's OK to be afraid of Them"). Othello himself recites his rise through the ranks of violence ("*feats of broil and battle*")[6] that brought him the title of general. Othello's downfall, convention suggests, comes not from his greed for status or acceptance or love (after all, who doesn't have such ambitions?) but the unwonted nature of his desires *given who he is*. ("*Rude am I in my speech*," Othello describes himself, "*And little bless'd with the soft phrase of peace.*"[7]) It is alright for him to battle the Turks on behalf of the Venetians to retain trade from Cyprus, but taking Desdemona as wife exceeds propriety. Had he stayed in his place, convention insinuates, both he and Desdemona would have remained safe. But Othello shows his "true" nature when venturing beyond his station. Shakespeare seems to agree. Lodovico laments at the end of the play: "*O thou Othello, thou wert once so good/Fall'n in the practise of a damned slave/What shall be said to thee?*"[8]

In a worldist context, Othello symbolizes the classical Subaltern Man. Always caught between the past and the future, constraints and possibilities, fury and love, Othello is, pardon the pun, "unmoored." He may be a great general but he cannot forget that he was once a slave. He may be hired to save the Venetians from the Turks in their fight for Cyprus, an entrepôt to lucrative trade between Europe and the Mediterranean,[9] but he cannot claim that he *is* a Venetian and not a *"malignant and turban'd Turk."*[10] He may have won the hand of the beautiful Desdemona but he cannot ascertain for sure that she loves and accepts him as he does her. *"Why did I marry?"* Othello cries in agony after hearing Iago's fabrications.[11] Cassio seems more like a "natural" match for Desdemona, Othello suspects. A "true" son of Venice, he is *almost damn'd in a fair wife,"* as Iago sneers.[12] Similarly, Desdemona is Venice's "true" daughter. She is *"[o]f her own clime, complexion, and degree."*[13]

We re-read Iago as well. A product of empire, Iago cannot accept a slave turned general. Othello is not *supposed* to succeed. He should not be in a position to promote or command Venetians, least of all marry them. After all, what is Othello but a Moor?

In our play, we find Othello in the Liminal Realm, that station after Death and before Life. He meets two historical figures: the third century BC Greek philosopher, Epicurus, and an eighteenth century Vietnamese feminist-poet, Hồ Xuân Hu'o'ng. Epicurus and Hồ persuade Othello to re-examine his life and understand it within the context of empire. Two additional characters – Cassandra, the Greek mythological figure who is gifted with foresight but cursed with no one believing her, and Lina, a professor of politics from the twenty-first century – join in to urge Othello not to erase himself for the narrow seductions of empire that fan power and insecurity, desire and violence, complicities both big and small, but to appreciate the wisdom and resilience offered by the multiple worlds that make him who and what he is.

Let us now turn to the play.

Lights dim. Music swells. Curtains rise . . .

⚙𝔱𝔥𝔢𝔩𝔩𝔬'𝔰 𝔍𝔬𝔲𝔯𝔫𝔢𝔶𝔰

MAIN CAST

(in order of appearance)

OTHELLO: seventeenth century lead character in Shakespeare's *Othello*
EPICURUS: third century BC Greek philosopher
HỒ XUÂN HU'O'NG: eighteenth century feminist poet from Vietnam
CASSANDRA: figure in Greek mythology, given the gift of prophecy but cursed with no one believing her
LINA: twenty-first century professor of politics

ACT I

"Recognition"

[*Stage left. Enter Othello, moaning with his hands over his head.*]
OTHELLO: O, miserable and eternal brute! I have killed that which I loved most.
Like the base Indian, I threw away a pearl that's richer than all his tribe.
And for what? To remonstrate with others that I am but one of them, a Man.
Yet I servic'd my state.
I smote that malignant Ottomite, the Turk,
For beating a Venetian and traducing the state!
Why canst it suffice?
I remain perplex'd in the extreme.[14]

EPICURUS: [*entering from the right, faces Othello, speaking softly and calmly*]. Brother, it was more than green-eyed Jealousy that undid you . . .
OTHELLO: [*startled, immediately draws his sword and roars*]. Who goes there?
HỒ: [*entering, behind Othello*]. You were seduced by another, bigger monster. It was dressed in gold and glory but fed on fear and possession.
OTHELLO: [*whipping around*]. What you?
HỒ: I was a celebrated poet in my own time, a century before the French came to a tropical land southeast of China, a place you've never heard of probably: Annam. I was known for bringing to light what others wanted to keep in the dark.
EPICURUS: And I was a philosopher who came of age during the time of Alexander the Great. Disciples have distilled my philosophy into a paean to pleasure but, I assure you, my thoughts had in them much more than that.
OTHELLO: What say you?

HÔ: We want to explore with you, brother, how you came to this state, what you call your "demise."

EPICURUS: So you are not doomed to eternal repetition. Know this: we have the capacity to transform ourselves, our environments, and our relations with others.

OTHELLO: Who are you to instruct *me*?

EPICURUS: Calm, brother, calm. We seek not to instruct but to engage with thee. Take from us what you will.

HÔ: We are you, brother Othello, and you are us. We are fellow travelers in and of multiple worlds.

OTHELLO: Multiple worlds?

HÔ: This idea will clarify as we go along but for now, know that in multiple worlds, you do not have to choose between being a Moor and a Venetian, a slave and a general, a subject and an object. You are these and more. You must face, also, that you are a lover and a murderer.

[*Othello groans and sinks onto a stone bench on stage left, devastated by his own history.*]

CHORUS: HE SEES NOT WHAT HE IS, YET HE SEES!

ACT II

"Alternatives"

EPICURUS: [*gesturing towards the air*]. A small repast to fuel our discourses! [*Food and wine appear on a massive oak table. All sit down. Epicurus pours everyone a goblet of wine.*] Tell us, brother, why did you smite the Turk for the Venetian?

OTHELLO: I was a great general. The toged consuls of Venice thought me best to battle the enemy. "[T]he fortitude of the place is best known to you," the Duke of Venice impressed upon me.[15] They wanted to secure trade with Cyprus. It had so enriched the Doge,[16] now eyed with envy by the Ottomites. [*He speaks more rapidly, excitedly.*] And I triumphed in Cyprus! For this soldier's strife, I won the fair hand of Desdemona, my love and daughter of a noble Venetian house.

EPICURUS: So you were a hired hand?

OTHELLO: Nay! I was master of my own fate. I thrash'd all that Fortune sent me. Why else would the Venetians commission me?

EPICURUS: What was your commitment to the Venetians' cause?

OTHELLO: Why, to win, of course!

EPICURUS: For whose benefit?

OTHELLO: Theirs but also, surely, *mine*!

HÔ: Yes, you gained fame and fortune and even love. But to what end and at what cost?

OTHELLO: I . . . I . . .

EPICURUS: And how is it that the Venetians got you to fight the Turk, your kin in religion and culture?

OTHELLO: [*clenching his fist, pounds the table, spilling wine*]. Fool was I, that I thought I could be one of them!

HÔ: No shame in being a hired hand, brother. Even an emperor is beholden to others. But you should understand who and what you were in their social order.

OTHELLO: I loved them. I loved them all! The battles, the sieges, the fortunes . . . Venice, Cyprus, Desdemona. All is lost to me forever.

EPICURUS: Nay, brother, judge not so harshly nor hastily. All of us are taught to desire what our gods tell us to, especially if it soars us to heights previously unimagined – and we all know that desire is but politics in disguise. Is not desire a social animal?

OTHELLO: Say'st thou desire a mean consumption, with no power to transform?

EPICURUS: Nay, nay. Desires are significant. But many times, they polarize and squeeze the creativity out of us, not allowing us to fully manifest our relations with others. Such desires become static idolatries because of a promise in certainty or in gold, as if life is and can always be simply captured and constantly exploited, just so empire can glorify in itself. You were not the first nor will you be the last to be seduced by empire.

[*At this point, Cassandra appears.*]

CASSANDRA: Greetings, all. I couldn't help overhear your fascinating discourse on desire and empire. May I interject a word or two, as I have experienced much with both?

EPICURUS AND HÔ: [*graciously*]. Please.

[*Cassandra joins them at table. Othello bows formally. He looks relieved. He needs the time and space to think.*]

CASSANDRA: In the battle at Troy, all thought Helen responsible. But I saw something else. Despite their differences and their war against each other, Troy and Argos shared a common deeper desire: each sought certainty over lands and men since they could not have it over the gods. And they grabbed it through any means possible: rapes, killings, and colonizing all that stood in the way. That's empire, my friends.

EPICURUS: We created those gods for every dimension of our existence and gave them our worlds so they could take care of us. We wanted them to protect us, to free us from war, to make it possible for us to fall in love, to make us wiser . . . Certainty, what an imaginary!

HÔ: Alas, certainty often turns into a nightmare like possession, especially of women and children, gold and glory, power and status. Rectification follows: that is, "correcting" all who are deemed different, especially how they see the world and act in it.

EPICURUS: [*nodding*]. Ay, certainty measures empire. Desire motivates it.

OTHELLO: What of love? Was my love for Desdemona imperial, too?

HÔ: Though a Moor, you shared with the Venetians what all patriarchs want: not a real person but a beautiful vessel, filled with intoxicating wine, to power your dreams of Manhood.

EPICURUS: And now you know its murderous consequences. Empire seduced you to conquer Desdemona, like Cyprus. But they were for the Venetians only. You were asked to fulfill these desires, not consummate them.

CASSANDRA: Your violence was not merely a single act. Much laid behind it, producing it.

OTHELLO: 'Twas Iago, that foul conjurer, who poisoned my heart to my lady's death!

CASSANDRA: He dangled the poison but how could he foresee its allure? Perhaps he, like you, had suffered too long from empire, soldiering a lifetime for others and their pleasures.

OTHELLO: [*thoughtfully*]. Ay, I saw Iago as a trusted friend turned monstrous fabricator but never a compatriot.

HỒ: More importantly, why thought you only of jealousy, rage, and murder? Why did other strategies not spring to mind for you *and* Desdemona?

EPICURUS: Empire harms in many ways but always through the same method. We fail to appreciate other ways of living and, in your case, dying.

CASSANDRA: You were annihilated thrice. By listening to Iago, you lost the general; by strangling Desdemona, you killed a great love; and by stabbing yourself, you deprived the world of Othello. In these moments, you annihilated parts of yourself bit by bit.

OTHELLO: [*jumps up from table, knocking over his chair*]. What else was before me?!

CHORUS: HE KNOWS NOT WHAT TO DO, YET HE DOES!

ACT III

"Knowing, Doing, Being"

HỒ: [*kindly*]. You were a slave yet you rose to become a great general.

OTHELLO: [*pacing back and forth*]. Ay, 'tis stories of my suffer'd youth that caught Desdemona's attentions later turned more tender. I spake of "disastrous chances" and "moving accidents" and "hair-breadth scapes."[17] Tho' imprisoned, and later sold into slavery, I found redemption through my travels' history. Each rough incident hewed a talent, a skill to lead men into battle and thence became I as he who stands before you: a valued general. 'Twas my knowledge, my education.

CASSANDRA: You were taught far more than that, brother. You were taught to fear because happiness meant colonizing territories and goods, skills and reputation, people and love. You came to believe that the undying quest for entering power echelons would secure you certainty. What many call "security." False dichotomies aided in that belief.

OTHELLO: But a soldier's life is simple and dichotomous. Win or lose, friend or foe, master or slave. Is it not?

CASSANDRA: It's more complicated than that, and so are you. It is not merely what we know but how we get to know what we know! Who teaches us to think and act the way we do, and why?

HỒ: A line from an eleventh century Song Dynasty poem comes to mind: *"zaxue er buzhi yu dao"* ("They studied all sorts of things and did not set their minds on the Way"). In other words, you may master skills but if you don't see the larger picture of what you are learning and why, you do not learn at all.

[*Lina enters.*]

LINA: Are you talking about education and world politics? My two favorite subjects!

HỒ: Ah, Lina, welcome! [*Hồ explains to Othello.*] She is a "professor of politics" from the twenty-first century. [*Othello bows gallantly.*]

LINA: [*sits down at table and takes a goblet of wine*]. Many scholars of world politics in my time, for example, mastered skills that they thought would free the world and themselves of violence. Yet the results often turned out to be just the opposite, sometimes painfully and destructively so. Yet they kept to the same education.

OTHELLO: They were obtuse, then?

LINA: They didn't think so! Many argued, for example, that passion was bad. It led to war and so on. So they pursued "science" and "objectivity" and "rationality" . . . and projected their passions onto Others whom they considered "alien": that is, those who looked or behaved or believed differently than they. Colonialism became a convenient canvas on which they could project all their passions. First it was for spices and trade, then lands and peoples, next raw materials and market shares, and in my time, "the Coke way of life"! [*Othello looks puzzled*] No, we need to speak honestly about our passions. It gives respect, finally, to those labeled irrational, underdeveloped, and uncivilized by the politics of elite, patriarchal, and colonial privilege. [*Othello strokes his beard*].

EPICURUS: We all have desires and want to devour them. There's nothing wrong with that. The trick is in asking: what are these desires about, where do they come from, and do they distract us from engaging one another, holding one another accountable?

CASSANDRA: Othello's life did not turn on a moment of passion, as Shakespeare would have us believe. Rather, it came from a lifetime of suppression and self-violence. I know it well, for empire's trick on me is similar. The gods gave me foresight but robbed me of voice. That is, the ability to engage with others on what is most relevant to what we experience and understand every day. Likewise, the empire Othello served did not allow him to trust and respect the insight already in him.

OTHELLO: "Insight?"

HỒ: The multiple worlds that gave birth to you and, though you denied them, nurtured you into the great general that you became.

OTHELLO: But does not such complexity lead to chaos?

HỒ: [*reciting*].

一人而千心，	"If a single person had a thousand minds,
內自相攫攦；	They would fight with each other inside him,
何暇能應物？	What time would he have to respond to things?
千手無一心；	But when a thousand arms have no single mind,
手手得其處。	Every arm attains its proper place.
稽首大悲尊，	I bow to the Revered One of Great Compassion,
願度一切眾，	Desiring also to save all living beings.
皆證無心法，	May each actualize the way of no-mind
皆具千手目。	And each acquire a thousand arms and eyes."[18]

You have a "thousand arms and eyes" at your beck and call. And you have benefited from each in the past, making you into who you are. Appreciate them.

EPICURUS: Reaching the no-mind, brother Othello, means freeing yourself of false anxieties and desires and, above all, false gods – especially those that come from the seduction of power, of glory, of possessing others, of certainty. Recognizing the multiple worlds from which we emerge, those entwinements that make us and to which we give life through our creativity is the first step to a just life. This checks the power of the gods to consume us – such as those to whom we give the power to become gods, and those who would force us to believe they are gods. Otherwise, we would have no recourse of our own.

OTHELLO: How do multiple worlds make a difference? How would they scythe the seductions of empire?

LINA: Multiple worlds remind us how crucial it is not to be chained to certainty. We succeed precisely by being fluid and dynamic, creative and syncretic, drawing from one world to give insight into another, enriching us all.

OTHELLO: How to stop pitting "friend" against "foe," pray?

LINA: Suspend judgment.

OTHELLO: What dost thou mean?

LINA: Each party needs to suspend judgment long enough to consider other strategies or methods of engaging the context that set "friend" against "foe." And these strategies are already there, developed through lifetimes of/ through/with/for/in multiple worlds.

OTHELLO: This requires another way of understanding the world —

LINA: Yes.

OTHELLO: —as well as being in the world.

LINA: [*nods*]. Yes.

OTHELLO: How to do it in everyday life?

LINA: [*smiling*]. That's up to you.

OTHELLO: [*murmurs*]. Hmmm . . .

HỒ: Perhaps a poem of mine might help:

Một vũng tang thương nước lộn trời.	[W]e see heaven upside-down in sad puddles.
Bể ái nghìn trùng khôn tát cạn.	Love's vast sea cannot be emptied.
Nguồn ân muôn trượng dễ khơi vơi.	And springs of grace flow easily everywhere.
Nào nào cực lạc là đâu tá?	Where is nirvana?
Cực lạc là đây, chín rõ mười.	Nirvana is here, nine times out of ten.[19]

OTHELLO: So not all is what it seems. Nor does all remain the same. And "love's vast sea" . . . is in me!

CHORUS: YES!

OTHELLO: Ay, a wonderful tonic are these multiple worlds . . . Where once weak and broken, I am strong and whole! [*He looks up and speaks softly.*] I am ready to face Desdemona now. 'Tis much overdue for the violence I did her – and myself. [*He straightens his shoulders.*] I am ready, too, for my brothers, Venetian and Turk. We each share in friend and foe alike, I suspect. [*He turns to the gathering on stage.*] Thank you, kind friends, for your wise and caring counsel. I will carry you with me forever. [*He sweeps a deep bow.*]

Lina, Cassandra, Hồ, and Epicurus: And we you!

CHORUS: HE HAS ARRIVED, YET HE IS ON HIS WAY!
AND SO ARE WE ALL!

THE JOURNEY CONTINUES . . .

Notes

Introduction, pp. 1–12

1 We consider "Self" and "Other" to be contingent, relational terms. However, we refrain from placing them in scare quotes throughout the text to make it easier to read.

2 This construction is evident regardless of location, culture, or issue in world politics: e.g., Hutus vs Tutsis in Central Africa, buyers vs trafficked persons in the world market, the European Union (EU) vs Turkey in talks on membership, the US vs al Qaeda in the "global war on terror."

3 Chalmers Johnson (2003) notes that the US strategy for hegemony since the end of World War II has centered on placing military bases or "mini-colonies" throughout the globe, even in allied countries.

4 The 2007/2008 annual report from the Bonn International Center for Conversion (BICC) (2008) finds that while prospects for nuclear disarmament remain promising, the trend toward worldwide rearmament of conventional weapons is continuing: "Global military expenditure increased by approximately 30 percent in real terms between 2001 and 2006 and totaled an estimated US $1,179 billion in 2006, the latest year for which detailed figures are available. Negotiations on disarmament have come to a standstill and there are even signs of a new arms race." Available HTTP: <http://www.bicc.de/publications/jahresbericht/2008/pressrelease_annual_report.php> (accessed 14 July 2008).

5 Again, we refrain from placing "whiteness" in scare quotes throughout the text for simplicity's sake. But this term should be read as historically contingent and constructed. See Agathangelou (2006) for how the neoliberal imperium draws on whiteness to "sell" and consolidate itself.

6 "President Bush Attends Veterans of Foreign Wars National Convention, Discusses War on Terror," Kansas City Convention and Entertainment Center, Kansas City, Missouri, 22 August 2007. Available HTTP: <http://www.whitehouse.gov/news/releases/2007/08/20070822-3.html> (accessed 1 June 2008).

7 We are aware of debates and contestations between (neo)colonial relations (i.e., aboriginal and indigenous) and postcolonial ones (see Smith 2005; Agathangelou *forthcoming*). What we underscore here are their common underpinnings in colonial power relations.

8 See, for example, Subaltern Studies Group (2002). Available HTTP: <http://www.postcolonialweb.org/poldiscourse/theosubaltern.html> (accessed 15 July 2008).

9 Here, we differ slightly from Nicholas Onuf's (1989) notion of "world-making." Whereas Onuf focuses on the rules and rule that make the world, we examine the social relations that make those rules and rule possible. Additionally, we look at how the rules and rule of one world interact with those of another world. For an early treatment of this latter comparison, see Ling (2002b).

10 Agathangelou (2008a: 2) argues that if we take a phenomenon like "globalization," we see how many "gestur[e] to the changes in world politics" which "hover
ambiguously between a *description* of the 'geopolitical marketplace' and a
performative articulation; thus establishing the geopolitical marketplace and
the position of the U.S. within it as a given truth and obscuring that the world
capitalist system has been changing dramatically." However, these attempts
are problematic as they are more descriptive in ways that make invisible that
"globalization" as a complex set of social relations "have to be brought about
instead of being accepted as given. To *grant this possibility* is a world apart from
saying that this is the best and most viable way to think and do social relations.
It is time for those of us who are interested in an alternative world to begin
thinking, planning, and embodying it now. Such an alternative [analysis and]
world [are] indeed necessary."

11 We use the term "reactive" to connote a narrow response to an action. It suggests that the respondent could not consider other options at the moment that
an event is happening. At the same time, being "reactive" suggests the possibility of rearranging the social relations that produced the event and the reaction
in the first place. This includes the people that come into contact with one
another and forming new relations. The term "reactionary" suggests a conservative
response that relies on established strategies and modes of interaction. The
two terms, "reactive" and "reactionary" thus indicate two kinds of agency.

12 This is the Coca Cola Company's advertising slogan for 2006 (Collect Cola 2008).
Available HTTP: <http://www.2collectcola.com/page/ACC/slogan> (accessed
14 July 2008).

13 See Chapter 6 of Agathangelou (2004b).

14 "Ottomite" was Shakespeare's term for Ottoman.

Chapter 1, pp. 15–30

1 We cite excerpts from Hammad's poem, "first writing since," because it
expresses, in another form and voice, what we are saying in this chapter. For
a complete text of the poem, see HTTP: <http://www.teachingforchange.
org/News%20Items/first_writing_since.htm> (accessed 29 April 2008). See
also Agathangelou and Killian (2006) for an in-depth analysis of Hammad's
poem. Suheir Hammad is also the author of *Born Palestinian, Born Black* and
other books.

2 Neta Crawford shows meticulously how ethical arguments on the abolition of
slavery and decolonization have changed norms and practices in international
institutions. Nonetheless, these arguments have stayed within the rhetoric and
discourses set by Western liberalism.

3 The Taliban housed the terrorists, their leader (Osama bin Ladin), and organization (al Qaeda) but the state of Afghanistan did not declare war, like Japan did
in 1941, against the US.

4 This figure does not include undocumented workers whose families were afraid
to register their missing loved ones with the government, especially in light of
federal crack-downs on illegal (or even) legal migrants.

5 All quotes from Powell's testimony are drawn from <http://www.whitehouse.
gov/news/releases/2003/02/20030205-1.html> (accessed 07 July 2008).

6 This transcript of the Iraqi ambassador's rebuttal to Colin Powell on 5 February 2003 comes from the following link: <http://www.emailthis.clickability.
com/et/emailThis?clickMap=viewThis&etMailToID=292460150&pt=Y> (accessed
07 July 2008).

7 "Iraq Address by his Excellency Dominique de Villepin, French Minister of Foreign
Affairs, before the United Nations Security Council 3/19/2003." Available HTTP:
<http://www.un.int/france/documents_anglais/030319_cs_villepin_irak.htm>
(accessed 14 July 2008).

8 The depictions in this section come from Chapters Two and Twelve in the Report. These speak most directly to Self/Other relations from the US perspective. Chapter Two examines the rise of bin Ladin and al Qaeda, and their appeal to the Muslim world. Chapter Twelve recommends preventive measures for the future.

9 Available HTTP: <http://www.swivel.com/data_sets/show/1007498> (accessed 07 March 2008).

10 Available HTTP: <http://www.antiwar.com/casualties/#count> (accessed 07 March 2008). Iraqi casualties, for both government and insurgent personnel, are harder to calculate but the same website estimates it is 1,173,743.

11 Available HTTP: <http://www.robert-fisk.com/text_of_usama_video_7october 2001.htm> (accessed 07 March 2008).

Chapter 2, pp. 31–47

1 See HTTP: <http://www.youtube.com/watch?v=MjpyskHMwRs> (accessed 05 July 2008).

2 Here, we focus on multilateral peacekeeping only, although our argument applies to peacekeeping by individual states as well. Peacekeeping activities include "military and police activities; protecting and delivering humanitarian assistance; offering negotiation and good offices; strengthening the rule of law; training and restructuring of local police forces; monitoring human rights; voter education and other electoral assistance; and disarmament, demobilization and reintegration of ex-combatants" (United Nations 2002: 75).

3 The same adulation does not apply to women leaders. "Paradoxically, while men have been released from tearlessness, it is increasingly expected of women . . . It's doubtful, in other words, that leaders like Condoleezza Rice or Hillary Rodham Clinton would get much sympathy if they welled up" (Wax 2001: 5). Hillary Rodham Clinton did well up during her campaign for Presidency in Spring 2008. Polls later showed a surge of support for her. She seemed more "human," many reported. But this occasion was not one of national crisis; it was more a moment of personal reflection.

4 Note, for example, HBO's highly-publicized multi-part series, "Band of Brothers." It details the trials and tribulations of a group of American soldiers ("E Company") battling Nazis in Europe. In conveying World War II through the eyes of an all-white, all-male cast, the series naturally creates an identification between the viewer and the characters such that World War II – and its eventual victory – becomes seen as a white man's only story. US defeat in Vietnam shattered this sense of racial and colonial superiority. For this reason, World War II has taken on an "anti-Vietnam syndrome" significance in American popular culture, despite the reversal in time of the two events. That former US Secretary of State, Colin Powell, and National Security Advisor, later Secretary of State herself, Condoleeza Rice, represented another racial/ethnic/ gender configuration does not efface this *cultural* valorization of white-male heroism since they both served as key advisors to and supporters of a hypermasculinized, white-male leader, George W. Bush.

5 At the same time, the Bush administration eroded its own commitment to federal agencies and offices devoted to women's issues (Lewin 2001).

6 The Bush administration rewarded the Taliban with $43 million when it announced a ban on opium production in July 2000 (Ehrenreich 2001).

7 Available HTTP: <http://www.workers.org/ww/2001/afghan0927.php> (accessed 08 July 2008).

8 According to the United Nations Development Fund for Women (UNIFEM), the Afghan government pledges to increase women's participation in government by 30%. See HTTP: <http://afghanistan.unifem.org/prog/MOWA/civilservice. html> (accessed 19 July 2008).

9 For this reason, female suicide bombers may not enjoy the same kind of approbation from their communities as their male counterparts.

10 Militarization is central to securing these global changes worldwide. Starting in the 1980s and especially with shifts in global market relations due to neo-liberal policies, militarization has been transnationalizing to secure conditions for capitalist expansion (Agathangelou 2008a). See also Enloe (1988, 2000) and Whitworth (2004).

11 The Philippines "ranked fourth among developing countries [in remittances] behind India ($25 billion), China ($24 billion) and Mexico ($24 billion)" Deparle (2007: 56).

12 Economic and Social Research Council (ESRC), "Our Society Today." Available HTTP: <http://www.esrcsocietytoday.ac.uk/ESRCInfoCentre/about/CI/CP/Our_Society_Today/globalisation/forces.aspx?ComponentId=15222&SourcePageId=16965> (accessed 08 July 2008).

13 For the latest investigations into these murders, see HTTP: <http://www.chavez.ucla.edu/maqui_murders/> (accessed 08 July 2008).

14 See, for example, "Private Investment in Chiapas up to 807mn Pesos Last Year," *Internet Securities*, January 2005. Available HTTP: <http://findarticles.com/p/articles/mi_hb5586/is_200501/ai_n23864500> (accessed 19 July 2008).

15 See also Amnesty International and Anti-Slavery International (2005) and the Council of Europe (2005). Data on sex trafficking are difficult to obtain given the criminalized nature of the industry. For recent data on sex trafficking in Asia, see Enriquez (2006).

16 In total, approximately 30 million children from Asia have been traded or trafficked in the past three decades (*BBC News*, 20 February 2003). Thai children, for example, are paid the equivalent of $5 for two hours of sexual contact (*Fox News*, 16 August 2006). UNICEF refers to this sex trade as a form of "slavery." See also Samarasinghe (2007).

17 The Association of Southeast Asian Nations (ASEAN) estimates that the region earned $153 billion from tourism in 2006, constituting 21% of global tourism earnings and a rise of 10% since 2005. Almost half of the visitors (49%) are from other ASEAN countries and a substantial portion of other travelers (28%) come from other Asian countries (e.g., South Korea, China, Japan, Taiwan) (Dodds and Farrington 2007).

18 Actual numbers of those trafficked by UN peacekeepers are hard to come by given the clandestine nature of the enterprise. Nonetheless, the International Organisation for Migration (IOM) has reported on peacekeepers' illicit activities in this area for different parts of the world, particularly Eastern Europe. See the IOM's website (http://www.iom.int/).

19 "UN Peacekeepers: Warriors or Victims?" *African Business* January 2001. Available HTTP: <http://findarticles.com/p/articles/mi_qa5327/is_200101/ai_n21467025> (accessed 09 July 2008).

20 Both gender and race figure in our definition of patriarchy. As a social order, patriarchy aims not only to valorize the rule of the father but also the father's claims over who belongs to his household, in what way, and who cannot even cross the threshold. Given certain historical and cultural contexts, this hegemonic practice carries connations for race and ethnicity as much as gender and sexuality.

Chapter 3, pp. 48–67

1 The English translation comes from Huỳnh (1996: 213); original Vietnamese from Balaban (2000: 20). The exact date of this poem is unknown. Hồ Xuân Hu'o'ng (1772–1822) was a feminist poet from Vietnam famous for her satirical poems on Confucian patriarchy.

2 Stoler notes, for example, a legal case in French-controlled Indochina where a French father sought clemency for his half-Vietnamese son but was refused on grounds of the son's insufficient "Frenchness." Yet other mixed-blood progeny were granted European status if they could demonstrate due "cultural competence" such as feeling alienated when placed among "natives."

3 Plenty more agents "live" inside and outside the House of IR (see Walker and Morton 2005). Our sample is necessarily limited and selective, given restrictions on scope and space. Nonetheless, we believe our argument of colonial household relations in IR knowledge production holds even if more schools of thought were included.

4 By realism, we refer to not one particular author or theory but rather "a family of arguments related by a common set of fundamental, if often unspoken, commitments" (Rupert 1995: 3).

5 Such claims are problematic historically and politically. One could ask in juxtaposition to violence against the Other that we have outlined above: What are the stakes behind this claim to a common history between "the West" and "ancient Greece"? See Agathangelou (2007).

6 See Ling (2002b) for alternative readings of Thucydides.

7 Arblaster (1984) notes, for instance, that the concept of tolerance in liberal thought allows only for the voicing of dissent, not attention to it.

8 The neoliberal imperium as an intellectual tradition, we propose, comes from a "feminized" position structured by the House of IR. But, as we show in the rest of the book, this characterization changes over time and as different elite interests rise.

9 For a presentation of standpoint feminism from one of its own, see Hartsock (1998).

10 Nussbaum proposes ten criteria to allow "a good human life:" i.e., life, bodily health and integrity, senses imagination, thought, emotions, practical reason, affiliation, other species, play, and, control over one's environment (Nussbaum 1999: 40–41).

11 To be sure, Nussbaum frequently cites non-Western thinkers like Rabindranath Tagore and Satyajit Ray. But these serve more as intellectual embellishments rather than integrations into her thinking.

12 For an alternative perspective on the role of women in third-world development, see Rai (2002).

13 Here, realist balance of power theory simulates neoclassical economic laws of supply and demand.

14 By "orderer," Waltz means a monopolistic world power or government like a monopoly in an economy.

15 Waltz effectively responds, "Hunh??" to Ashley's extensive critique of neorealism. "I find Richard K. Ashley difficult to deal with. Reading his essay is like entering a maze. I never know quite where I am or how to get out" (Waltz 1986: 337). This exchange exemplifies the deafening silence that has passed for debate between neorealists and their critics in the discipline. This lack of attention is especially egregious for neorealists given their claim to scientific objectivity.

16 Stories abound in our discipline of departments that have disassembled due to ideological/methodological disputes between neorealist/rational choice advocates, on one side, and the rest on the other. Yet the former continue to dominate both institutionally and intellectually (see Green and Shapiro 1994).

17 A scan of mainstream IR journals like *International Studies Quarterly, International Organization*, and *Journal of Conflict Resolution* would affirm the dominance of neorealist/rational choice approaches. Related to the above point, these journals carry more weight in hiring/promotion/grant decisions than journals that publish a variety of ideological/methodological approaches.

18 Pragmatists in IR, for instance, claim to offer a "multiperspectival" approach. Yet their concepts all come from Anglo-American-European sources (see *Millennium* 2002).

19 Neither postmodernism nor constructivism in IR is monolithic. Our critique concentrates on these two sources, respectively, due to their representativeness.

20 On individualism and empiricism, see Chapters 1, 2, and 3 in Arblaster (1984).

21 For another angle to the same conclusion that Wendt seeks the approval of pater realism, if not brother neorealism, see Palan (2000).

22 "The state is pre-social relative to other states in the same way that the human body is pre-social" (Wendt 1999: 198).

23 Nonetheless, neoliberal capital eagerly embraces the homosexual market even while neoliberal theory argues against queerness (Alexander 1998; Agathangelou, Bassichis and Spira 2008).

24 See, for example, "Feminist Theories in IR," in the *Brown Journal of World Affairs* 10(11), Tickner (2004). See, also, Carpenter (2002). Most members of the House of IR prefer to deal with identity in a less revelatory manner (see Lapid and Kratochwil 1997).

25 In contrast, former Dutch employers often remember their Indonesian servants with romantic, sometimes sensual, nostalgia. See Chapter 7 in Stoler (2002).

26 For example, such "recalcitrants" could fail to receive all those rewards the academy usually bestows upon its valorized subjects: e.g., publications, raises, grants, promotions, media coverage. They could also suffer immediate acts of disciplining: e.g., failure to obtain employment, denial of tenure, dismissal even with tenure.

27 For instance, Germany is buying major public industries in Greece such as ETA (Hellenic Telecommunications Organisation) in the name of "EU economic progress." Public debates on these firesales, moreover, have accused the Greek political leadership of failing to serve as an exemplar of capitalism as it has been running some of these industries in the red (Agathangelou 2008b).

28 These economies can follow all the neoliberal rules and demands and yet still be characterized as "backward" due to the violence and marginalization that such a system requires. See, for example, Ong and Collier (2005).

29 Cosmo Man could not enact his "cosmopolitanism" without capitalist and imperialist structures of privilege to support him. These designate him to be white and masculine in effect, even though anyone could inhabit this persona in body.

30 Note, for instance, Harvard University's recent curriculum change, the first in thirty years, to reflect this orientation. It will put new emphasis on "sensitive religious and cultural issues, the sciences and overcoming U.S. 'parochialism'" (Szep 2007).

31 See McPherson and Schapiro (1999) for a more detailed analysis of economic and other structural pressures faced by US liberal arts colleges and universities.

32 Between 1991–98 in political science, the umbrella discipline for international relations, African-American and Asian female doctorates in political science exceeded their male cohorts by 6.9% compared to 4.3%, respectively, for the former, 3.4% to 2.7%, respectively, for the latter (Brandes *et al.* 2001: 321). Hispanic female doctorates lagged slightly behind their male cohorts with 2.9% compared to 3.7%, respectively; American Indian male and female doctorates had 0.5% each (Brandes *et al.* 2001: 321). Nonetheless, political science has the lowest proportion of minority students in graduate programs within the social sciences, lagging behind the natural sciences and engineering (Babco 2000: 297).

33 The *Chronicle of Higher Education* reports that full-time employment declined by 1% from 1991–95; part-time employment, in contrast, rose by 18%, and part-time faculty at two-year colleges surged from 19% to 31% of faculty totals (Schneider 1997).

34 Available HTTP: <http://www.polity.co.uk/global/realism.htm> (accessed 01 April 2004).

35 See also Panitch and Gindin (2004).

Chapter 4, pp. 68–82

1 A.M. Agathangelou's translation from the original Greek (Nikas 2003). Manos Hatjidakis was a writer, singer, and intellectual in Greece. See also, Ling (2004) for an examination of the monster theme in the current war on terror as reflected in popular culture icons like Fu Manchu and Hannibal Lecter.

2 Westphalia's claim to introducing the inter-state system is open to debate. For instance, theorists like Teschke (2002: 5) argue that the "decisive break to international modernity comes with the rise of the first modern state – England."

3 We treat terms like "progress," "modernity," "market rationalism," "consumer choice," "individual happiness," and "democratic politics" as historically and contextually contingent. But we refrain from placing them in quotes throughout the text to save it from being flooded by these markers.

4 Interview with Mark Twain, "Society of Sceptred Thieves," 9 May 1907, *Baltimore News*. Available HTTP: <http://www.boondocksnet.com/ai/twain/mtws_stupendous_joke.html> (accessed 18 November 2005).

5 According to Genevieve Lloyd (1993), Western intellectual thought never considered women capable of rationality defined as reason – the necessary criterion for entering into the social contract. Only men could transcend the profane shackles of the Body to soar into the heavenly realm of Reason.

6 See, for example, this commercial for "Nestles Crunch" made and shown in the 1990s: <http://youtube.com/watch?v=o8T2JQizPaM> (accessed 09 July 2008).

7 "Coca Cola Advertising Slogans by Year." Available HTTP: <http://www.2collectcola.com/page/ACC/slogan> (accessed 09 July 2008).

8 Kipling knew this price personally. His son died in a foreign war.

9 "'The White Man's Burden': Kipling's Hymn to U.S. Imperialism." Available HTTP: <http://historymatters.gmu.edu/d/5478/> (accessed 18 November 2005).

10 Interview with Mark Twain, "The Funniest Thing," *Baltimore Sun*, 9 May 1907. Available HTTP: <http://www.boondocksnet.com/ai/twain/mtws_stupendous_joke.html> (accessed 18 November 2005).

11 "Anti-Imperialist League, Collected Records, 1899–1919," Swarthmore Peace Collection. Available HTTP: <http://www.swarthmore.edu/Library/peace/CDGA.A-L/antiimperialistleague.htm> (accessed 18 November 2005).

12 It is telling that there is no record of a poem from or about "brown" women.

13 "Kipling, The White Man's Burden, and US Imperialism," *Monthly Review* November 2003. Available HTTP: <http://www.findarticles.com/p/articles/mi_m1132/is_6_55/ai_111269066> (accessed 12 July 2008).

14 *Ibid.*

15 "America and Empire: Manifest Destiny Warmed Up?" *The Economist* 14 August 2003. Available HTTP: <http://www.economist.com/printedition/displayStory.cfm?Story_ID=1988940> (accessed 12 July 2008).

16 *Ibid.*

17 *Ibid.*

18 *Ibid.*

19 Available HTTP: <http://www.usip.org/isg/iraq_study_group_report/report/1206/iraq_study_group_report.pdf> (accessed 12 July 2008).

20 There were exceptions like Johnson (1998).

21 Available HTTP: <http://www.aseansec.org/21104.pdf> (accessed 14 July 2008).

22 ASEAN initiated swapping foreign currency reserves in 1977 but it was limited to a small scale, particularly as ASEAN did not have the huge reserves that China, Japan, and South Korea have today.

23 See, for example, the Center for Public Integrity. Available HTTP: <http://www.openairwaves.org/wow/bio.aspx?act=pro> (accessed 07 March 2008).

Chapter 5, pp. 85–98

1 Rushdie (1992: 394), original emphasis.

2 Here, we denote the postcolonial distinction by writing the terms "selves" and "others" in plural form and lower-case in contrast to the neoliberal universalization of the "Self" vs "Other" binary usually written in the singular form with upper-case letters.

3 For example, once the Soviet Union could no longer maintain its fiction as a superpower, it had to resort to another story to recuperate itself: i.e., "perestroika" and "glasnost" (see Duffy, Frederking, and Tucker 1998).

4 For other examples of such postcolonial retelling of national narratives, see Nandy (1988), Prakash (1999), Chakrabarty (2000), Chowdhry and Nair (2002), and Franklin (2005).

5 For example, some patriarchies rely on the clan and/or family as the central, deciding unit whereas global capital emphasizes individual entrepreneurship and independence. Yet evidence abounds that these supposed oppositions are reconciled and reconstituted every day. One prominent example comes from the proliferation of family-owned firms in Asia, especially among the ethnic Chinese diaspora well-known for their patriarchal forms of organization (see Peng 2002).

6 For a critique and extension of subaltern mimicry, see Ling (2002a).

7 Rupert (1995) argues that social ontologies refer to processes of self-creation. Agathangelou (2009) expands upon this idea to argue for other kinds of creations: for example, how do we (re)create the ecologies and languages of everyday life without "othering" social ontologies that contest and problematize imperial capitalist formations (e.g., aestheticizing violence through film or other forms of popular culture)?

8 Here, we refer to "tradition" as a live, growing, and organic part of multiple worlds. We do not abide by the European Enlightenment's differentiation between "modernity," defined as dynamic and emancipatory, and "tradition," as stagnant and imprisoning. Our notion of "tradition" conveys more of a "way of life."

9 For more on the pre-Confucian worldview, see Hwang and Ling (2008).

10 For a survey of primary materials on Chinese elites' struggles with the European Enlightenment as well as Westphalian inter-state power politics, see Teng and Fairbank (1979). For a postcolonial analysis of European Enlightenment science in India, see Prakash (1999).

11 Other international movements like the Bandung Conference of 1955 or the New International Economic Order (NIEO) of the 1970s centered more on anti-colonial, anti-imperialist solidarity for economic development among Afro-Asian states, rather than any consideration of "civilizations."

12 In this effort, Alker had worked with Tahir Amin, Thomas J. Biersteker, and Takashi Inoguchi on their forthcoming book, *The Dialectics of World Orders*. See also the Alker archive at HTTP: <http://www-rcf.usc.edu/~alker/index. html> (accessed 12 July 2008).

13 Tom Biersteker, one of the authors of the DWO project, agrees. Private communication (6 June 2008). See also, Biersteker (2008).

Chapter 6, pp. 99–117

1 In the novel, this couplet is written on both sides of an archway marked "The Land of Illusion," the gateway to the human world of "red dust" (Cao 1973: 55).

2 These manuscripts were transmitted by others and mostly copied after Cao's death (Wu 2006: 224–225).

3 From this term comes the "red" in *Dream of the Red Chamber*.

4 Louise Edwards argues that *Honglou meng* slips in a "phallogocentric binary" that "valorizes the male character as the active one" and subjugates women and femininity to passivity (Edwards 1990: 78). This rendition of sexuality and sexual play, however, misunderstands the dialectical interplays in the novel between masculinity and femininity, heterosexuality and homosexuality, Baoyu and others.

5 Another romantic drama, the seventeenth-century *The Peony Pavilion* (*Mudan ting*), serves a similar purpose in the Prospect Garden but a discussion of it is beyond our scope here.

6 Typically, Nuwa symbolizes fertility and reproduction.
7 Even cell phones and computers with cameras require access to a certain level of funding not accessible to large segments of the world's population (see Corbett 2008).
8 Dimoulas neither intended nor inspired our political and methodological interpretations. Rather, we draw on her poetry to articulate our worldist principles.
9 Available HTTP: <http://greece.poetryinternational.org/cwolk/view/17918> (accessed 14 July 2008).
10 *Ibid.*
11 *Ibid.*

Chapter 7, pp. 118–135

1 "*Os poetas do Ceará e a seca,*" quoted in Arons (2004: 91).
2 We put the word "peacekeeping" in quotes to question the institution's ability to keep "peace" as opposed to maintaining relations of oppression and violence. For simplicity's sake, we refrain from placing "peacekeeping" in quotes in each instance of its use.
3 This section draws from Agathangelou (1997, 2000, 2004b, 2006, and forthcoming).
4 See also Fisher (2001), Güney (2004), Eralp and Beriker (2005), Kalyoncu and Yucel (2005).
5 For a definition of "white but not quite" and the ways these relations unfold in Cyprus, Greece, and Turkey under the neoliberal imperium, see Agathangelou (2004b).
6 Historically, "*barbaros*" did not have a negative connotation. Homer used this word in the compound form, "*barbarophonos,*" to describe some Trojan allies whose speech was foreign, hence "barbaric." Thus the word, as used in fifth century BC, simply denoted a linguistic difference.
7 The Greeks were the first to "liberate" themselves racially/ethnically from the Ottoman Empire.
8 For a fuller discussion of these "discursive hooks," see Agathangelou and Ling (1997).
9 In 1974, all economic links between north and south Cyprus were severed and the island started to import extensively: e.g., food and natural resources, fuels, most raw materials, heavy machinery, transportation equipment and other luxury kinds of goods.
10 See HTTP: <http://www.cyprus-un-plan.org> (accessed 14 July 2008).
11 It is not a coincidence that both the UN and the EU intervened simultaneously in Cyprus. Interim agreement deadlines culminated in the two communities setting up referenda "16 days before the signing of the EU Accession Treaty and eventually took place a week before the formal accession of Cyprus. The Annan effort also incorporated Greece and Turkey into negotiations initially at a track two level (UN S/2003/398: para 50) and later in the second phase of the 13 February Agreement process in Bürgenstock (UN S/2004/437: para. 30–41)" (Michael 2006: 12).
12 These formulations are drawn specifically from Agathangelou (forthcoming).
13 The "Eastern Question" refers to the problem of European territory controlled by the Ottoman Empire from the eighteenth to early twentieth centuries.
14 Still, these reworkings are not without their contradictions or tensions. Local social movements may disrupt the dominant idea of Self vs Other but they also reinsert this binary regionally on the question of Turkey's entry into the EU. Local solidarities also challenge the notion of what it means to be political in Cyprus but these efforts are being guided by the UN towards the "right" solution.
15 For an analysis of the historical and geographical relations of Cyprus see Hadjidemetriou (1987).

16 Neither the Greek nor Turkish "governments" recognize these marriages. Nevertheless, villagers continue to intermarry and their children participate in the social rituals of both Greeks and Turks (interviews in Potamia, Agathangelou 1997). Recently, the law has changed whereby Greek and Turkish Cypriots can marry through civil law.

17 In 1996, the UN Committee on the Elimination of Discrimination Against Women (CEDAW) found that Cypriot women kept primarily to the roles of wife and mother (CEDAW Report, 1993–1995; available HTTP: <http://www.unhchr. ch/tbs/doc.nsf/0/b2a8e68f2fbeb9dec12572c2003dd065/$FILE/N9680066.pdf> [accessed 08 May 2008]). The Family Law in the Republic of Cyprus, for example, prohibited women from joining the same clubs or groups as their husbands (CEDAW/C/CYP1-2: 4 May 1995: 25; available HTTP: <http://www.bayefsky.com/ reports/cyprus_cedaw_c_cyp_1-2_1994.php> [accessed 3 August 2008]). Women who worked outside the home were restricted, typically, to low-paying, low-skilled, low-mobility work. Rural women, in particular, worked without well-defined hours, breaks, or modern appliances (CEDAW/C/CYP1-2: 1993–1995: 116; available HTTP: see above). They also missed out on benefits like pensions and health care granted to other women workers. Yet rural women, at 17% of the country's population, comprised 25% of the female labor force nationwide and contributed more than 50% to their family's income through sales of handicrafts and other small-scale activities during the off-season from farming (CEDAW/C/CYP1-2, 1993–1995: 115; available HTTP: see above). More heinously, laws overlooked violence against women and, by extension, children. This included rape and battery within the household and in society at large (CEDAW/C/CYP: 1–2: 4 May 1995: 41–43; available HTTP: http://www. bayefsky.com/reports/cyprus_cedaw_c_cyp_1-2_1994.php [accessed 3 August 2008]).

18 In 2004, women in the south received 34% less in wages than their male counterparts (Cyprus Survey Data Report, March 2007). Available HTTP: <http:// www.fr.eurofound.eu.int/working/surveyreports/CY0608019D/CY0608019D_3. htm> (accessed 10 June 2008).

19 The same report notes, however, that women were more likely to be employed in junior positions. Only 32% of women in the workforce qualified as heads of businesses (e.g., chief executives, directors and managers of small businesses).

20 See for instance, stories by participants in the bi-communal movements, available HTTP: <http://www.cyprus-conflict.net/oztoprak.htm> (accessed 10 June 2008).

21 Since Christofias's election, there has been a move to forge alliances between Greek and Turkish Cypriots by reaching a decision on the creation of a bi-communal, bi-zonal federation with two equal polities.

22 This section draws from Ling (2008).

23 See, also, *Newsweek*'s cover story "China 2008: The Rise of a Fierce Yet Fragile Superpower." Available HTTP: <http://www.newsweek.com/id/81588> (accessed 14 July 2008), and Curtis (2007).

24 NBR started out as the National Bureau of Asian Research, focused specifically on Cold War strategies for Asia. Banerjee and Ling (2006: 4) note that current members of the board of *NBR Analysis* come from "mega-corporations (e.g., Unocal, Coca Cola, Corning, Microsoft, Boeing, Ford) and their elite associates in the military (e.g., former joint chiefs of staff John M. Shalikashvili), industry (e.g., Virginia Mason Medical Center), and academia (e.g., American Enterprise Institute, Woodrow Wilson Center)."

25 See HTTP: <http://chess.about.com/od/history/p/aa06a14.htm> (accessed 14 July 2008).

26 For more on the non-aligned movement and its contemporary aspirations, see HTTP: <http://www.nam.gov.za/background/background.htm#1.1%20History> (accessed 14 July 2008).

27 For a sampling of this history, see Orleans (1896), Chapin (1944), and Cleaves (1949).

28 Interest in the Southern Silk Road is rising today, particularly from those in the regions involved. Note, for example, a conference on "The Southern Silk Route: Historical Links and Contemporary Convergences," sponsored by the Asian Scholarship Foundation, originally slated for the University of Yunnan at Kunming, China but rescheduled for the University of Calcutta, from 2–5 August 2008, due to the Olympics in China at the same time.

29 See HTTP: <http://www.hinduonnet.com/fline/fl1707/17070980.htm> (accessed 14 July 2008).

30 In 2006, bilateral trade between Yunnan province and Bangladesh reached $40 million; for Yunnan and India, $124 million (Aiyar 2006). Tourism in Yunnan has doubled the average income in the past decade to almost $1,000. In 2005, tourism contributed to 20% of the province's $45 billion gross domestic product (GDP).

31 More evidence needs to be unearthed about how ordinary people experienced life in the borderlands. This is currently underway, for example, with the International Dunhuang Project (IDP) located in the United Kingdom (http://idp.bl.uk/) (accessed 14 July 2008).

32 Some may critique this as simply creating charities. However, given that social welfare at the time depended solely on the family, leaving orphans and widows, for example, with no recourse, Su's efforts improved the lot for many.

Chapter 8, pp. 134–146

1 Act V, Scene II.

2 Smith identified ten assumptions in mainstream IR that comply with elite power plays in world politics: (a) "the state as the unit of analysis, rather than either humanity as a whole or the individual," (b) "distinction between the inside and the outside of the state," (c) "distinction between economics and politics," (d) "the notion of a common progression of humanity towards one end-state as exemplified in most accounts of globalization," (e) "absence of considerations of gender and ethnicity from the main theories," (f) "definition of violence [as] war," (g) "stress on structure over agency," (h) "the idea of one, universal rationality," (i) "underplaying of the importance of issues of identity in theories of international relations," and (j) "the search for explanation rather than understanding" (Smith 2004: 499–515).

3 See, for example, the type of "social entrepreneurship" undertaken by Ashoka Fellows. Available HTTPS: <www.ashoka.org> (accessed 14 July 2008).

4 Iago describes himself as a tried-and-true soldier whose "eyes had seen the proof/At Rhodes, at Cyprus and on other grounds/Christian and heathen" (Act I, Scene I).

5 Act V, Scene III.

6 Act I, Scene III.

7 *Ibid.*

8 Act V, Scene III.

9 The Turks attacked Cyprus in 1570 (Bradley 1991: 171).

10 Act V, Scene II.

11 Act III, Scene III.

12 Act I, Scene I.

13 Act I, Scene III.

14 With apologies to Shakespeare, we excerpt some phrases and images from the original *Othello* to make the Moor's speech seem more in keeping with his character and time.

15 Act I, Scene III.

16 "Doge" or Duke of Venice. He was the city-state's chief aristocrat and magistrate.

17 Act III, Scene III.
18 This is an excerpt from an encomium written by the Song Dynasty poet-official, Su Shi, on the Buddhist notion of "no-mind" (*wu-xin*) (Su, quoted in Egan 1994: 151). "'No-mind' does not mean that one is mindless like a rock or tree. 'No-mind' means that one is freed from false anxieties and cravings so that one's 'true mind' may be recovered . . . [N]o-mind serves to enhance rather than to diminish the individual's responsiveness to the world" (Egan 1994: 153–154).
19 Balaban (2000: 115).

References

9/11 Commission Report. (2004) *The Final Report of the National Commission on Terrorist Attacks Upon the United States*, Authorized Edition, New York: W.W. Norton.

Addario, L. (2001) "Jihad's Women," *New York Times Magazine*, 21 October: 38–41.

Adler, L. and Ling, L.H.M. (1995) "From Practice to Theory: Toward a Dissident-Feminist Reconstruction of Nonviolence," *Gandhi Marg: Journal of the Gandhi Peace Foundation* 16(4) January/March: 462–480.

AFP. (2008) "South American Nations to Launch Bank as Rival to IMF." Available HTTP: <http://www.democraticunderground.com/discuss/duboard.php?az=view_all&address=102x3029862> (accessed 17 July 2008).

Agathangelou, Anna M. (1997) *The Cypriot "Ethnic" Conflict in the Production of Global Power*, PhD Dissertation, Department of Political Science, Maxwell School of Citizenship and Public Affairs, Syracuse University.

Agathangelou, Anna M. (2002) "Sexing 'Globalization' in International Relations: Migrant Sex and Domestic Workers in Cyprus, Greece, and Turkey," in Geeta Chowdhry and Sheila Nair (eds) *Power, Postcolonialism and International Relations: Reading Race, Gender and Class*, New York: Routledge, pp. 142–49.

Agathangelou, Anna M. (2004a) "Gender, Race, Militarization, and Economic Restructuring in the Former Yugoslavia and at the U.S.-Mexico Border," in D.D. Aguilar and Anne Lacsamana (eds) *Women and Globalization*, New York: Humanity Books.

Agathangelou, Anna M. (2004b) *The Global Political Economy of Sex: Desire, Violence, and Insecurity in the Mediterranean Nation-States*, London: Palgrave Macmillan.

Agathangelou, Anna M. (2006) "Ontologies of Desires, Empire, and Capital: Recolonizations, 'Security' and the 'Near East,'" invited by the Institute of Political Science, National Sun Yat-sen University, Taiwan, paper presented at the International Academic Conference, "Asian Security Facing Hegemony: Nationalism, Immigration and Humanity," 2 June 2006.

Agathangelou, Anna M. (2007) "Desire, Violence, and the World Politics: Epicurus, the Melian, Dialogue, and Empire," invited presenter at the New School, Graduate Program in International Affairs, New York, 19 April 2007.

Agathangelou, Anna M. (2008a) "Seductions of Imperialism: Incapacitating Life, Fetishizing Death and Catastrophizing Ecologies," *Human Rights and Human Welfare Roundtable*, Joel R. Pruce, Roundtable Editor, University of Denver.

Agathangelou, Anna M. (2008b) "Neoliberal and Terror-Necrotic Regimes and the New World Order: Sacrifice Economies, Insecurities and Eurasia," paper presented at Globalization, Difference and Human Security, A Major International Conference, at Osaka University Nakanoshima Center, organized by Global COE "A Research Base for Conflict Studies in the Humanities," and Global Collaboration Center (GLOCOL) Osaka University, Osaka, Japan, 12–14 March 2008.

Anna M. Agathangelou. (2009) "Economies of Blackness and Sacrifice of (Homo) Virilities: Bodies, Accumulations, Disaster(s) and Slaughterhouses," in Shampa Biswas and Sheila Nair (eds) *Margins, Peripheries and Excluded Bodies: International Relations and States of Exception*, New York: Routledge.

Agathangelou, Anna M., Bassichis, Daniel, and Spira, Tamara. (2008) "Intimate Investments: Homonormativity, Global Lockdown, and Seductions of Empire," *Radical History Review* 100 (Winter): 120–143.

Agathangelou, Anna M. and Killian, Kyle D. (2006) "Epistemologies of Peace: Poetics, Globalization, and the Social Justice Movement," *Globalizations* 3(4): 459–483.

Agathangelou, Anna M. and Ling, L.H.M. (1997) "Postcolonial Dissidence within Dissident IR: Transforming Master Narratives of Sovereignty in Greco-Turkish Cyprus," *Studies in Political Economy* 54(1) September: 7–38.

Agathangelou, Anna M. and Spira, Tamara. (2007) "Sacrifice, Abandonment, and Interventions for Sustainable Feminism(s): The Non-Profit Organization Industry and Transbordered Substantive Democracy," in Sonita Sarker (ed.) *Sustainable Feminism(s)* USA: JAI Press, Elsevier Limited, pp. 95–123.

Ahmad, Aijaz. (1992) *In Theory: Classes, Nations, Literatures*, London: Verso.

Ahn, Mi-Young. (2007) "New Labour Law Hurts More Than Helps Women." Available HTTP: <http://ipsnews.net/news.asp?idnews=38951> (accessed 3 July 2008).

Aiyar, Pallavi. (2006) "Yunnan Model," *Frontline, India's National Magazine* 23(21) 21 October–3 November. Available HTTP: <http://www.hinduonnet.com/fline/fl2321/stories/20061103000306300.htm> (accessed 14 July 2008).

Albert, M., Kessler, O., and Stetter, S. (2008) "On order and conflict: International relations and the 'communicative turn'," *Review of International Studies*, 34: 43–67.

Alexander, Jacqui M. (1998) "Imperial Desire/Sexual Utopias: White Gay Capital and Transnational Tourism," in Ella Shohat (ed.) *Talking Visions: Multicultural Feminism in a Transnational Age*, New York and Massachusetts: The MIT Press.

Alexander, Jacqui M. (2005) *Pedagogies of Crossing: Meditations on Feminism, Sexual Politics, Memory, and the Sacred*, Durham, NC: Duke University Press.

Alexander, Jacqui M. and Mohanty, Chandra. (1997) *Feminist Genealogies, Colonial Legacies, Democratic Futures*. New York: Routledge.

Alker, Hayward R. (1995) "If not Huntington's Civilizations, then Whose?" *Review* 18(4) Fall: 533–562.

American Political Science Association Report. (2005) "APSA Releases Report on Women in PS: *Women's Advancement in Political Science*, July 2005." Available HTTP: <http://www.apsanet.org/content_18107.cfm> (accessed 17 July 2008).

Amin, Samir. (2004) *The Liberal Virus: Permanent War and the Americanisation of the World*, New York: Monthly Review Press.

Amin, Samir. (1989) *Eurocentrism*. New York: Monthly Review Press.

Amin, Tahir. (2008) "World Orders in Central Asia," paper presented at the conference in memory of Hayward R. Alker, Watson Institute of International Studies, Brown University, 6–7 June.

Amnesty International and Anti-Slavery International. (2005) "Amnesty International and Anti-Slavery International Call on European States to Ratify the Council of Europe Convention Against Trafficking,". Available HTTP: <http:www.Antislavery.org/archive/press/pressrelease2005maycoe.htm> (accessed 17 July 2008).

Anastasiou, Harry. (2006) "The EU as a Peace Building System: Deconstructing Nationalism in an Era of Globalization," paper presented at the annual meeting of the International Studies Association, Town & Country Resort and Convention Center, San Diego, California, 22 March 2006.

Annual Report. (1994) Central Bank of Cyprus, Eurosystem, Nicosia, Cyprus. Available HTTP: <http://www.centralbank.gov.cy/nqcontent.cfm?a_id=2592&lang=en> (accessed 18 June 2008).

Anthias, F. (1989) "Women and Nationalism in Cyprus," in N. Yuval-Davis and F. Anthias (eds) *Woman-Nation-State*, New York: St. Martin's Press.

Anthias, F. and Ayres, R. (1983) "Ethnicity and Class in Cyprus," *Race and Class* 25(1): 59–76.

"Anti-Imperialist League, Collected Records, 1899–1919." Swarthmore Peace Collection. Available HTTP: <http://www.swarthmore.edu/Library/peace/CDGA.A-L/antiimperialistleague.htm> (accessed 18 November 2007).

Arblaster, Anthony. (1984) *The Rise and Decline of Western Liberalism*, New York: Basil Blackwell.

Arons, Nicholas Gabriel. (2004) *Waiting for Rain: The Politics and Poetry of Drought in Northeast Brazil*, Tucson: University of Arizona Press.

Ashcroft, Bill, Griffiths, Gareth, and Tiffin, Helen. (eds) (1995) *The Post-Colonial Studies Reader*, London: Routledge.

Association of American University Professors (AAUP). (1993) *The Status of Non-Tenure-Track Faculty*, Washington, D.C.: American Association of University Professors.

Ayoob, Mohammed. (1992) *The Third World Security Predicament: State-Making, Regional Conflict, and the International System*, Boulder: Lynne Reinner.

Ayoob, Mohammed. (2002) "Inequality and Theorizing in International Relations: The Case for Subaltern Realism," *International Studies Review* 4(3) Fall: 27–48.

Babco, E. (2000) *Professional Women and Minorities: A Total Human Resources Data Compendium*, 13th edition, Washington, D.C.: Commission on Professionals in Science and Technology.

Balaban, John (trans.) (2000) *Spring Essence: The Poetry of Hồ Xuân Hu'o'ng*, Port Townsend: Copper Canyon Press.

Banerjee, Payal. (2006) "Indian Information Technology (IT) Workers in the U.S.: The H-1B Visa, Flexible Production, and the Racialization of Labor," *Critical Sociology* 32(2–3): 427–447.

Banerjee, Payal and Ling, L.H.M. (2006) "Hypermasculine War Games: Triangulating US-India-China," paper presented at the Institute for Malaysian and International Affairs (IKMAS) (Kuala Lumpur), Institute of Defence and Strategic Studies (IDSS) (Singapore), National Taiwan University (Taipei), and National Sun Yat-sen University (Kaohsiung), 25 May–3 June.

Banuri, Tariq. (1990) "Modernisation and its Discontents: A Cultural Perspective on the Theories of Development," in Frederique Apfel Marglin and Stephen A. Marglin (eds) *Dominating Knowledge*, Oxford: Clarendon Press.

Batchell, John. (2004) "Winds of change sweep Cyprus," *People's Weekly World Newspaper*, 21 February. Available HTTP: <http://www.pww.org/article/articleview/4809/1/144/> (accessed 10 June 2008).

BBC News. (2003) "Asia's Sex Trade is Slavery," 20 February. Available HTTP: <http://news.bbc.co.uk/2/hi/asia-pacific/2783655.stm> (accessed 08 July 2008).

Bellas, Marcia. (2002) *Faculty Salary and Faculty Distribution Fact Sheet, 2000–2001*, Washington, D.C.: Association of American University Professors (AAUP).

Bello, W. (2002) "Perspective: A Rerun of the 1930s?" *Businessworld* 19 August 2002.

Bello, Walden. (2007) "All Fall Down: Ten Years After the Asian Financial Crisis," *Znet* 13 August 2007. Available HTTP: <http://www.zmag.org/content/showarticle.cfm?ItemID=13518> (accessed 07 March 2008).

Berger, Mark and Beeson, Mark. (1998) "Lineages of Liberalism and Miracles of Modernisation: The World Bank, the East Asian Trajectory and the International Development Debate," *Third World Quarterly* 19(3): 487–504.

Bernal, Martin. (1987) *Black Athena: the Afroasiatic Roots of Classical Civilization (The Fabrication of Ancient Greece 1765–1985, Volume 1)*, New Jersey: Rutgers University Press.

Berrigan, Frida and Hartung, William D., with Heffel, Leslie. (2005) *US Weapons at War 2005: Promoting Freedom or Fueling Conflict? U.S. Military Aid and Arms Transfers Since September 11*, New York: A World Policy Institute Special Report, New School University, June. Available HTTP: <http://www.worldpolicy.org/projects/arms/reports/wawjune2005.html#execsum> (accessed 14 July 2008).

Bertsch, C. (2002) "Interview with Wendy Brown," in J. Schalit (ed.) *The Anti-Capitalism Reader: Imagining a Geography of Opposition*, New York: Akashic Books.

Bhabha, Homi. (1994) *The Location of Culture*. London: Routledge.

Biersteker, Thomas J. (2008) "Concluding the Dialectics of World Orders: Things Seen, Things Foreseen, and Things Not," paper presented at the Alker Memorial Conference, 6–7 June 2008, Brown University.

bin Ladin, O. (2001a.) March 11. Available HTTP: <http://users.skynet.be/terrorism/html/laden_statement_3.htm> (accessed 06 June 2005).

bin Ladin, O. (2001b) October 7. Available HTTP: <http://users.skynet.be/terrorism/html/laden_statement.htm> (accessed 06 June 2005).

Bleiker, Roland (ed.) (2000) "Editor's Introduction," *Alternatives* 25(3): 271–272.

Boal, Augusto. (1985) *Theatre of the Oppressed*; trans. Charles A. & Maria-Odilia Leal McBride, New York: Theatre Communications Group, Inc.

Bolukbasi, S. (1995) "Bhoutros-Gali's Cyprus Initiative in 1992: Why Did it Fail?" *Middle Eastern Studies* 31/3 (July): 460–482.

Boxer, S. (2001) "Banality of Terror: Dreams of Holy War over a Quiet Evening," *New York Times Week in Review* 16 December: 1, 5.

Bradley, A.C. (1991) *Shakespearean Tragedy: Lectures on Hamlet, Othello, King Learn and MacBeth*, London: Penguin Books.

Bradsher, Keith. (2007) "10 Years After Asia's Financial Crisis, Worries Remain," *International Herald Tribune* 27 June 2007. Available HTTP: <http://www.iht.com/articles/2007/06/27/business/crisis.php> (accessed 07 March 2008).

Brandes, Lisa, *et al.* (2001) "The Status of Women in Political Science: Female Participation in the Professoriate and the Study of Women and Politics in the Discipline," *PS: Political Science & Politics* 34(2): 319–326.

Bridger, Sue, Kay, Rebecca, and Pinnick, Kathryn. (1996) *No More Heroines?* London: Routledge.

Brininstool, E.A. (1899) "The White Woman's Burden," *Los Angeles Times* 6 March 1899. Available HTTP: <http://www.boondocksnet.com/ai/kipling/brininstool_kipling.html> (accessed 6 June 2005).

Brown, Eleanor. (2007) "The Ties that Bind: Migration and Trafficking of Women and Girls for Sexual Exploitation in Cambodia," Geneva: International Organisation for Migration. Available HTTP: <http://www.humantrafficking.org/publications/595> (accessed 08 July 2008).

Brown, P.L. (2001) "Heavy Lifting Required: The Return of Manly Men," *New York Times Sunday Week in Review* 28 October 2001: 5.

Bull, Hedley. (1966) "Society and Anarchy in International Relations," in Herbert Butterfield and Martin Wight (eds) *Diplomatic Investigations: Essays in the Theory of International Relations*, Cambridge: Harvard University Press.

Bumiller, E. (2001a) "First Lady to Speak About Afghan Women," *New York Times* 16 November 2001: B2.

Bumiller, E. (2001b) "The Politics of Plight and the Gender Gap," *New York Times* 19 November 2001: B2.

Burns, J.F. (2002) "Bin Laden Stirs Struggle on Meaning of Jihad," *New York Times* 27 January 2002: A1, A15.

Buruma, Ian and Avishai Margalit. (2002) *Occidentalism: the West in the Eyes of its Enemies*, New York: Penguin Press.

Bush, G.W. (2001a) "Bush's Speech to Congress," *New York Times* 21 September 2001: B4.

Bush, G.W. (2001b) "President Discusses War on Terrorism, In Address to the Nation, World Congress Center, Atlanta, Georgia," 8 November 2001. Available HTTP: <http://www.whitehouse.gov/news/releases/2001/11/20011108-13.html> (accessed 6 June 2005).

Byrne, Bridget, Marcus, Rachel, and Power-Stevens, Tanya. (1996) "Gender, Conflict, and Development, Vol II, Case Studies: Cambodia, Rwanda, Kosovo, Algeria, Somalia, Guatemala and Eritrea," *Bridge Report No. 35*, 12, Ministry of Foreign Affairs: The Hague, The Netherlands.

Calaguas, Mark. (2006) "Military Privatization: Efficiency or Anarchy?" *Chicago-Kent Journal of Comparative Law* 6: 58–81.

Calame, J. and Charlesworth, E. (2003) "No Man's Land: A Spatial Anatomy of Five Divided Cities," paper presented at the 6th US/ICOMOS International Symposium, "Managing Conflict & Conservation in Historic Cities," April 24–27, 2003 in Annapolis, Maryland. Available HTTP: <http://www.icomos.org/usicomos/Symposium/SYMP03/Calame.htmland> (accessed 6 June 2005).

Cameron, Angus and Palan, Ronen. (2004) *The Imagined Economies of Globalisation*, London: Sage.

Cao, Xueqin. (1973) *The Story of the Stone, Volume 1*; trans. David Hawkes, London: Penguin Books.

Captive Daughters. (2005) "Conference on Pornography and International Sex Trafficking." Available HTTP: <http://findarticles.com/p/articles/mi_qa3693/is_200507/ai_n15665844/pg_12> (accessed 14 July 2008).

Cardoso, Fernando Henrique and Enzo, Faletto. (1979) *Dependency and Development in Latin America*, Berkeley: University of California Press.

Carney, B.M. (2002) "Scandals Show America's Strength," *Wall Street Journal* 24 July 2002.

Carpenter, Charli R. (2002) "Gender Theory in World Politics: Contributions of a Nonfeminist Standpoint?" *International Studies Review* 4(3) Fall: 153–165.

Catalyst. (2007) "The Double-Bind Dilemma for Women in Leadership: Damned If You Do, Doomed If You Don't," 17 July 2007. Available HTTP: <https://www.catalyst.org/xcart/product.php?productid=16182&cat=248&bestseller> (accessed 07 March 2008).

Cavafy, C.P. (2003) *Poems*, Athens: Ikaros.

Cavaluzzo, Jean Smith. (2004) "The Corporation: More than 'A Few Bad Apples'," *Catholic New Times* 29 February 2004. Available HTTP: <http://findarticles.com/p/articles/mi_m0MKY/is_4_28/ai_n13455691> (accessed 07 March 2008).

CBS News. (2003) "All In the Family: Company Official Defends No-Bid Army Contract," 21 September 2003. Available HTTP: <http://www.cbsnews.com/stories/2003/04/25/60minutes/main551091.shtml> (accessed 08 March 2008).

Chakrabarty, Dipesh. (2000) *Povincializing Europe: Postcolonial Thought and Historical Difference*, Princeton, NJ: Princeton University Press.

Chang, K. and Ling, L.H.M. (2000) "Globalization and its Intimate Other: Filipina Domestic Workers in Hong Kong," in Marianne Marchand and Anne Sisson Runyan (eds) *Gender and Global Restructuring: Sightings, Sites, and Resistances*, London: Routledge.

Chapin, Helen B. (1944) "Yunnanese Images of Avalokitesvara," *Harvard Journal of Asiatic Studies* 8(2) August: 131–186.

Chatterjee, Partha. (1998) "Beyond the Nation? Or Within?" *Social Text* 56(16)3: 57–69.

Cho, Sumi. (1997) "Converging Stereotypes in Racialized Sexual Harassment: Where the Model Minority Meets Suzie Wong," in A.K. Wing (ed.) *Critical Race Feminism: A Reader*, New York: New York University Press.

Chomsky, Noam. (2003) *Hegemony or Survival: America's Quest for Global Dominance*, New York: Henry Holt & Co.

Chow, Kai-wing, Ng, On-cho, and Henderson, John B. (eds) (1999) *Imagining Boundaries: Changing Confucian Doctrines, Texts, and Hermeneutics*, Albany: State University of New York Press.

Chow, Rey. (2003) "Where Have All the Natives Gone?" in Lewis, Reina and Mills, Sara (eds) *Feminist Postcolonial Theory: A Reader*, New York: Routledge.

Chowdhry, Geeta. (2007) "Edward Said and Contrapuntal Reading: Implications for Critical Interventions in International Relations," *Millennium: Journal of International Studies*, 36(1): 101–116.

Chowdhry, G. and Nair, S. (eds) (2002) *Power in a Postcolonial World: Race, Gender and Class in International Relations*, London: Routledge.

Christofias, D. (2008) "Cyprus President: Reunification Is Only Option On Table," Dow Jones Newswire, Dow Jones & Company Inc, July 8. Available HTTP: <http://news.morningstar.com/newsnet/ViewNews.aspx?article=/DJ/200807080754D OWJONESDJONLINE000249_univ.xml> (accessed 14 July 2008).

Churchill, Ward. (1998) *A Little Matter of Genocide: Holocaust and Denial in the Americas from 1492 to the Present*, San Francisco: City Lights Books.

Cleaves, Francis W. (1949) "The Sino-Mongolian Inscription of 1362 in Memory of Prince Hindu," *Harvard Journal of Asiatic Studies* 12(1/2): 1–133.

CNN. (2002) "Money Morning," 07:00 am, EST, 2 December 2002. (Transcript # 120201cb.l29.).

Cockburn, Cynthia. (2004) *The Line: Women, Partition, and the Gender Order in Cyprus*. London and New York: Zed Books.

Coile, Zachary. (2003) "Rep. Stark Blasts Bush on Iraq War," *San Francisco Chronicle*, 19 March 2003. Available HTTP: <http://www.commondreams.org/ headlines03/0319-05.htm> (accessed 26 June 2008).

Connell, R.W. (1995) *Masculinities*, Cambridge: Polity Press.

Corbett, Sara. (2008) "Can the Cellphone Help End Global Poverty?" *The New York Times Magazine* 13 April 2008: 35–41.

Cordesman, Anthony H. (2007) "Success or Failure? Iraq's Insurgency and Civil Violence and US Strategy: Developments through June 2007," Working Draft, Center for Strategic and International Studies, 9 July. Available HTTP: <http:// www.csis.org/media/csis/pubs/070709_iraqinsurgupdate.pdf> (accessed 8 March 2008).

Costantinou, C. (2000) "Poetics of Security," *Alternatives* 25(3) July-September: 287–306.

Council of Europe. (2005) "Council of Europe Convention on Action Against Trafficking in Human Beings." Available HTTP: <http://Volumes/SECURE%

20II/MA%20coursework/Council%20of)20Europe)20-%20Council%20of%20Europe)
20Convention> (accessed 6 June 2005).

Cox, Robert. (1986) "Social Forces, States, and World Orders: Beyond International Relations Theory," in Robert O. Keohane (ed.) *Neorealism and Its Critics*, New York: Columbia University Press.

Cox, Robert. (1987) *Production, Power, and World-Order*, New York: Columbia University Press.

Crawford, Neta S. (2000) "The Passion of World Politics: Propositions on Emotion and Emotional Relationships," *International Security* 24(4): 116–156.

Crawford, Neta S. (2002) *Argument and Change in World Politics: Ethics, Decolonization, and Humanitarian Intervention*, Cambridge: Cambridge University Press.

Curtis, Lisa. (2007) "India's Expanding Role in Asia: Adapting to Rising Power Status," *The Heritage Foundation* 20 February. Available HTTP: <http://www.heritage.org/Research/AsiaandthePacific/bg2008.cfm> (accessed 14 July 2008).

Dalglish, Sarah. (2003) "Former Trustee at Center of Corporate Scandal," *The Tufts Daily*, 17 January. Available HTTP: <http://tuftsdaily.lunarpages.com/articleDisplay.jsp?a_id=1008> (accessed 6 June 2005).

Darby, Phillip. (2004) "Pursuing the Political: A Postcolonial Rethinking of Relations International," *Millennium: Journal of International Studies* 33(1):1–32.

Deleuze, G. (1988) *Foucault*, Minneapolis: University of Minnesota Press.

DeParle, Jason. (2007) "Migrant Money Flow: A \$300 Billion Current," *The New York Times* 18 November 2007. Available HTTP: <http://www.nytimes.com/2007/11/18/weekinreview/18deparle.html> (accessed 17 July 2008).

Der Derian, James and Shapiro, Michael J. (1989) *International/Intertextual Relations: Postmodern Readings of World Politics*, Toronto: Lexington Books.

Detienne, Marcel. (1996) *The Masters of Truth in Archaic Greece*; trans. Janet Lloyd, New York: Zone Books.

Devahuti, D. (2002) "Ancient Central-Asia and India," in Rahman, A. (ed.) *History of Science, Philosophy and Culture in Indian Civilization, Volume III, Part 2*. New Delhi: Oxford University Press.

Dienstag, Joshua Foa. (1996) "Serving God and Mammon: The Lockean Sympathy in Early American Political Thought," *American Political Science Review* 90(3) September: 497–511.

Dodds, Anita and Farrington, Anneka. (2007) "2007 ASEAN Child-Sex Tourism Review: An Outcome of the Annual Meeting of the ASEAN Regional Taskforce to Combat the Sexual Exploitation of Children in Tourism Destinations." August. Available HTTP:<http://childwise.net/uploads/Child%20Sex%20Tourism%20Review.pdf> (accessed 08 July 2008).

Doucette, Jamie. (2007) "South Korea: Labour Strife Escalates as New Labour Law Comes into Effect," *Znet* 19 July2007. Available HTTP: <http://www.zmag.org/content/showarticle.cfm?ItemID=13329> (accessed 08 March 2008).

Drezner, Daniel W. (2007) "The New New World Order," *Foreign Affairs* March/April. Available HTTP: <http://www.foreignaffairs.org/20070301faessay86203/daniel-w-drezner/the-new-new-world-order.html> (accessed 14 July 2008).

Droushiotis, Makarios. (1996) *The Invasion of Junta in Cyprus* (Η "Εισβολή" της Χούντας στην Κύπρο), Athens: Stahi.

Duffy, Gavan, Frederking, Brian, and Tucker, Seth. (1998) "Language Games: Dialogical Analysis of INF Negotiations," *International Studies Quarterly* (42): 271–294.

Dyson, M.E. (2002) *The Michael Eric Dyson Reader*. New York: Basic Civitas Books.

Ebert, Teresa M. (1999) "Globalization, Internationalism, and the Class Politics of Cynical Reason," *Nature, Society, and Thought* 12(4): 389–410. Available HTTP: <http://www.autodidactproject.org/other/cynebert.html> (accessed 6 June 2005).

Economist, The. (2003) "Special Report: America and Empire: Manifest Destiny Warmed Up?" 14 August 2003. Available HTTP: <http://www.economist.com/printedition/displayStory.cfm?Story_ID=1988940> (accessed 6 June 2005).

Edkins, Jenny. (2003) *Trauma and the Memory of Politics*, Cambridge: Cambridge University Press.

Edwards, Louise. (1990) "Gender Imperatives in Honglou meng: Baoyu's Bisexuality," *Chinese Literature: Essays, Articles, Reviews* (CLEAR) 12 (December): 69–81.

Egan, R.D. (2002) "Anthrax," in J. Collins and R. Glover (eds) *Collateral Language: A User's Guide to America's New War*, New York: New York University Press.

Egan, Ronald C. (1994) *Word, Image, and Deed in the Life of Su Shi*, Cambridge: Harvard University Press.

Ehrenreich, B. (2001) "Veiled Threat," *Los Angeles Times* 4 November: 1, Opinion Desk.

Eisenstein, Zillah. (2004) *Against Empire: Feminisms, Racism, and "the" West*, London: Zed Books.

Embassy of Cyprus. (1995) *Newsletter* 6 September 1995. Washington, D.C.: Embassy of Cyprus Press & Information Office.

Enloe, Cynthia. (1988) *Does Khaki Become You? The Militarization of Women's Lives*, London, Pandora Press.

Enloe, Cynthia. (1990) *Bananas, beaches, and bases*, Berkeley, CA: University of California Press.

Enloe, Cynthia. (2000) *Maneuvers: The International Politics of Militarizing Women's Lives*, Berkeley, CA: University of California Press.

Enriquez, Jean. (2006) "Globalization, Militarism, and Sex Trafficking," talk given at the International Meeting of Women World March, in Lima, Peru, 4–9 July 2006. Available HTTP: <http://sisyphe.org/article.php3?id_article=2475> (accessed 08 July 2008).

Eralp, Doğa Ulaş and Nimet Beriker. (2005) "Assessing the Conflict Resolution Potential of the EU: The Cyprus Conflict and Accession Negotiations," *Security Dialogue*, 36(2): 175–192.

Escobar, Arturo. (1995) *Encountering Development: The Making and Unmaking of the Third World*, Princeton, NJ: Princeton University Press.

European Commission. (2008) "Women and Men in Decision-Making 2007: An Analysis of the Situation and Trends," European Commission, Directorate General for Employment, Social Affairs and Equal Opportunities, Luxembourg: European Commission, Office for Official Publications of the EU Communities.

Farley, P.A. (1997) "The Black Body as Fetish Object," *Oregon Law Review* 76(3): 457–535.

Farmanfarmaian, A. (1992) "Did You Measure Up? The Role of Race and Sexuality in the Gulf War," in C. Peters (ed.) *Collateral Damage: The New World Order at Home and Abroad*, Boston: South End Press.

Feldman, Noah. (2004) *What We Owe Iraq: War and the Ethics of Nation Building*, Princeton, NJ: Princeton University Press.

Femia, Joseph V. (1987) *Gramsci's Political Thought*, Oxford: Clarendon Press.

Fierke, Karin and Knud Jorgenson (eds) (2001) *Constructing International Relations: The Next Generation*, Armonk, NY: M.E. Sharpe.

Firat, A.F. and Dholakia, N. (2000) *Consuming People: From Political Economy to Theaters of Consumption*, New York and London: Routledge.

Fisher, R.J. (2001) "Cyprus: The Failure in Mediation and the Escalation of an Identity Based Conflict to Adversarial Social Impasse," *Journal of Peace Research* 38(3): 307–326.

Foucault, Michel. (1994) *Power: Essential Works of Foucault 1954–1984*, series editor Paul Rabinow, Vol. 3, New York: The New Press.

Fox News. (2006) "Child Sex Trafficking Thrives in Thailand," 16 August. Available HTTP: <http://www.foxnews.com/story/0,2933,208800,00.html> (accessed 08 July 2008).

Franklin, Marianne I. (2005) *Postcolonial Politics, the Internet, and Everyday Life: Pacific Traversals Online*, London: Routledge.

Friedman, Thomas. (2005) *The World is Flat: A Brief History of the Twenty-First Century* (Updated and Expanded), New York: Farrar, Strauss and Giroux.

Fukuyama, Francis. (1989) "The End of History?" *The National Interest* (Summer): 3–18.

Fukuyama, Francis. (2002) "History and September 11," in Ken Booth and Tim Dunne (eds) *Worlds in Collision: Terror and the Future of Global Order*, London: Palgrave Macmillan.

Garamone, Jim. (2007) "Task Force Analyzes Detainee's Motivation in Iraq," American Forces Press Service, US Department of Defense, 6 August. Available HTTP: <http://www.defenselink.mil/news/newsnewsarticle.aspx?id=46961> (accessed 8 March 2008).

Garst, Daniel. (1989) "Thucydides and Neorealism," *International Studies Quarterly* 33(1): 3–27.

Gartzke, Erik. (2007) "The Capitalist Peace," *American Journal of Political Science* 51(1): 166–191.

Garver, John W. (2002) "The China-India-U.S Triangle: Strategic Relations in the Post-cold War Era," *NBR Analysis* 13(5) October. Available HTTP: <http://unpan1.un.org/intradoc/groups/public/documents/APCITY/UNPAN015790.pdf> (accessed 1 May 2006).

Gaudin, Colette. (1987) *On Poetic Imagination and Reverie: Selections from Gaston Bachelard*, Dallas, TX: Spring Publications, Inc.

Ghebali, Victor-Yves. (2007) "The United Nations and the Dilemma of Outsourcing Peacekeeping Operations," in Alan Bryden and Marina Caparini (eds) *Private Actors and Security Governance*, Geneva: Geneva Centre for Democratic Control of Armed Forces.

Gibney, Frank. (1998) "Culture of Deceit," *Time*, 26 January 1998: 54.

Gilpin, Robert. (1987) *The Political Economy of International Relations*, Princeton, NJ: Princeton University Press.

Gilroy, P. (1993) *The Black Atlantic: Modernity and Double Consciousness*, Cambridge: Harvard University Press.

Glanz, James and Tavernise, Sabrina. (2007) "Security Firm Faces Criminal Charges in Iraq," *The New York Times* 23 September 2007. Available HTTP: <http://www.nytimes.com/2007/09/23/world/middleeast/23blackwater.html> (accessed 8 March 2008).

Glenn, David. (2008) "Gender Gap in Academic Wages is Linked to Type of Institution, Researcher Says," *The Chronicle of Higher Education* 25 March 2008. Available HTTP: <http://www.nyu.edu/diversity/pdf/Chronicle%20article%20Women%20Wages.pdf> (accessed 15 July 2008).

Goto-Jones, Christopher S. (2005) *Political Philosophy in Japan: Nishida, the Kyoto School and Co-Prosperity*, London: Routledge.

Green, Donald P. and Shapiro, Ian. (1994) *Pathologies of Rational Choice Theory: A Critique of Applications in Political Science*, New Haven: Yale University Press.

Gregory, Donna M. (1989) "Foreword," in James Der Derian and Michael J. Shapiro (eds) *International/Intertextual Relations: Postmodern Readings of World Politics*, Toronto: Lexington Books.

Guardian, The. (2008) "US Jobs Figures Down for 6th Consecutive Month," 3 July 2008. Available HTTP: <http://blogs.guardian.co.uk/markets/2008/07/the_key_us_unemployment_figure.html> (accessed 05 July 2008).

Güney, Aylin. (2004) "The USA's Role in Mediating the Cyprus Conflict: A Story of Success or Failure?" *Security Dialogue* 35(1): 27–42.

Hadjidemetriou, K. (1987) *History of Cyprus*. Nicosia, Cyprus: Co-op.

Hadjipavlou, Maria and Cynthia Cockburn. (2006) "Women in projects of co-operation for peace: Methodologies of external intervention in Cyprus," *Women's Studies International Forum* 29(5): 521–533.

Hadjri, Karim. (2008) "Building Partnership for the Future: An overview of bi-communal initiatives in Cyprus," paper presented at the Multi-disciplinary Workshop, 20–21 May 2008, Belfast Queen's University Belfast, UK.

Haggard, Stephan. (1999) "Governance and Growth: Lessons from the Asian Economic Crisis," *Asia-Pacific Economic Literature* 13(2): 30–42.

Hall, Tony. (1997) "Who Silenced Clayton Matchee? We Did," *Canadian Forum* April: 5–6.

Hall, Zac. (2008) "Interrogating Whiteness: Realist IR, US State Torture and (Re)Producing Race and Gender Power Relations in Iraq and the 'Global War on Terror'." Master's thesis, Graduate Program in International Affairs, The New School.

Hamilton, Clive. (2007) "Building on Kyoto," *New Left Review* 45 (May June): 91–103.

Hammad, Suheir. (2001) "First Writing Since." Available HTTP: <http://www.camden.rutgers.edu/RUCAM/events/Perspectives1poem.html> (accessed 6 June 2005).

Han, Jong Woo and Ling, L.H.M. (1998) "Authoritarianism in the Hypermasculinized State: Hybridity, Patriarchy, and Capitalism in Korea," *International Studies Quarterly* 42(1): 53–78.

Harding, Sandra. (1991) *Whose Science? Whose Knowledge? Thinking from Women's Lives*, New York: Cornell University Press.

Hardt, Michael and Negri, Antonio. (2000) *Empire*, Cambridge: Cambridge University Press.

Hartsock, Nancy C.M. (1998) *The Feminist Standpoint Revisited and Other Essays*, Boulder: Westview Press.

Held, David. (1995) *Democracy and the Global Order*, Stanford: Stanford University Press.

Hider, James. (2005) "Iraqi Insurgents Now Outnumber Coalition Forces," *Times-On-Line* 4 January 2005. Available HTTP: <http://www.timesonline.co.uk/tol/news/world/iraq/article408134.ece> (accessed 08 March 08).

Hirschman, Albert O. (1970) *Exit, Voice, and Loyalty: Responses to Decline in Firms, Organizations, and States*, Cambridge: Harvard University Press.

Hirschman, Albert O. (1977) *The Passions and the Interests*, Princeton, NJ: Princeton University Press.

Hodges, L. (2007) "Little Accord on the Island," *The Independent* 8 November 2007. Available HTTP: <http://findarticles.com/p/articles/mi_qn4158/is_20071108/ai_n21105950> (accessed 8 March 2008).

Hoffmann, Stanley. (1995) "An American Social Science: International Relations," in James Der Derian (ed.) *International Theory: Critical Investigations*, New York: New York University Press.

Holston, J. and Appadurai, A. (1996) "Cities and Citizenship," *Public Culture* 8: 187–204.

Hooper, C. (2001) *Manly States: Masculinities, International Relations, and Gender Politics*, New York: Columbia University Press.

Hughes, Donna M. (2000) "The 'Natasha' Trade: the Transnational Shadow Market of Trafficking in Women," *Journal of International Affairs* 53(2): 625–651.

Hunt, Michael. (1987) *Ideology and US Foreign Policy*, New Haven: Yale University Press.

Huntington, Samuel P. (1993) "The Clash of Civilizations?" *Foreign Affairs* 72(3): 22–49.

Huntington, Samuel P. (1996) *The Clash of Civilisations and Remaking of World Order*. New York: Simon and Schuster.

Huntington, Samuel P. (2004) *Who Are We? The Challenges to America's National Identity*. New York: Simon and Schuster.

Huỳnh Sanh Thông (ed.) (1996) *An Anthology of Vietnamese Poems: From the Eleventh through the Twentieth Centuries*, New Haven: Yale University Press.

Hwa, Yol Jung. (1969) "Confucianism and Existentialism: Intersubjectivity as the Way of Man," *Philosophy and the Phenomenological Research* 30(2) December: 186–202.

Hwang, C.C. and Ling, L.H.M. (2008) "The Kitsch of War: Misappropriating Sun Tzu for an American Imperial Hypermasculinity," in Bina D'Costa and Katrina Lee-Koo (eds) *Gender and Global Politics in the Asia Pacific*, London: Palgrave Macmillan.

Hyam, Ronald. (1991) *Empire and Sexuality: the British Experience*, London: Palgrave Macmillan.

Hyland, Julie. (2000) "Explosive Growth Internationally in Trafficking of Women and Children for Sex Trade," *World Socialist Website* 8 June 2000. Available HTTP: <http://www.wwws.org/articles/2000/jun2000/trafj08.shtml> (accessed 6 June 2005).

Ikenberry, G. John. (2004) "Illusions of Empire: Defining the New American Order," *Foreign Affairs* March/April 83(2). Available HTTP: <http://www.foreignaffairs.org/20040301fareviewessay83212b/g-john-ikenberry/illusions-of-empire-defining-the-new-american-order.html> (accessed 6 June 2005).

Inayatullah, Naeem and Blaney, David L. (2004) *International Relations and the Problem of Difference*, New York/London: Routledge.

INEK-PEO. (2007) "Informative activities against racism, nationalism, religion and age," (in Greek 'Δραστηριότητες ενημέρωσης κατά των διακρίσεων στη βάση της φυλής, εθνότητας, θρησκείας και ηλικίας'), Nicosia: Cyprus: Institute of Labor, Cyprus.

Iraq Study Group. (2006) Available HTTP: <http://www.usip.org/isg/iraq_study_group_report/report/1206/iraq_study_group_report.pdf> (accessed 12 July 2008).

Jansson, P. (1997) "Identity-Defining Practices in Thucydides' *History of the Peloponnesian War*," *European Journal of International Studies* 3(2): 147–165.

Jeffords, Susan. (1991) "Rape and the New World Order," *Cultural Critique* 19 (Autumn): 203–215.

Johnson, Chalmers. (1998) "Cold War Economics Melt Asia," *The Nation* 23 February 1998: 16–19.

Johnson, Chalmers. (2003) *The Sorrows of Empire: How the Americans Lost Their Country*, New York: Metropolitan Books.

Johnston, Alastair Iain. (1995) *Cultural Realism: Strategic Culture and Grand Strategy in Chinese History*. Princeton, NJ: Princeton University Press.

Johnston, David Kay. (2007) "Income Gap is Widening, Data Shows," *The New York Times* 29 March 2007. Available HTTP: <http://www.nytimes.com/2007/03/29/business/29tax.html> (accessed 05 July 2008).

Joseph, S. Joseph. (1997) *Cyprus: Ethnic Conflict and International Politics, from Independence to the Threshold of the European Union*, London/New York: Macmillan Press/St. Martin's.

Kalyoncu, Huseyin and Yucel, Fatih. (2005) "An analytical approach on defense expenditure and economic growth: the case of Turkey and Greece," MPRA Paper 4262, University Library of Munich, Germany.

Kelmendi, Adriatik. (2001) "Kosovo Prostitution Flourishes: UN Struggles to Break Up Lucrative Prostitution Racket," *BCR* (230), 28 March 2001.

Keohane, Robert. (1984) *After Hegemony: Cooperation and Discord in the World Political Economy*, Princeton, NJ: Princeton University Press.

Keohane, Robert (ed.) (1986) *Neorealism and its Critics*, New York: Columbia University Press.

Keohane, Robert. (1989) "International Relations Theory: Contributions of a Feminist Standpoint," *Millennium* 18: 245–253.

Keohane, Robert and Joseph Nye. (2000) *Power and Interdependence*, 3rd edition, Boston: Little Brown.

Khatami, Mohamed. (1998) Transcript of Interview with Iranian President Mohammad Khatami with Christiane Amanpour, CNN Interactive.

Kindleberger, Charles P. (1973) *The World in Depression, 1929–1939*, Berkeley, CA: University of California Press.

King, Gary, Keohane, Robert O., and Verba, Sidney. (1994) *Designing Social Inquiry: Scientific Inference in Qualitative Research*, Princeton, NJ: Princeton University Press.

Kipling, Rudyard. (1899) " 'The White Man's Burden': Kipling's Hymn to U.S. Imperialism." Available HTTP: <http://historymatters.gmu.edu/d/5478/> (accessed 6 June 2005).

Klein, Naomi. (2005) "The Rise of Disaster Capitalism," *The Nation*. Available HTTP: <http://thenation.com/doc/20050502/klein> (accessed 07 February 2008).

Kole, William J. and Cerkez-Robinson, Aida. (2001) "UN Police Accused of Involvement in Prostitution in Bosnia," *Associated Press* 28 June 2001.

Krishna, Sankaran. (2006) "Race, Amnesia, and the Education of International Relations," in Branwen Gruffydd Jones (ed.) *Decolonizing International Relations*, London: Rowman & Littlefield.

Labouchère, Henry. (1899) "The Brown Man's Burden," *Truth* (London); reprinted in *Literary Digest* 18, 25 February. Available HTTP: <http://www.boondocksnet.com/ai/kipling/labouche.html> (accessed 18 November 2005).

Labour Force Survey. (2004) "Labour Force Survey in the EU, Candidate and EFTA Countries," Luxembourg: European Commission, Office for Official Publications of the EU Communities, 2006.

Lacayo, R. (1997) "IMF to the Rescue," *Time* 8 December 1997: 36.

Lander, Mark and Cowell, Alan. (2003) "U.S. Secretary of State dismisses UN's Iraq Report," *The New York Times* 27 January 2003. Available HTTP: <http://www.nytimes.com/2003/01/27/international/middleeast/27IRAQ.html> (accessed 6 June 2005).

Lapid, Josef. (1989) "The Third Debate: On the Prospects of International Theory in a Post-Positivist Era," *International Studies Quarterly* 33(3): 235–251.

Lapid, Josef and Friedrich Kratochwil (eds) (1997) *The Return of Culture and Identity in IR Theory*, Boulder: Lynne Rienner.

Lavelle, Marianne. (2008) "Exxon's Profits: Measuring a Record Windfall," *US News & World Report*, 1 February 2008. Available HTTP: <http://www.usnews.com/articles/business/economy/2008/02/01/exxons-profits-measuring-a-record-windfall.html> (accessed 5 July 2008).

Leadbeater, C. (2002) "A Series of Mini-Accidents Always in Progress; Does Our Global Economy Offer Us the Option of a New Capitalism?" *New Statesman* 15 July 2002.

Lebow, R.N. and Strauss, Barry S. (1991) *Hegemonic Rivalry: From Thucydides to the Nuclear Age*, London: Blackwell Publishers.

Leeson, P.T. (2002) "In America, Capitalism is the Great Uniter," *Chicago Sun-Times* (Editorial) 22 August 2002.

Lelyveld, J. (2001) "All Suicide Bombers Are Not Alike: A Journey to Gaza, Cairo and Hamburg in Search of What Really Made Sept. 11 Possible," *The New York Times Magazine* 28 October 2001: 49–53, 62, 78–79.

Lewin, T. (2001) "Bush May End Offices Dealing with Women's Issues, Groups Say," *The New York Times* 19 December 2001: A23.

Lewis, Reina and Mills, Sara (eds) (2003) *Feminist Postcolonial Theory: A Reader*, New York: Routledge.

Lijphart, Arend. (1971) "Comparative Politics and the Comparative Method," *The American Political Science Review* 65(3) September: 682–693.

Lim, Lin Lean (ed.) (1998) *The Sex Sector*, Geneva: International Labour Office.

Lindo, V.R. (2006) "The Trafficking of Persons into the European Union for Sexual Exploitation: Why it persists and suggestions to compel implementation and enforcement of legal remedies in non-complying member states," *HeinOnline*, 135–150.

Lindstrom, Nicole. (2004) "Regional Sex Trafficking in the Balkans: Trans-national Networks in Enlarged Europe," *Problems of Post-Communism* 51(3): 45–52.

Ling, L.H.M. (1994) "Rationalizations for State Violence in Chinese Politics: The Hegemony of Parental Governance," *Journal of Peace Research* 31(4) November: 393–405.

Ling, L.H.M. (1999) "Sex Machine: Global Hypermasculinity and Images of the Asian Woman in Modernity," *positions: east asia cultures critique* 72(2) November: 1–30; reprinted in D. Pettman (ed.) (2004) *Internationalizing Cultural Studies*, London: Blackwell.

Ling, L.H.M. (2002a) "Cultural Chauvinism and the Liberal International Order: 'West versus Rest' in Asia's Financial Crisis," in Geeta Chowdhry and Sheila Nair (eds) *Power, Postcolonialism, and International Relations: Reading Race, Gender, Class*, London: Routledge.

Ling, L.H.M. (2002b) *Postcolonial International Relations: Conquest and Desire between Asia and the West*, London: Palgrave Macmillan.

Ling, L.H.M. (2004) "The Monster Within: What Fu Manchu and Hannibal Lecter Can Tell Us about Terror and Desire in a Post-9/11 World," *positions: east asia cultures critique* 12(2) Fall: 377–400.

Ling, L.H.M. (2005) "Neoliberal Neocolonialism: Comparing Enron with Asia's 'Crony Capitalism'," in Dirk Wiemann, Agata Stopinska, Anke Bartels and Johannes Angermüller (eds) *Discourses of Violence – Violence of Discourses: Critical*

Interventions, Transgressive Readings and Postnational Negotiations, Frankfurt/ Main: Peter Lang.

Ling, L.H.M. (2008) "Borderlands: A Postcolonial-Feminist Approach to Self/ Other Relations under the Neoliberal Imperium," in Heike Brandt, Bettina Bross, and Susanne Zwingel (eds) *Mehrheit am Rand*, Berlin: VS Verlag.

Linklater, Andrew, and Suganami, Hidemi. (2006) *The English School of International Relations: A Contemporary Reassessment*, Cambridge: Cambridge University Press.

Liu, Lydia H. (2004) *The Clash of Empires: The Invention of China in Modern World Making*, Cambridge: Harvard University Press.

Lloyd, Genevieve. (1993) *Man of Reason*, Minneapolis: University of Minnesota Press.

Luke, Brian. (1998) "Violent Love: Hunting, Heterosexuality, and the Erotics of Men's Predation," *Feminist Studies* 24(3): 627–655.

Marx, K. (1968, 1988) *Economic and Philosophic Manuscripts of 1844 and the Communist Manifesto*; trans. Martin Milligan, New York: Prometheus Books.

Marx, K. (1978) The Marx-Engels Reader, Robert C. Tucker (ed.), 2nd edn., New York: W.W. Norton.

McClintock, Anne. (1995) *Imperial Leather: Race, Gender and Sexuality in the Colonial Context*, New York: Routledge.

McPherson, Michael S. and Morton O. Schapiro. (1999) "The Future Economic Challenges for the Liberal Arts Colleges," *Daedalus* 128(1): 47–76.

Mehta, Uday S. (1997) "Liberal Strategies of Exclusion," in Frederick Cooper and Ann Laura Stoler (eds) *Tensions of Empire: Colonial Cultures in a Bourgeois World*, Berkeley, CA: University of California Press.

Michael, Michális S. (2006) "The Cyprus Peace Talks: A Critical Appraisal, Centre for Dialogue," Working Papers Series no. 1., LaTrobe University Centre for Dialogue, Victoria, Australia.

Mignolo, Walter D. (2000) *Local Histories/Global Designs: Coloniality, Subaltern Knowledges, and Border Thinking*, Princeton, NJ: Princeton University Press.

Millennium. (2002) Pragmatism in International Relations Theory, *Special Issue* 31(3).

Miller, Judith and Preston, Julia. (2003) "Blix Says He Saw Nothing to Prompt a War," *The New York Times* 31 January 2003. Available HTTP: <http:// www.nytimes.com/2003/01/31/international/middleeast/31BLIX.html> (accessed 6 June 2005).

Mitchell, Timothy. (1991) *Colonizing Egypt*, New York: Cambridge University Press.

Moallem, M. (1999) "Transnationalism, Feminism, and Fundamentalism," in Caren Kaplan, Normal Alarcon, and Minoo Moallem (eds) *Between Woman and Nation: Nationalism, Transnational Feminisms, and the State*, Durham, NC: Duke University Press.

Molloy, Patricia. (1999) "Desiring Security/Securing Desire: (Re)Re-Thinking Alterity in Security Discourse," *Cultural Values* 3(3): 304–328.

Monroe, Kristen, Saba Ozyurt, Ted Wrigley, and Amy Alexander Kristen. (2008) "Gender Equality in Academia: Bad News from the Trenches, and Some Possible Solutions," *Perspectives on Politics* 6(2): 25–233.

Monten, Jonathan. (2006) "Thucydides and Modern Realism," *International Studies Quarterly* 50(1): 3–26.

Monthly Review. (2003) *Special Issue.* November.

Moon, Katharine H.S. (1997) *Sex among allies*, New York: Columbia University Press.

Moraga, Cherrie and Anzaldua, Gloria (eds) (1983) *This Bridge Called My Back: Writings by Radical Women of Color*, New York: Kitchen Table, Women of Color Press.

Mullings, Beverley. (2000) "Fantasy tours: exploring the global consumption of caribbean sex tourisms," in Mark Gottdiener (ed.) *New Forms of Consumption: Consumers, Culture, and Commodification*, Boulder, Co: Rowman & Littlefield Publishers Inc.

Nandy, Ashis. (1988) *The Intimate Enemy: The Psychology of Colonialism*, Delhi: Oxford.

Narayan, Uma. (1997) *Dislocating Cultures*, New York: Routledge.

National Center for Education Statistics (NCES) Report. (1997) "Projections of Education Statistics to 2007," Washington, D.C.: Government Printing Office.

National Center for Education Statistics (NCES) Report. (2004) "Trends in Educational Equity of Girls and Women – 2004," Washington, D.C.: Government Printing Office. Available HTTP: <http://nces.ed.gov/pubs2005/equity/> (accessed 15 July 2008).

National Center for Education Statistics (NCES) Report. (2008) "The Condition of Education – Indicator 27 – 2008," Washington, D.C.: Government Printing Office. Available HTTP: <http://nces.ed.gov/programs/coe/2008/section3/indicator27.asp> (accessed 15 July 2008).

Nepali, Purna (ed.) (2003) *Gandharwa: Sangeet Ra Sanskriti* (*Marginalised: Songs and Culture*). Kathmandu: UNESCO.

New Republic, The (TNR) (1998) "Tocqueville and the Mullah," 2 February 1998.

Nguyen, Thanh D. (2003) "What If There Had Been No Mahathir?" *Jakarta Post* 23 November 2003. Available HTTP: <http://thangthecolumnist.blogspot.com/2005/05/what-if-there-had-been-no-mahathir.html> (accessed 08 March 2008).

Nikas, G. (2003) *Other Lyricists* ("Ξένοι Λυρικοί"), Athens: Potamos. (In Greek.)

Norwegian Refugee Council. (2001) "Global Internally Displaced People Database," December.

Nussbaum, Martha. (1999) *Sex and Social Justice*, Oxford: Oxford University Press.

Nussbaum, Martha. (2000) *Women and Human Development: the Capabilities Approach*, Cambridge: Cambridge University Press.

Nye Jr., Joseph S. (2004) "Soft Power and American Foreign Policy," *Political Science Quarterly* 119(2): 255–270.

O'Gorman, Edmundo. (1961) *The Invention of America: An Inquiry into the Historical Nature of the New World and the Meaning of Its History*, Bloomington, IN: Indiana University Press.

Olson, Mancur. (1993) "Dictatorship, Democracy, and Development," *American Political Science Review* 87(3): 567–576.

Olsson, Louise and Tryggestad, Torum (eds) (2001) *Women and International Peacekeeping*, London: Frank Cass.

Ong, Aihwa and Collier, Stephen J. (eds) (2005) *Global Assemblages: Technology, Politics, and Ethics as Anthropological Problems*, Malden, MA: Blackwell.

Onuf, Nicholas J. (1989) *World of Our Making*, Columbia, SC: University of South Carolina Press.

Orleans, Prince Henry of. (1896) "From Yun-nan to British India," *Geographical Journal* 7(3) March: 300–309.

Oztoprak, Canan. (2000) "The Experience of Bi-Communal Contacts Through the Eyes of a Turkish Cypriot: Facts and Fictions," paper presented at an international conference in California in the summer of 2000, a conference convened in part by a former Fulbright scholar, Marco Turk. Available HTTP: <http://www.cyprus-conflict.net/oztoprak.htm> (accessed 05 May 2008).

Palan, Ronen. (2000) "A World of their Making: an Evaluation of the Constructivist Critique in International Relations," *Review of International Studies* 26(4) October: 575–598.

Panitch, L. and Gindin, S. (2004) *Global Capitalism and American Empire*, London: Merlin.

Paolini, Albert J. (1999) *Navigating Modernity: Postcolonialism, Identity, and International Relations*, Boulder: Lynne Rienner Publishers.

Parry, Milman. (1971) *The Making of Homeric Verse: The Collected Papers of Milman Parry*; (ed.) Adam Parry, Oxford: Clarendon Rpt 1987.

Pateman, Carole. (1988) *The Sexual Contract*, Stanford: Stanford University Press.

Pavlou, S. (2005) "Equal Opportunity Policy in Cyprus," For the Mediterranean Institute of Gender Studies, Nicosia, Cyprus. Available HTTP: <http://www.rosadoc.be/site/maineng/pdf/athena%20papers/pavlou.pdf> (accessed 08 March 2008).

Peng, Dajin. 2002. "Invisible Linkages: A Regional Perspective of East Asian Political Economy," *International Studies Quarterly* 46: 423–447.

Persaud, R.B. (2001) *Counter-Hegemony and Foreign Policy: The Dialectics of Marginalized and Global Forces in Jamaica*, Albany, NY: State University of New York Press.

Pettman, Jindy Jan. (1996) *Worlding Women*, London: Routledge.

Polanyi, Karl. (1944) *The Great Transformation*, New York: Farrar and Rinehart, Inc.

Pollack, Andrew. (1997) "South Korea Says IMF Has Agreed to Huge Bailout," *The New York Times* 1 December 1997. Available HTTP: <http://query.nytimes.com/gst/fullpage.html?res=9E00E3DC1F3AF932A35751C1A961958260> (accessed 07 March 2008).

Porteus, Liza. (2005) "UN Not at Peace with its 'Blue Helmets'," *Fox News* 24 March 2005. Available HTTP: <http://www.foxnews.com/story/0,2933,151310,00.html> (accessed 17 July 2008).

positions: east asia cultures critique. (1997) Special issue on "The comfort women: colonialism, war, and sex," 5(1) Spring.

Prakash, Gyan. (1999) *Another Reason: Science and the Imagination of Modern India*, Princeton, NJ: Princeton University Press.

Rai, Shirin. (2003) *Gender and the Political Economy of Development: from Nationalism to Globalization*, Cambridge, UK: Polity.

Rajaram, P.K. (2006) "Dystopic Geographies of Empire," *Alternatives Global, Local, Political* 31(4) October–December: 475–506.

Ramazani, Vaheed K. (2001) "September 11: Masculinity, Justice, and the Politics of Empathy," *Comparative Studies of South Asia, Africa, and the Middle East* 21(1–2): 118–124.

Rao, V.V. Bhanoji. (1998) "East Asian Economies: The Crisis of 1997–98," *Economic and Political Weekly* 6 June: 1397–1416.

Razack, Sherene. (2000) "From the 'Clean Snows of Petawawa': The Violence of Canadian Peacekeepers in Somalia," *Cultural Anthropology* 15(1): 127–163.

Razack, Sherene. (2004) *Dark Threats and White Knights: The Somalia Affair, Peacekeeping, and the New Imperialism*, Toronto: University of Toronto Press.

Revolutionary Association of the Women of Afghanistan (RAWA). (2001) "Afghani Women's Resistance Organization: bin Laden is not Afghanistan," 14

September. Available HTTP: <http://www.ucolick.org/~de/WTChit/RAWA. html> (accessed 6 June 2005).

Robinson, Adam. (2002) *Bin Laden: Behind the Mask of the Terrorist*, Edinburgh and London: Mainstream Publishing.

Rochas, Grauber. [1965] (1983) "The Aesthetics of Hunger," in Michael Chanan (ed.) *25 Years of the New Latin American Cinema*, London, 1983.

Rohde, David and Sanger, David E. (2007) "How the 'Good War' in Afghanistan Went Bad'," *The New York Times*, 12 August 2007: 1, 12–13.

Rosenau, James (ed.) (1993) *Global Voices: Dialogues in International Relations*, Boulder: Westview Press.

Rubin, Elizabeth. (2008) "Battle Company is Out There," *The New York Times Magazine* 24 February 2008: 38–45, 64, 82.

Rumelili, Bahar. (2003) "Liminality and the Perpetuation of Conflicts: Turkish-Greek Relations in the Context of Community Building by the EU," *European Journal of Intnernational Relations* 9(2): 213–248.

Rupert, Mark. (1995) *Producing Hegemony*, London: Cambridge University Press.

Rushdie, Salman. (1992) "In Good Faith," in *Imaginary Homelands: Essays and Criticism 1981–91*, London: Granta Books.

Said, Edward. (1979) *Orientalism*, New York: Vintage.

Said, Edward. (1988) "Identity, Negation and Violence," *New Left Review* 171: 46–60.

Said, Edward. (1994) *Culture and Imperialism*, New York: Alfred A. Knopf.

Sakamoto, Y. (1991) "Introduction: the Global Context of Democratization," *Alternatives* 16(2): 119–127.

Samarasinghe, Vidyamali. (2007) *Female Sex Trafficking in Asia: The Resilience of Patriarchy in a Changing World*, London: Routledge.

Sanger, David E. (1998) "Greenspan Sees Asian Crisis Moving World to Western Capitalism," *The New York Times* 13 February 1998: D1.

Sassen, Saskia. (1998) *Globalization and its Discontents*, New York: The New Press.

Sayyid, Salman. (2006) "After Babel: Dialogue, Difference and Demons," *Social Identities* 12(1) January: 5–15.

Schneider, Alison. (1997) "Proportion of Minority Professors Up to About 10%," *The Chronicle of Higher Education* 20 June: A12.

Sen, Sudipta. (1998) *Empire of Free Trade: The East India Company and the Making of the Colonial Marketplace*, Philadelphia: University of Pennsylvania Press.

Sen, Tansen. (2006) "The Travel Records of Chinese Pilgrims Faxian, Xuangzang, and Yijing: Sources for Cross-Cultural Encounters between Ancient China and Ancient India," *Education About Asia* 11(3): 24–33.

Shapiro, Michael J. (1992) *Reading the Postmodern Polity*, Minneapolis: University of Minnesota Press.

Shilliam, R. (2008) "The 'Human' as Interpolated Subject: Maori Struggles In New Zealand and the Antinomies of 'Human Security' as a Concept," paper presented at Globalization, Difference and Human Security, A Major International Conference March 12–14, 2008, at Osaka University Nakanoshima Center, organized by Global COE "A Research Base for Conflict Studies in the Humanities," and Global Collaboration Center (GLOCOL), Osaka University.

Shohat, Ella and Stam, Robert. (1994) *Unthinking Eurocentrism: Multiculturalism and the Media*, London and New York: Routledge.

Singh, Ajit and Weisse, Bruce A. (1999) "The Asian Model: A Crisis Foretold?" *International Social Science Journal* June: 203–216.

Smith, Adam. (1776) *The Wealth of Nations*, Oxford: Oxford University Press.

Smith, Andrea. (2005) *Conquest: Sexual Violence and American Indian Genocide*, Cambridge: South End Press.

Smith, Steve. (2004) "Singing Our World into Existence: International Relations Theory and September 11," *International Studies Quarterly* September: 499–515.

Soguk, Nevzat. (2006) "Splinters of Hegemony: Ontopoetical Visions in International Relations," *Alternatives* 31: 377–404.

Spivak, Gayatri Chakravorty. (1999) *A Critique of Post-Colonial Reason: Toward a History of the Vanishing Present*, Cambridge: Harvard University Press.

Spivak, Gayatri. (1999) "Letter to the Editor," *The New Republic* 220.16 (19 April): 43.

Staudt, Kathleen. (2006) "Violence and Activism at the Border: Gender, Fear and Everyday Life in in Ciudad Juárez Women and Maquiladoras," *Public Culture* 11(3): 453–74.

Stein, Arthur A. (1984) "The Hegemon's Dilemma: Great Britain, the United States, and the International Economic Order," *International Organization* 38: 355–86.

Stoler, Ann Laura. (2002) *Carnal Knowledge and Imperial Power: Race and the Intimate in Colonial Rule*, Berkeley: University of California Press.

Subramanian, K. (2006) "Has the IMF Lost its Relevance?" *The Hindu Business Line, International Edition* 27 January. Available HTTP: <http://www.thehindubusinessline.com/2006/01/27/stories/2006012700221100.htm> (accessed 20 June 2008).

Surkiewicz, Joe. (2004) "Dickensian Horrors in Baltimore: Inside the City Detention Center," *Counterpunch* May 15–16. Available HTTP: <http://counterpunch.org/surkiewicz05152004.html> (accessed 6 June 2005).

Sylvester, Christine. (1993) "Reconstituting a Gender Eclipsed Dialogue," in James Rosenau (ed.) *Global Voices: Dialogues in International Relations*, Boulder: Westview Press.

Sylvester, Christine. (2001) "Art, Abstraction, and International Relations," *Millennium: Journal of International Studies* 30: 535–554.

Szep, Jason. (2007) "Harvard Oks Biggest Curriculum Change in 30 Years," Reuters. Available HTTP: <http://www.reuters.com/article/domesticNews/idUSN1545816720070515?pageNumber=1&virtualBrandChannel=0> (accessed 15 July 2008).

Tan, Chung. (2002) "India and China: A Saga of Sharing Historical Heritage," in Rahman, A. (ed.) "Part 2: India's interaction with China, Central and West Asia," *History of Science, Philosophy and Culture in Indian Civilization, Volume III*, New Delhi: Oxford University Press.

Taylor, Howard S. (1899) "The Poor Man's Burden," *The Public* 1, 18 February. Available HTTP: <http://www.boondocksnet.com/ai/kipling/taylor.html> (accessed 18 November 2005).

Teng, Ssu-yu and Fairbank, John K. (1979) *China's Response to the West: A Documentary Survey, 1839–1923*, Cambridge: Harvard University Press.

Teschke, B.G. (2002) "Theorising the Westphalian System of States: International Relations from Absolutism to Capitalism," *European Journal of International Relations* 8(1): 5–48.

Thakur, Ravni and Tan, Chung. (1998) "Enchantment and Disenchantment: A Sino-Indian Introspection," in Tan Chung (ed.) *Across the Himalayan Gap: An Indian Quest for Understanding China*, New Delhi: Gyan Publishing House and Indira Gandhi National Centre for the Arts.

Tickner, Ann J. (1997) "You Just Don't Understand: Troubled Engagements between Feminists and IR Theorists," *International Studies Quarterly* 41(4): 611–632.

Tickner, Ann J. (2004) "The Growth and Future of Feminist Theories in International Relations," An Interview, *Brown Journal of World Affairs* Winter/Spring: 47–57.

Times of India. (2001) "UN Peacekeepers Fuelling Women Trafficking," 11 April.

Todorov, Tzvetan. (1984) *The Conquest of America: The Question of the Other.* New York: Harper and Row.

Trafficking in Persons Report. (2005) US Department of State. Available HTTP: <http://www.state.gov/documents/organization/47255.pdf> (accessed 2 February 2007).

Trimikliniotis *et al.* (2005) "Ανεργία, Υποαπασχόληση και Ετεροαπασχόληση: Μια Έρευνα για την Εργασιακή Αβεβαιότητα και Ανασφάλεια των Νέων στη Κύπρο," [Unemployment, Underemployment and other-employment: Research on working uncertainty and precariousness of youth in Cyprus], research commissioned by the Cyprus Youth Board, INEK. Available HTTP: <http://www.netinfocms.com/youthboard/pdf/Anergia_Ypoapasxolisi_Eteroapasxolisi.pdf> (accessed 08 March 2008).

Truong, Thanh-Dam. (1990) *Sex, Money, and Morality,* London: Zed Books.

Truong, Thanh-Dam. (1999) "The Underbelly of the Tiger: Gender and the Demystification of the Asian Miracle," *Review of International Political Economy* 6(2): 133–165.

Truong, Thanh-Dam. (2000) "Globalisation, Criminal Capital and Gender: An Inquiry into Human Trafficking," paper presented at the Institute of Social Studies, January.

Tsiolis, Ioannis. (1997) "Poiisi ke Politiki: To Elliniko Politismiko Dilimma Simera," in C. Nadia Seremetakis (ed.) *Diaschizontas to soma: o politismos istoria ke phylo sten Ellada*, Athens: Nea Synora Ekdotikos Organismos Livane.

United Nations. (2002) *Women, Peace, and Security.* New York: United Nations Publications.

von Zielbauer, Paul. (2007) "Rape of Iraqi Girl and Killing of Family Gets G.I. 110 Years," *The New York Times* 5 August 2007.

Wade, Robert. (1996) "The World Bank and the Art of Paradigm Maintenance: the East Asian Miracle in Political Perspective," *New Left Review* 217: 3–36.

Wade, Robert. (2007) "Global Finance: The New Global Financial Architecture?" *New Left Review.* Available HTTP: <http://www.forliberation.org/site/archive/issue0807/article060807.htm> (accessed 9 July 2008).

Walker, Thomas C. and Jeffrey S. Morton. (2005) "Re-Assessing the 'Power of Power Politics' Thesis: Is Realism Still Dominant?" *International Studies Review* 7(2) June: 342–356.

Wallerstein, Immanuel. (1974) *The Modern World-System I: Capitalist Agriculture and the Origins of the European World-Economy in the Sixteenth Century,* New York: Academic Press, Inc.

Wallerstein, Immanuel. (1980) *The Modern World-System II: Mercantilism and the Consolidation of the European World-Economy, 1600–1750,* New York: Academic Press, Inc.

Wallerstein, Immanuel. (1989) *The Modern World-System III: The Second Era of Great Expansion of the Capitalist World-Economy, 1730–1840s,* New York: Academic Press, Inc.

Waltz, Kenneth. (1979) *Theory of International Politics,* Reading: Addison-Wesley.

Waltz, Kenneth. (1986) "Reflections on *Theory of International Politics*: A Response to My Critics," in Robert O. Keohane (ed.) *Neorealism and its Critics*, New York: Columbia University Press.

Wang, Guowei. (1987) *Wang Guowei wenxue meixue lunzhu*, Taiyuan: Beiyuewenyi chubanshe.

Wax, N. (2001) "Not to Worry. Real Men Can Cry," *New York Times Sunday Week in Review* 28 October: 5.

Weatherford, Jack. (2004) *Genghis Khan and the Making of the Modern World*, New York: Three Rivers Press.

Weber, Cynthia. (1994) "Good Girls, Little Girls and Bad Girls," *Millennium* 23(2): 337–348.

Weber, Cynthia. (1999) *Faking It: U.S. Hegemony in a "Post-Phallic" Era*, Minneapolis: University of Minnesota Press.

Weber, Cynthia. (2002) "Flying Planes Can Be Dangerous," *Millennium: Journal of International Studies* 31(1): 129–147.

Weber, Max. (1951) *The Religion of China: Confucianism and Taoism*, New York: The Free Press.

Weber, Max. (1958) *The Protestant Ethic and the Spirit of Capitalism*, New York: Scribner's Press.

Wendt, Alexander. (1999) *Social Theory of International Politics*, Cambridge: Cambridge University Press.

Wendt, Alexander. (2005) "The State as Person in International Theory," *Review of International Studies* 30(2): 289–316.

Whitworth, Sandra. (2004) "Militarized Masculinities and the Politics of Peace-keeping: the Canadian Case," in Ken Booth (ed.) *Security, Community, Emancipation*, Boulder: Lynne Rienner Publishers.

Willman-Navarro, Alys. (2006) "Making it at the Margins: The Criminalization of Nicaraguan Women's Labor under Structural Reform," *International Feminist Journal of Politics* 8(2): 243–266.

Wilson, Rodney. (1992) *Cyprus and the International Economy*. London: St. Martin's Press.

Wilson, Rodney. (1994) "Regional Disparities Between the North and South of Cyprus: A Challenge for Re-Integration" *European Urban and Regional Studies* 1(1): 69–71.

Winichakul, Thongchai. (1994) *Siam Mapped: A History of the Geo-body of a Nation*, Honolulu: Hawaii University Press.

Winslow, Donna. (1997) "The Canadian Airborne Regiment in Somalia: A Socio-Cultural Inquiry," A Study Prepared for the Commission of Inquiry into the Deployment of Canadian Forces to Somali, Ottawa: Minister of Public Works and Government Services Canada.

World Bank. (1993) *The East Asian Miracle*, New York: Oxford University Press.

Wu, I-Hsien. (2006) "The Journey of the Stone: Experience, Writing, and Enlightenment," PhD Dissertation, Graduate School of Arts and Sciences, Columbia University.

Yashin, Neshe. (1995) *Which Half in Nicosia?*, Nicosia, Cyprus: Thegona.

Yoshiaki, Yoshimi. (1999) *Comfort Women*, New York: Columbia University Press.

Yoto, Adriana. (2008) "Get Away Any Day: The Mall as a Frontline for Consumerist Citizenship," Master's thesis, Graduate Program in International Affairs, The New School, May 2008.

Young, Robert. (2004) *White Mythologies: Writing History and the West*, 2nd edn, London: Routledge.

Yu, Ying-shih. (1978) *Honglou meng de liangge shijie*, Taipei: Lianjing.

Zakaria, Fareed. (2006) "India Rising," *Newsweek* 6 March 2006. Available HTTP: <http://www.fareedzakaria.com/articles/newsweek/030606.html> (accessed 14 July 2008).

Zuehlke, Eric. (2008) "Spend More, But Wisely: Discourse, Politics and Power in Thailand's Sufficiency Economy," Master's thesis, Graduate Program in International Affairs (GPIA), The New School.

Zweigenhaft, Richard L. and Domhoff, William G. (1998) "The New Power Elite," *Mother Jones* March/April. Available HTTP: <http://www.motherjones.com/news/feature/1998/03/zweigenhaft.html> (accessed 07 March 2008).

Index

eBooks – at www.eBookstore.tandf.co.uk

A library at your fingertips!

eBooks are electronic versions of printed books. You can store them on your PC/laptop or browse them online.

They have advantages for anyone needing rapid access to a wide variety of published, copyright information.

eBooks can help your research by enabling you to bookmark chapters, annotate text and use instant searches to find specific words or phrases. Several eBook files would fit on even a small laptop or PDA.

NEW: Save money by eSubscribing: cheap, online access to any eBook for as long as you need it.

Annual subscription packages

We now offer special low-cost bulk subscriptions to packages of eBooks in certain subject areas. These are available to libraries or to individuals.

For more information please contact webmaster.ebooks@tandf.co.uk

We're continually developing the eBook concept, so keep up to date by visiting the website.

www.eBookstore.tandf.co.uk

Printed in Great Britain
by Amazon